Straight Skin, Gay Masks a to Be Gay on Screen

Straight Skin, Gay Masks and Pretending to Be Gay on Screen examines cinematic depictions of pretending-to-be-gay, assessing performances that not only reflect heteronormative and explicitly homophobic attitudes, but also offer depictions of gay selfhood with more nuanced multidirectional identifications.

The case of straight protagonists pretending to be gay on screen is the ideal context in which to study unanticipated progressivity and dissidence in regard to cultural construction of human sexualities in the face of theatricalized epistemological collapse. Teasing apart the dynamics of depictions of both sexual stability *and* fluidity in cinematic images of men pretending to be gay offers new insights into such salient issues as sexual vulnerability and dynamics and long-term queer visibility in a politically complicated mass culture which is mostly produced in a heteronormative and even hostile cultural environment. Additionally, this book initially examines queer uses of sexuality masquerade in Alternate Gay World Cinema that allegorically features a world pretending to be gay, in which straights are harassed and persecuted, in order to expose the tragic consequences of sexual intolerance. Films and TV series examined as part of the analysis include *The Gay Deceivers*, *Victor/Victoria*, *Happy Texas*, William Friedkin's *Cruising* and many other straight *and* gay screens.

This is a fascinating and important study relevant to students and researchers in Film Studies, Media Studies, Gender Studies, Queer Studies, Sexuality Studies, Communication Studies and Cultural Studies.

Dr. Gilad Padva is a film, popular culture, men's studies and queer theory scholar. He is the author of *Queer Nostalgia in Cinema and Pop Culture* (2014) and co-editor of *Sensational Pleasures in Cinema, Literature and Visual Culture: The Phallic Eye* (2014), *Intimate Relationships in Cinema, Literature and Visual Culture* (2017) and *Leisure and Cultural Change in Israeli Society* (2020). He also publishes extensively in international academic journals, international collections and international encyclopedias. He currently teaches men's studies and popular culture at the Program for Women and Gender Studies with the NCJW at Tel Aviv University, Tel Aviv, Israel.

Research in Sexualities

The Body in French Queer Thought from Wittig to Preciado
Queer Permeability
Elliot Evans

Straight Skin, Gay Masks and Pretending to be Gay on Screen
Gilad Padva

https://www.routledge.com/Research-in-Sexualities/book-series/RIS

Straight Skin, Gay Masks and Pretending to Be Gay on Screen

Gilad Padva

Routledge
Taylor & Francis Group

LONDON AND NEW YORK

First published 2020 by Routledge

2 Park Square, Milton Park, Abingdon, Oxon OX14 4RN
605 Third Avenue, New York, NY 10017

Routledge is an imprint of the Taylor & Francis Group, an informa business

First issued in paperback 2022

Publisher's Note

The publisher has gone to great lengths to ensure the quality of this reprint but points out that some imperfections in the original copies may be apparent.

British Library Cataloguing-in-Publication Data
A catalogue record for this book is available from the British Library

Library of Congress Cataloging-in-Publication Data
A catalog record has been requested for this book

ISBN: 978-0-367-24774-4 (hbk)
ISBN: 978-1-03-233622-0 (pbk)
DOI: 10.4324/9780429287442

Typeset in Sabon
by Deanta Global Publishing Services, Chennai, India

Contents

Figures

Acknowledgments

I acknowledge that this book has been written in a particularly challenging time for me. Writing this book was a ray of light for me at the heart of darkness, shining in all colors of the rainbow. This project has given me new hopes, new insights, new ideas, new experiences and a new perspective on the place of sincerities, authenticities and reliabilities in our reality and psychic landscapes, as much as the immense power of voluntary and involuntary masquerades we use for daily survival, experimentation, development, erotic pleasures and better understanding of the Other inside and outside ourselves.

I am thankful to my family, friends, colleagues and mentors for their encouragement and sustained support. I am grateful to Professor Moshe Zuckermann, Professor Dafna Lemish, Professor Dafna Hacker (the Chair of the Program in Women's and Gender Studies with the NCJW at Tel Aviv University), and Dr. Elisabetta Girelli.

I am grateful to my devoted students whose insights and fresh ideas are always inspiring.

I'm thankful to my Routledge editors, Alexandra McGregor and Eleanor Catchpole Simmons, for believing in this project. I deeply appreciate their creative cooperation, professionalism, collegiality and kindness.

The final stages of the production of this book are conducted in the shadow of the Coronavirus COVID-19 pandemic. My deepest sympathies go out to those who lost their love ones. My heart is with those who struggle every day with this disease under devastating personal and economic circumstances. I hope the world will soon overcome this catastrophe and its subsequent multiple violations of human rights. We all deserve wellbeing, freedom, sexual pluralism and, of course, fabulous *masks* and beautiful *skin*.

Introduction

Fabricated screens: sexual authenticity, flamboyant masquerade and the queer epistemology of pretending-to-be-gay films

Why would a straight man want to pretend he is gay? Why would a man who belongs to the privileged majority wish to impersonate a member of a minority whose very identity ("homo!", "queer!", "faggot!") is still considered offensive in the eyes of hundreds of millions of people in a highly intolerant and bigoted world? Why would a man, who is perceived as a hetero-masculine guy, want to be considered effeminate in a world in which flaming men are often subjected to daily harassment, abuse and degradation in their neighborhood, schoolyard, family, workplace and many social institutions (e.g., barracks, prisons and boarding schools)? In other words, why would a man wish to play it like a sissy, despite the devastating hardships that many gay men regularly experience?

In a popular 2011 episode of the Israeli TV satire show *The Nation's Situation* (aka *Matzav Ha'Umah*) (inspired by the American TV series *Saturday Night Live*), the straight-identified Israeli TV star Guri Alfi performs the controversial Hebrew musical number "Does It Make Me Gay?!"[1] Before his singing, he speaks about the sensational coming-out of the Israeli popstar Harel Skaat, a few months after the latter represented Israel at the Eurovision Song Contest in Norway in 2010. After the tuxedoed Alfi surprisingly proves to be a connoisseur of this song contest, which is often associated with gay male fandom,[2] the other participants at this entertainers' panel look at him suspiciously. Alfi whispers, "It doesn't mean anything..." The host comments in a sinister voice: "That means a bit." Another of his colleagues, an openly lesbian comedian, nods affirmatively in solidarity with the host's remark.

Alfi gets upset: "You laugh at a friend, and it's at my expense, and that's just..." He tearfully gets up from his seat and runs into the spotlight. His lesbian colleague whispers off screen, "Wow! He is really offended!" before Alfi starts singing melodramatically, pretending that he is a married guy who likes shopping with his wife, wearing fashionable sweaters, keeping on diets, obsessively working-out at the gym and whistling show tunes. The audience at the studio laughs out loud every time Alfi wonders, "Does it make me gay?"

In his effeminate voice, Alfi sissifies this gay man (who is married to a woman), presenting him as a childish guy who collects colorful napkins and corks and bursts into tears while watching *Titanic* because of Leonardo DiCaprio's unlikable outfits. Alfi also typifies this character as submissive to his ruling mother and a nice guy who considers himself a sensitive, romantic and sympathetic man. Then this guy dramatically confesses about a discreet sexual encounter he had with a stranger in a hotel room, in which the guy shoved a green dildo into the speaker's ass while sitting on the latter's face (a tremendously acrobatic sexual position indeed). Alfi wonders "Does it make me gay?" while dancing flamboyantly in a theatrical Broadway style (see Figure 0.1).

In its vulgar defamatory way, Alfi's song "Does It Make Me Gay?" connotes gayness with effeminacy, immaturity, obsessiveness, promiscuity, permeability, perversity, adultery and fakery. Significantly, this ostensibly homophobic musical number reflects a dichotomous and hierarchical perception of homo- and heterosexualities. This song reaffirms the infamous opposition between the hegemonic heteronormative masculinity and gayness (see Table 0.1).

Conspicuously, a straight man is gay-acting here in order to entertain his straight audience. His performance reflects not only what many straight people still think about gay men but also a particular politics of pleasure that primarily reconstitutes straight supremacy. Michael Kimmel explains that one definition of manhood continues to remain the standard against which other forms of manhood are measured and evaluated.[3] In particular, the heteronormative masculinity is contrasted with gay masculinity in a culture in which the boy becomes gendered (masculine) and heterosexual at the same time.[4] Unsurprisingly, the schoolyard bully who abuses a supposedly gay student, for example, is the *least* secure about his manhood. Thus, he is constantly trying to prove it. But he "proves" it by choosing opponents he is absolutely certain he can defeat.[5]

Figure 0.1 Guri Alfi sings and dances in the musical number "Does It Make Me Gay?!" in *The Nation's Situation* (aka *Matzav Ha'Umah*) (TV satire series) (Israel 2011) (film still).

Table 0.1 Gayness vs. straightness – dichotomous distinction

Gay	Straight
pervert	normal
invert	natural
effeminate	manly
neat	rough
tidy	unkempt
fashionable	casual
whiner	tough
complainer	firmed
fragile	hardened
drama queen	laid-back
sensitive	strong
permeable	invasive
pervious	phallic
penetrated	penetrator
bottom	top
masochist	sadist
defeatist	triumphant
subdued	dominant
promiscuous	moral
adulterer	loyal
liar	sincere
untrustworthy	trustworthy
dubious	reliable
delicate	resilient
mama's boy	father's son
softy	cocky
limbed	erected
sissy	macho
cultivated	rough
gentle	tough
needy	self-reliant
dependent	independent
obsessive	stable
capricious	reasonable
melodramatic	realistic
artistic	mundane
exceptional	common
Other	standard
peculiar	ordinary
bizarre	conventional
eccentric	regular
erratic	self-controlled

Pleasure, abuse and mockery are interwoven in this musical number. The straight clientele of this grotesque clownish cry-boy do not laugh because a real gay man is singing and dancing in front of them. Epistemologically, the straight people enjoy his song because they know that (1) Alfi is a straight man who only pretends to be gay; (2) the gay character is mockingly theatricalized and caricatured; (3) Alfi's stereotypical gay mask reaffirms his apparently homophobic beliefs about the sexual Other; and consequently (4) the song "Does It Make Me Gay?" never destabilizes or challenges homophobia.

According to the twisted logics of this musical number, it's okay to be gay as long as the gay is inferior. The gay is framed and perverted here as a colorful pariah who is neat and childish, stylized and capricious, connoisseurial and effeminate, adulterous and permeable, and as a drama queen and a slut who is vividly penetrated by a green dildo. Such demonization guarantees that playing it like a sissy is not risky for straight-identified Alfi. In mocking the gay man and his assumed effeminacy, this heterosexual entertainer pleases his (mostly) straight audience. He doesn't challenge but reconfirms his hetero-normalcy and heteronormativity.

Notably, Alfi is *petit*, i.e. a short and thin man with an innocent face. It is hard to believe that he would ever play the role of an unscrupulous criminal, a violent policeman, an underworld arbitrator or a ruthless serial killer. He is definitely not a macho. Yet, he is perceived by his many straight fans as a straight guy. Although he often mocks his own somewhat effeminate masculinity, assuring his audience that he's certainly not a macho man, he is known as a straight artist who is married (to a woman) with children. Although Alfi *is* very convincing in playing a hyper-effeminate guy, the audience laughs *with* him, never laughs *at* him, when he viciously scorns gay men. The straight viewers are expected to identify with Alfi's representation of gay authenticity that he primarily connotes with promiscuity, dishonesty and sassy effeminacy.

Acting gay, mediating stereotypes

Authenticity, however, is constrained by inescapable frameworks of the self in moral space. There is always a crucial sense of a path that is right for us that enables us to see our life projects either as filled with self-deception or as authentic, proper to us, or our own. We can sense when we are going wrong and feel motivated to get straightened out only because we have some sense of what is proper to us or what is our own.[6] Hence, the facts about who I am are inseparable from a deep sense of what I should be.[7]

However, there is nothing wrong with one's pretending to be someone else, as long as it is not forced by oppressive regimes that do not respect plurality, otherness and multiculturalism. Compulsory pretense is deeply disturbing, morally. Where there is injustice, we all have a duty to combat it, rather than cooperating with it by reinforcing its institutions and expectations.[8] Despite the moral demand for emancipated authenticity, however, hundreds of films feature gay male characters pretending to be straight, at least in a certain phase of their coming to terms with their homosexuality.[9] These films reflect diverse and even contradicted approaches toward sexual minorities. Yet they all represent gayness, i.e. gay cultures, styles, attitudes and sensibilities. Whether they fairly or unfairly portray sexual minorities, they mediate gayness to broad audiences and intensively formulate the public image of what it means to be gay. John M. Clum suggests in his book *Still Acting Gay* that we may not choose to be attracted to members of the same sex, but, to a large extent, we choose our *signs of gayness*, our *gay* "act": "Leather or drag, camp or jock, or some combination with different elements dominant in different contexts."[10] There are many ways of acting gay, and we all choose some acts and reject others.

Mainstream cinematic articulations of men pretending to be gay, however, tend to perpetuate a limited scale of roles of gay men, who are conventionally depicted as miserable scapegoats, campy buffoons, sassy designers and other kinds of flamboyantly submissive servants of the straight majority. These discriminatory mechanisms reflect the significant role of homophobia in the construction of heterosexual masculine identity in patriarchal societies.[11] However, the research of mass consumption of homophobic cinematic imageries paints a complex picture which may not be readily accounted for through single-factor explanations.

The cultural phenomenon of pretending-to-be-gay films, in particular, often eschew linear interpretations, operating through juxtaposition, assortment, hybridity and collage, and challenge the production of fixed or single meanings or reading positions. Although heteronormative screens portray diverse motivations for pretending to be gay (see Table 0.2), playing it like a gay – from the late 1960s to the late 2010s – mostly means playing it like a sissy.

Like the popular infamous "blackface" or minstrel shows in America in the 19th century and early 20th century, in which white actors in make-up or blackface mockingly played the role of black people, the pretending-to-be-gay films are a sort of "gayface" show that are continuously produced and consumed by members of a discriminative mass culture.

Notably, the title of this book, *Straight Skin, Gay Masks*, rephrases the title of Frantz Fanon's postcolonial book *Black Skin, White Masks*.[12] Referring to Fanon's title is based on the idea that racism and homophobia, although they do differ from each other in numerous aspects, both are societal prejudices that involve bigotry, hate, stigmatization, discrimination, ostracism and persecution and are symbolic of even physical annihilation. Fanon claims that the white man had woven him out of a thousand details, anecdotes and stories. He initially believed that what he had in hand was a need to construct a physiological self, to balance space, to localize sensations. But then he experienced a devastating encounter with members of the white hegemony:

"Look, a Negro!" It was an external stimulus that flicked over me as I passed by. I made a tight smile.
"Look, a Negro!" It was true. It amused me.

Table 0.2 Predominant motivations in significant pretending-to-be-gay films and television series

Motivation for pretending to be gay	Year	Film	Director	Country
Dodging military recruitment	1969	Gay Deceivers	Bruce Kessler	USA
	1978	Big Wednesday	John Milius	USA
Legitimizing a lease agreement	1976–1984	Three's Company	ABC network	USA
	2008	Dostana	Tarun Mansukhani	India/USA
Developing a professional career	1982	Victor Victoria	Blake Edwards	USA
	1997	Heads or Tails	Claude Fournier	Canada
	2004	Connie and Carla	Michael Lembeck	USA
	2016	Macho	Antonio Serrano	Mexico
Catching a gay (serial) killer	1980	Cruising	William Friedkin	USA
	1982	Partners	James Burrows	USA
	2014	Death in Buenos Aires	Natalia Meta	Argentina
	2015	Aquarius (episode: "Cease to Exist")	NBC network	USA
Escaping the mafia	1976	The Ritz	Richard Lester	USA
Attracting straight women	1974	How to Seduce a Woman	Charles Martin	USA
	1994	Friends (episode: "The One with the Baby on the Bus")	NBC network	USA
	2000	If You Only Knew	David Snedeker	Germany/USA
	2002	Boat Trip	Mort Nathan	USA
	2004	Dog Gone Love	Rob Lundsgaard	USA
	2004	Freshman Orientation	Ryan Shiraki	USA
	2005	Kenny vs. Spenny (episode: "Who Can Kiss More Women?")	Showcase network	Canada
Escaping the police	1984	The Ladies' Hairdresser	Ze'ev Revach	Israel
	1999	Happy, Texas	Mark Illsley	USA
Committing a (hate) crime	2002	The Matthew Shepard Story	Roger Spottiswoode	USA
	2017	Beach Rats	Eliza Hittman	USA

Scenario	Year	Title	Director / Network	Country
Preventing dismissal	2001	*The Closet*	Francis Veber	France
Winning a reality TV contest	2003	*Boy Meets Boy* (reality TV series)	Bravo network	USA
Adopting metrosexual aesthetics	2003	*South Park* (episode: "South Park Is Gay")	Comedy Central network	USA
Surviving an alternate gay world / gay sphere	2004	*Different*	Tyrrell Shaffner	USA
	2005	*Almost Normal*	Marc Moody	USA
	2000	*3rd Rock from the Sun* (episode: "Frankie Goes to Rutherford")	NBC network	USA
	2012	*Love Is All You Need?* (short film)	Kim Rocco Shields	USA
	2016	*Love Is All You Need?* (aka *Love Is Love*) (long film)	Kim Rocco Shields	USA
Receiving domestic partner benefits	2004	*Strange Bedfellows*	Dean Murphy	Australia
	2007	*I Now Pronounce You Chuck & Larry*	Dennis Dugan	USA
Returning to an ex-girlfriend	2009	*Plan B*	Marco Berger	Argentina
Helping a first-degree relative	2013	*Bromance: My Brother's Romance*	Wenn V. Deramas	Philippines
Forced by the mafia	2014	*Kicking Out Shoshana*	Shay Kanot	Israel

"Look, a Negro!" The circle was drawing a bit tighter. I made no secret of
   my amusement.
"Mama, see the Negro! I'm frightened!" Frightened! Frightened! Now they
   were beginning to be afraid of me. I made up my mind to laugh myself
   to tears, but laughter had become impossible.
I could no longer laugh, because I already knew that there were legends, stories, history [...] Then, assailed at various points, the corporeal schema
   crumbled, its place taken by a racial epidermal schema. In the train it
   was no longer a question of being aware of my body in the third person
   but in a triple person. In the train I was given not one but two, three
   places. I had already stopped being amused.[13]

Both black studies and LGBT studies, as interdisciplinary studies, have
grown as a response to the absence of inquiry into race and sexuality in
traditionally bounded disciplines. These fields of research have been constituted out of a similar logic of identity-based scholarship. Yet there are
significant differences between ethnic and sexual minorities. In LGBT studies, questions of race and racialization tend to be subordinate to analyses
of sexuality. In the scholarship on race, with a few notable exceptions,
there has been a general critical tendency to minimize the role of sexuality, and particularly homosexuality.[14] Hence, the challenge, according to
Siobhan Somerville's *Queering the Color Line: Race and the Invention of
Homosexuality in American Culture* (2000), is to recognize "the instability
of multiple categories of difference simultaneously rather than to assume the
fixity of one to establish the complexity of another."[15]

This book's title *Straight Skin, Gay Masks and Pretending to be Gay
on Screen* reflects a multifaceted and often ambivalent approach toward
these relations between ethnic minorities studies and sexual minorities studies. Despite significant historical, political, intercultural and epistemological
differences, these fields are both involved with critical research of bigotry,
discrimination, objectification, persecution, submission, dissidence, emancipation, dehumanization, heritage, legacy, collective memory, communality,
activism, and self- and public image.[16]

In terms of public visibility and popular representation, in particular, a
person's gayness is usually easier to hide than one's blackness. Although
minorities share a common media fate of relative invisibility and demeaning stereotypes, there are differences as well as similarities in the ways in
which various minorities are treated by cinema and other mass media. And,
because there are important differences in the conditions that they face in
our society, the effects of their media images are different for members of
the various minority groups.[17]

Despite the currently growing number of LGBT families, most queers
are still not born into minority communities in which parents or siblings
share their minority status. In contrast to racial minorities, lesbians, bisexu-
als and gay men are a self-identified minority and generally only recognize

or announce their status at adolescence, or later. Women are surrounded by other women, blacks by other blacks, and so forth, and they can observe the variety of choices and fates facing those who are like them. In contrast, lesbians and gay men are a self-identifying minority. Gross explains:

> We are presumed to be straight, and are treated as such, until we recognize that we are not what we have been told. But how are we to understand and deal with that difference? We only have limited direct experience with those who are sufficiently close to the accepted stereotypes to be labeled publicly as queer, faggots, dykes, and so on and we all – gay or straight – have little choice but to accept media stereotypes which we imagine to be typical of all lesbians and gay men.[18]

Whereas types are instances which indicate those who live by the rules of society (social types), stereotypes indicate those for whom the rules are designed to exclude. Thus, in stereotypes a few traits are foregrounded and change, or "development" is kept to a minimum. Dyer suggests that for this reason, stereotypes are also more rigid than social types.[19] Stereotypes are not provisional and flexible, or they do not create the sense of freedom, choice or self-definition for those within the boundaries of normalcy. They are characteristically fixed, clear-cut and unchangeable. One appears to choose his or her social type in some measure, whereas he or she is condemned to a stereotype. Dyer claims:

> Just think of the line-up – the butch dyke and the camp queen, the lesbian vampire and the sadistic queer, the predatory schoolmistress and the neurotic faggot, and all the rest. The amount of hatred, fear, ridicule and disgust packed into those images is unmistakable.[20]

The pretending-to-be-gay films employ highly traditional stereotyping of gay men, though. They predominantly connote gayness with effeminate behavior, permeable male body, sexually compulsive behavior or, alternatively, with phallic and ultra-virile regalia and performance. Even same-sex partnership, a common theme in some of these films, is often misrepresented on screen as a primarily opportunistic and pretentious financial device which is not based on true love or any sort of (same-sex) attraction, romance and devotion. In this respect, the protagonists wear their gay mask in order to conceal their sexual authenticity, not for freeing their mind and exploring new sexual possibilities and delights.

Faking faggotry, negotiating perversities

Claudia Mills contends that pretense is morally problematic because it is a species of lying. While sometimes pretense can involve only the refusal not to be forthcoming with information, and the willingness to let others' misperceptions of one's identity stand uncorrected, often pretense makes use of a direct and explicit falsehood. "This may seem enough for us to say that great pretenders are equally great liars."[21] The pretending-to-be gay films, however, involve intricate, multidimensional and multidirectional masquerade strategies. In many cinematic representations of masqueraded straightness, as I am going to show in the following chapters, social and sexual boundaries are often blurred and challenged rather than reaffirmed.

Notably, this research concentrates on men pretending to be gay rather than women pretending to be lesbians, mainly because of the conspicuous rarity of films about women who pretend to be homosexual. The inequality in cinematic representations of gay male deceivers versus lesbian deceivers is possibly interrelated with the popularity of gay male mannerisms which are perceived by mass audiences as more comic than stereotypical lesbian mannerisms. Further, the boundaries between male hetero- and homosexuality are traditionally perceived as more rigid than the boundaries between female hetero- and homosexuality. Men pretending to be gay are usually perceived by mainstream cinemas as funnier than women pretending to be lesbians.[22]

Mainstream cinematic depictions of pretending-to-be-gay typically stigmatize the (faked) gayness as sensationally promiscuous, unleashed and bacchanalian marginality. In his discussion of the politics of marginalization, Erving Goffman refers to a "stigmaphile" space of *the stigmatized among themselves* (and those who are sympathetic and supportive) and the "stigmaphobe" world of the normal people. He contends that the stigmaphile space is where we find a commonality with those who suffer from stigma, and in this alternative realm learn to value the very things the rest of the world marginalizes – not just because the world marginalizes them, but because the world's pseudo-morality is a phobic and inauthentic way of life. Goffman refers here to the intolerant and narrow-minded stigmaphobic world, which is characterized by its hypocritical and narrow-minded approach toward social, ethnic, gender and sexual minorities.[23] In the dominant culture, conformity is ensured through the fear of stigma.[24]

John Champaign notes that in its refusal to obey the strictures of procreative heterosexuality, homosexuality, in particular, presents as desirable an inappropriate and undisciplined use of the body, including the perilous pleasures of pornography, for example, that advertises, conveys and implants the pleasures of polymorphous perversity.[25] Dennis Altman, in his book *Homosexual Oppression and Liberation*, criticizes the repression of a polymorphous perversity that would permit the release of sexuality from opposite-gendered configurations or any gendered configurations.[26] The discussed pretending-to-be-gay films are acting-out polymorphous perversities, mainly to entertain their straight viewers, while demonstrating a powerful epistemology of sexual (mis)identifications that critically reconsiders and undermines cultural and countercultural validities, axioms, vulnerabilities and stabilities.

The pretending-to-be-gay films embody contested pleasures of masqueraded identities. Charles Taylor notes that we define our identity always in dialogue with, sometimes in struggle against, the identities our significant others want to recognize in us.[27] According to Kwame Anthony Appiah, identities are complex and multiple and grow out of a history of changing responses to economic, political and cultural forces almost always in opposition to other identities.[28] In screening gay men pretending to be gay from the 1960s to 2010s, in particular, the protagonists' gayness is often misrepresented as an entertaining device which is always contested with heteronormative identities.

Whether fake gayness is cinematically synonymous with flamboyantly effeminate faggotry or, alternatively, excessive and theatrical machismo, the protagonist is primarily portrayed as a fraudster. In concealing his straightness the pretender both enjoys the gap between authenticity and fakery, and his new opportunity to fill this gap by self-experiencing subcultural pleasures and latent transgressive desires. In this respect, masquerade is a situation that concomitantly enforces and theatricalizes the dichotomy between heteronormativity and gayness. The pretense produces some precious moments of self-discovery, including possible erotic and romantic same-sex experimentations. In other words, the mask simultaneously separates *and* merges the authentic self and his camouflage.

Deborah Bell suggests that the mask and masquerade assign meaning and a categorical place in a universe that does not offer labels. Consequently masquerade is always reconstituting itself. While the cognitive side of our brain does not recognize essential hidden truths in the universe, the art of masquerade invariably provokes opportunities for reflecting on our world – outside of its own sphere – as well as within it.[29] Ultimately the universal agency of masquerade has the immense potential to invent and constantly re-invent the essential fabric of culture. Whether masquerade functions to create a sense of renewal, address controversial topics with anonymity, control human behavior, acknowledge and celebrate human rites-of-passage or simply reflect on the human experience, we all regularly – and increasingly – experience masquerade's power and variations.[30]

Nunley *et al.* stresses that masking at all times, both traditionally and now, has dealt with sliding and multiple identities – even when these masquerading identities are considered rather fixed. An identity which is not fixed tends to gnaw at a traditional definition of masking and is fueled with ambivalence and ambiguity.[31] Yet sliding and multiple identities are found in both traditional and contemporary societies and can become the bridge for traditional and new ways of thinking about the significant role of masks and masquerades, as much as removing masks, in sexual identifications, experiences, experimentations, coming to terms and coming-out.[32]

In particular, the premise of sliding and multiple sexual identities and multiple identifications with sexual communities inherent in sexual masquerade offers new opportunities to think about disguised, transient and transforming sexual identities and their sexual carnalities and voluptuous embodiments. Whether sexual masquerade is voluntary or imposed by personal and social circumstances, it is a powerfully constructed falsification of one's most intimate, innate and inherent aspects of personal identity.

Interestingly, males-pretending-to-be-gay is mostly popular in comedies and sitcoms. These genres typically involve expressions of the carnivalesque, whereby the social world is temporarily turned upside down and where transgressive behavior and queer play are celebrated.[33] The romantic comedy, in particular, often deals with such risk-taking in gendered, sexual and libidinal contexts. Although the genre typically focuses on heterosexual couples, comedies typically challenge traditional gender roles *and* the heteronormative behaviors they entail.

Comedies alleviate the provocative characters of transgressive gender and sexual phenomena, moderating their dramatic consequences while the audience, failing to fully absorb the implications, understands these phenomena as merely funny, and therefore consider them non-threatening to their presumptions about "the natural."[34] In a way, "fake gay" bodies remap sexuality and its relations to gender, libido and cultural (cross)identification as bodies that are often (mis)represented as grotesque or that represent a play of desires. These liminal bodies vivaciously disrupt the dichotomized sexual identities by provoking traditional visual, aural, vocal, and haptic codes and systems.

The dissident working within multiple masquerades, incongruities, ironies, paradoxes, contradictions and absurdities is a common feature of both postmodernism and queer theory.[35] Dealing with hetero- and homosexual vulnerabilities and resilience in regard to hegemonic and marginalized communities is timely and relevant in contemporary multicultural dynamics. It is especially intriguing to focus this discussion on "gay" masquerade in films that aim at straight audiences who have limited accessibility to progressive sexual knowledge about the gay community's subcultures, venues, folklore, heritage, dilemmas, angsts and perilous pleasures. For heterosexual audiences, the screening of "faked" gayness is a popular resource for (mis)information about this sexual community.

Strange bedfellows and their melodramatic straightness

Jane Ward, in her book *Not Gay: Sex between Straight White Men*, however, distinguishes *heteroflexibility* – straight-identified men's interest in occasional sex with other men – from *gayness*.[36] Heteroflexibility involves engaging in same-sex sexuality while distancing oneself from the lesbian and gay movement. Yet Ward admits that this characterization could use a bit more nuance, as many sexually fluid straight people *do* identify as allies to the LGBT movement, or even loosely as "queer."

Notably, people who identify as heterosexual, unlike gay men and lesbians, are generally content with *straight culture*, or heteronormativity; they enjoy heterosexual sex, and more importantly, they enjoy heterosexual culture: "Simply put, being sexually 'normal' suits them. It feels good; it feels like home."[37] Hence, these men who have sex with men, without recognizing themselves as gays, distinguish between same-sex erotic pleasures and gay culture. They consider themselves as straight men despite their occasional (homo)sexual acts.

Interestingly, the male protagonists in most of the pretending-to-be-gay films hardly or never have sex with other men. They are involved with gayness as long as it does not comprise sexual practices. Like "heteroflexible" men who have sex with other men without identifying themselves as gays, the cinematic pretenders distance themselves from both homosexuality (romantic, erotic and sexual attraction to members of the same sex, including sexual relationship) and gayness (countercultural folklore, language, performance and ideality).

In avoiding gay sex, the pretenders conspicuously maintain their status as deceivers who are authentically attracted to women and merely pretend to be gay. In pretending to be temporary members of the gay culture, who never have sex with other men, they maintain heteronormativity. Furthermore, in the pretending-to-be-gay films, gayness is synonymous with faggotry, i.e. caricatured effeminacy, grotesque flamboyancy, loathed sissyness and various degrees of ridiculed androgyny. In the straight mind, faggots are not real men or, at least, their masculinity is dubious and questionable.

Yet this book suggests that the heteronormative obsession with re-imagining and caricaturing faggotry exposes some subterranean tendencies, effects, nuances and subtleties that complicate the dichotomous distinction between "masculine" straightness and "effeminate" faggotry. Some unanticipated pleasures, gratifications and emancipations of the men pretending-to-be-gay on screen vividly disrupt and undermine sexual binaries and taboos. This book shows how the fear of faggotry is often intermixed in these films with libidinal anxieties, stimulating curiosities and unforeseen emancipations. Cinematic disruptions of the rigid boundaries between firmed straightness and festive faggotry, for over four decades of pretending-to-be-gay films, have anticipated, in a way, the contemporary post-gay and post-queer politics.[38]

Although a significant part of these films reflect heterocentric attitudes, they often demonstrate some more nuanced intricacies, multiplicities and multidirectional identifications that challenge heteronormative conventionality. This book's exploration of intriguing subversive elements in mainstream cinema is inspired by Barbara Klinger's reevaluation of progressivity and resistance within the extremely formulated and systemized Hollywood cinema. Her critical examination of signifying practices of dominant cinema involves critical identification of a series of "rebel" texts within the Hollywood empire. These texts, while firmly entrenched within the system, display certain textual features which are critically deemed as combative to the conventions governing the "typical" classic text. Ideological criticism, which has so entertained the variability of textual politics within mainstream production, has distinguished a category of films referred to as "progressive" or "subversive."[39]

The case of straight protagonists pretending to be gay on screen, however, is the ideal context in which to study unanticipated progressivity and dissidence in regard to cultural construction of human sexualities in the face of theatricalized epistemological collapse: Firstly because it is a unique inversion of conventional representation of closeted gay men who anxiously camouflage their true identity in a heteronormatively driven world, and secondly because of the prolific discussion generated by such unprecedented masquerade that uncovers hidden aspects and consequences of the intricacy, complexity, variability, polymorphous perversity and imaginative dynamics of the human sexuality and its ideological construction and its contested cultural manifestations and artistic expressions.

Flamboyant deceivers in a performative third space

The broad goal of this book is to tease out the dynamics of the screening of both sexual stability *and* fluidity in cinematic images of men pretending-to-be-gay with high levels of sociocultural complexity and epistemological ingenuity, through the application of a hermeneutic cinematic research. Selecting as a case study the pretending-to-be-gay films provides a unique opportunity to examine the interaction among such salient issues as sexual vulnerability and dynamics and long-term queer visibility in a politically complicated mass culture, mostly produced in a heteronormative and even a hostile cultural environment and in the context of dramatized epistemological crisis.

Notably, preliminary academic researches on cinematic representations of men who pretend to be gay are conspicuously rare. One of a very few studies of this intriguing cultural phenomenon is Diane Raymond's examination of popular culture and queer representation which addresses, among other things, the issue of pretending to be gay on screen. Raymond suggests that the trope of gay pretender has been a staple of situation comedies ever since Jack Tripper in *Three's Company*[40] posed as gay so that his uptight landlord would let him live with two attractive women. This sort of masquerade has been also deployed by *Frasier*,[41] *Three Sisters*,[42] *M.A.S.H.*[43] and the soap opera *Days of Our Lives*,[44] which includes an episode in which the male protagonist "outs" himself to Greta so as not to hurt her feelings and confesses that he is not attracted to her.

In this way, this straight man reaffirms the heteronormative pattern. His faked gayness is merely an excuse for his unattraction to the straight woman. Raymond notes that, on the one hand, these examples of gender and sexuality play may be consistent with a progressive queer agenda that suggests either that we're all queer or that there's a little queer in each of us.[45]

Yet Raymond contends that there is never any suggestion whatsoever of any temptation or questioning on the part of the "straight" character; that firmness of resolve serves once again not only to reinforce a strict binary of gay/straight but also to suggest that solid and impermeable boundaries frame one's sexuality.[46] I suggest, however, that the "gay pretender" trope indicates much more elusive, multifaceted, multidirectional, ambiguous, subtle, contradicted and conflicted meanings, and ideological tendencies. Conspicuously, the pretending-to-be-gay films (mis)represent multiple gay subcultures: flaming effeminacy and campiness, drag shows, political activism, gym cult and body fascism, fetish and BDSM, and different sorts of straight-acting lifestyles and bourgeois practices. I believe that investigating pretending-to-be-gay films and TV series in terms of performativity, theatricality, campiness,[47] queerness, polymorphous perversity and intricate sexual epistemology can expose some unexpected progressivity and subversions in these hegemonic televisual and cinematic texts.

In approaching films as cultural texts and looking at their empowering, productive as well as renewing potential to promote semantic innovation and social change, this book is highly inspired by Eve Kosofsky Sedgwick's groundbreaking reconsideration of the epistemology of the closet, the particularities of coming-out as performative revelation of perilous knowledge and complicated politics of authenticity and its validation.[48] Sedgwick suggests that categories presented in a culture as symmetrical binary oppositions – heterosexual/homosexual, in this case – actually subsist in a more unsettled and dynamic tacit relation.

The term "homosexual" is not symmetrical with but subordinated to the term "heterosexual." Yet, for its meaning, the "heterosexual" actually depends on the simultaneous subsumption and exclusion of the homosexual. Hence, the question of priority between the supposed central and the supposed marginal category of each dyad is irresolvably unstable, an instability caused by the fact that the homosexual is constituted as at once internal and external to the heterosexual.[49] In exploring "semiotic excess"[50] in these films and TV episodes, however, with their notorious theatricality, carnivalesque flamboyancy and passionate spectacles, I hope to unveil the subtleties of unanticipated hybrid forms, third spaces and fusions that challenge the heterosexual/homosexual binary and evade the hegemonic surveillance, providing precious opportunities for broadening the spectrum of sexual negotiations and identifications.

In negotiating the subversive queer potentialities of the pretending-to-be-gay films, I am particularly inspired by José Esteban Muñoz's vision of queerness. Muñoz stresses that queerness is an ideality and that we may never touch queerness, but we can feel it as the warm illumination of a horizon imbued with potentiality – queerness which is distilled from the past[51] (in this case, queer representations in films made in previous decades) and which is used to imagine a future (better understanding of the role of popular culture in shaping the intricate relationships between stereotyping and current sexualities). Here, I agree with Amy Villarejo's consideration of queer stereotype *as a temporal structure*, a way to register existential and affective connection as well as a form of temporal production of queer life.[52] Villarejo's insight complicates the interrelations between stereotypes, temporality, structuralism and queerness, and inspires reconsideration of sexual epistemologies formulated and mediated by heteronormative, often defamatory, screens.

This book attempts to explore diverse ideological aspects and to decode aesthetic mechanisms in pretending-to-be-gay films. The critical analysis of these films aims to examine their contribution to affirmative and subversive visualizations of "faked" gayness and its intricate interrelations with "authentic" straightness.

The first chapter, "Staging effeminacy: screening the perilous pleasures of pretending to be a sissy," is concerned with (mis)representations of camp subculture, stylishness, extravagance and flamboyancy in pretending-to-be-gay films like *The Gay Deceivers*,[53] *The Ritz*,[54] *Victor Victoria*,[55] *Happy, Texas*,[56] *Macho*[57] and *Kicking Out Shoshana* (aka *Shoshana Halutz Merkazi*),[58] as well as in the episode "South Park Is Gay" from the animated TV series *South Park*.[59] These films and episodes theatricalize a broad scale of ideological perspectives on the intricate interrelations between gender, sexuality, effeminacy and sex roles. This intersection is examined in this chapter in regard to the politics of contempt and the interconnected homophobia and effeminophobia, the fear *and* lure of festivity and flamboyancy. This chapter also elaborates the possibility of male "homeovestism," a subversive masquerade in which a man is not masked as a woman but rather reiterates a theatrically stylish and playfully transgressive version of masculinity.

The second chapter, "Take it like a man: cruising machismo in Leatherland," reevaluates the gay masquerade in the controversial "gay serial killer" thriller *Cruising*[60] and the semi-documentary film *Interior. Leather Bar*[61] that dramatizes James Franco's attempts to reconstruct a mythically censored 40-minute segment of *Cruising*. Unlike most cinematic representations of gay-acting straight men, however, these films focus on hypermasculinity rather than effeminacy. Conspicuously, gayness is connoted in this sort of cinema with ruthless machismo, perverted brutality, monstrous sadism, delirious masochism and uninhibited phallic instincts. The deployment of such signifiers of masculinity produces an intricate and intriguingly contradicted "drag macho" who is theatrically demonized and demonically theatricalized. These cinematic cabinets of curiosities display sadomasochistic interrelations between disguise and disgust in order to fascinate their straight viewers. They embody a multilayered cinematic sexual epistemology in which a straight man plays as a straight cop pretending to be gay[62] or rather a straight actor plays as a reflectively straight-identified actor who plays as a straight cop who is pretending to be gay.[63] These epistemologies are problematized, however, by their interactions with sadomasochistic role playing in a voracious culture industry that oscillates between carnival and cannibal.

The third chapter, "Pretending to be allies? Straight women, their pretending-to-be-gay admirers and sexual authentication," unmasks the particularities and peculiarities of screening straight women's friendship with the gay deceivers and these women–men alliances and unanticipated attraction to each other. This chapter initially distinguishes between (1) Gay Male Manipulator Films, like *How to Seduce a Woman*,[64] *If You Only Knew*,[65] *Dog Gone Love*[66] and, particularly, *Boat Trip*,[67] in which the pretender adopts a gay identity only to fulfill his desire and love for a straight woman; (2) Straight Female Manipulator Films, like *Freshman Orientation*,[68] in which the straight woman manipulates a man whom she mistakenly perceives as gay; and (3) Gay Authentication Films, like *Plan B*,[69] that overtly challenge heteronormativity and present the pretenders as closeted gay men whose gay masquerade stimulates their coming to terms with their authentic same-sex desire. This chapter complicates the cinematic articulations of masqueraded lustfulness and attractiveness that queerly transgress heteronormative sexual boundaries and disrupt conventional perceptions of sexual sincerities, authenticities and scripted pleasures.

The fourth chapter, "Odd couples, queer partnerships and gay marriages in pretending-to-be-gay films," focuses on the oddities of faking romantic and marital relationships between men on screen. Although films like *The Gay Deceivers*,[70] *Strange Bedfellows*[71] and *I Now Pronounce You Chuck & Larry*[72] apparently demonstrate an anti-gay backlash against the political struggle for legal gay marriage, these films challenge, in different ways, the powerful heterosexual hegemony. These films vividly prove that sexuality is highly variable over the life span. They center on straight protagonists who socialized into stereotypically colorful and flamboyant gay communities. As cinematic grotesques, however, they uncover the excessiveness and ruthless arbitrariness of conventional power relations between sexual majorities and minorities, as much as the grotesque nature of homophobia. These films' commercial imperative to primarily satisfy the straight eye is significantly challenged by the frivolous, unruly and disruptive nature of the grotesque. Whereas the grotesque and its absurdities, paradoxes and farcicalities are essential to any masquerade, the "dark masquerade" in these films uncontrollably subverts itself, insatiably consuming its ridiculed objects *and* itself.

The fifth chapter, "Screening compulsory homosexuality: the perilous pleasures of parodying heteronormativity and fantasizing a topsy-turvy martyrdom," focuses on cinematic representations of closeted straight boys and girls in alternate gay worlds. Films about a world pretending-to-be-gay, like the short film *Different*,[73] the short and long versions of *Love Is All You Need?*[74] and the feature film *Almost Normal*,[75] fantasize a world in which gays are the majority and straights are a persecuted minority, often degraded as "breeders." This chapter problematizes these allegorical cinematic carnivals, with their diverse ideological attitudes toward the relationship between reality and fantasy, oppression and dissidence, authenticity and pretense. In particular, this chapter criticizes the screenings of dichotomized alternate gay worlds that perpetuate a traditional distinction between hetero- and homosexualities and relentlessly glorify public coming-out of agonized martyrs in an atrociously intolerant world. Like grotesque, however, martyrdom is explored in this chapter as a powerful rhetorical device that flamboyantly exceeds itself, unmasking the mundane brutality of everyday life, and transgressing, in its unruly, unanticipated and often melodramatic way, the oppressive conventionalities of both majorities and minorities.

My hope is that *Straight Skin, Gay Masks and Pretending to Be Gay on Screen* will open up a critical discussion of persistent stereotypes and sexual defamations, as much as emancipatory strategies and subversive disruptions of the heteronormative sexual order in contemporary mainstream cinema and television. Although a significant part of the pretending-to-be-gay films apparently demonstrate a backlash against the social, political and cultural achievements of the gay liberation movement, this book aims to explore their protagonists' elusive desire for experimentation of transgressive desires and perilous sexual pleasures. Hence, this book aims to critically expose and problematize the pretending-to-be-gay films' disruptive, provocative, stimulating and occasionally surprising identity politics.

As Freddie Mercury suggests, in his cover version of The Platters' hit song "The Great Pretender," "too real is this feeling of make believe/too real when one feels what his heart can't conceal."[76]

Notes

1 *The Nation's Situation* (aka *Matzav Ha'Umah*) 2011; this episode is available at YouTube Internet website: https://www.youtube.com/watch?v=lDXmAAFC Q5c.
2 Lemish 2004.
3 Kimmel 2001: 271.
4 Kimmel 2001: 273.
5 Kimmel 2001: 274.
6 Taylor 1989: 207.
7 Guignon 2013: 206.
8 Mills 1999: 48.
9 Among the cinematic pretenders, closeted gay children and preadolescents (e.g., *For a Lost Soldier*, *My Friend Rachid* and *Billy Elliot*), closeted teenagers (e.g., *Beautiful Thing*, *Get Real*, *Edge of Seventeen*, *Handsome Devil*, *The Way He Looks*, *Boys*, *Call Me by Your Name*, *Beach Rats* and *Love, Simon*), closeted young adults (e.g., *Shelter*, *Weekend* and *4th Man Out*), closeted middle-aged men (e.g., *The Lost Language of Cranes*, *I Now Pronounce You Chuck & Larry*, *Pride* and *Jonathan*), closeted old men (e.g., *Love and Death on Long Island* and *Beginners*), closeted Mormons (e.g., *Latter Days*, *G.B.F.* and *The Falls*) and closeted prisoners (e.g., *Locked Up* and *I Love You Phillip Morris*).
10 Clum 1992: vii.
11 Kimmel 2001.
12 Fanon 1952.
13 Fanon 1988 (1952): 91.
14 Somerville 2000: 4.
15 Somerville 2000: 5.
16 Icard 1986; Mercer 1991; Diawara 1996; Gates 2002; Miller 2008; Moradi *et al* 2010; Martin Jr. 2014; Barnard 2018.

17 Gross 1989, 1994, 1998.
18 Gross 1998: 91.
19 Dyer 1999 (1977).
20 Dyer 1999 (1977): 297.
21 Mills 1999: 30.
22 Various emotional and intimate expressions between women are highly tolerated by heteronormativity, whereas male bonding is highly restricted and constrained by the fear of homosexuality.
23 Goffman 1986 (1963).
24 Warner 1999.
25 Champaign 2000.
26 Altman 1993 (1971).
27 Taylor 1991: 33.
28 Appiah 1992: 178.
29 Bell 2015: 5.
30 In a way, life, identity and meaning are all understood as consisting of nothing more than language games, exercises in role playing. It is only through relishing the role one plays can a person find any sense of satisfaction (Mackay 2001). Consequently, as we search to validate identities no longer relevant for our ever-expanding cultural sensibilities, we find the art of masquerade in multiple contexts – including mainstream cinema – as a handy (and frequently crucial) panacea, as much as embodiment of paradoxical pleasures, transformational power and attendant dangers (see Bell 2015).
31 Nunley *et al.* 1999.
32 Padva 2004.
33 Hines 2009: 119.
34 Carver 2009: 128.
35 Hennessy 1993; Stein and Plummer 1994; Dilley 1999; Plummer 2003; Edwards and Jones 2009; McCluskey 2009.
36 Ward 2015.
37 Ward 2015: 28.
38 Murray 2015; Alderson 2016; Mathers, Sumerau and Cragun 2018.
39 Klinger 1984.
40 *Three's Company* 1976–1984.
41 *Frasier* 1993–2004.
42 *Three Sisters* 2001–2002.
43 *M.A.S.H.* 1972–1983.
44 *Days of Our Lives* 1965–present.
45 Raymond 2003.
46 Raymond 2003.
47 Padva 2000.
48 Sedgwick 1990.
49 Sedgwick 190: 9–10.
50 Fiske 1986.
51 Muñoz 2009.
52 Villarejo 2014.
53 *Gay Deceivers* 1969.
54 *The Ritz* 1976.
55 *Victor Victoria* 1982.
56 *Happy, Texas* 1999.
57 *Macho* 2016.
58 *Kicking Out Shoshana* 2014.
59 "South Park Is Gay!" (*South Park*, 7th Season, 8th episode) 2003.

60 *Cruising* 1980.
61 *Interior. Leather Bar* 2013.
62 *Cruising* 1980.
63 *Interior. Leather Bar* 2013.
64 *How to Seduce a Woman* 1974.
65 *If You Only Knew* 2000.
66 *Dog Gone Love* 2004.
67 *Boat Trip* 2002.
68 *Freshman Orientation* 2004.
69 *Plan B* 2009.
70 *The Gay Deceivers* 1969.
71 *Strange Bedfellows* 2004.
72 *I Now Pronounce You Chuck & Larry* 2007.
73 *Different* 2004.
74 *Love Is All You Need?* 2012; *Love Is All You Need?* (aka *Love Is Love?*) 2016.
75 *Almost Normal* 2005.
76 "The Great Pretender" 1987 (originally recorded in 1955).

1 Staging effeminacy
Screening the perilous pleasures of pretending to be a sissy

In the straight mind, and in some masculinist gay men's minds too, the sissy is still synonymous with defenseless maleness (baby, crybaby, mamma's boy), negative characteristics (cuckold, coward, namby-pamby, milksop, pushover, wimp, wuss, yellow-belly, softy, milquetoast, pussy whipped, prissy, dopey, wisecracker), fragile animals (chicken, jellyfish, fraidy-cat), festive animals (peacock, gold fish, puddle, hoopoe, angora kitten), delicate flowers (daisy), delightful foods (cream puff), girly first names (Nelly, Chrissy, Trixie, Roxie, Tillie, Josie, Suzy, Gertie, Dotty, Dolly, Britney, Madonna, Celine, Joanie, Loretta, Maggie, Margo, Molly, Velma) and, unsurprisingly, iconic faggotry (pansy, pantywaist, half ass, queenie).

Yet sissyness plays a significant role in queer culture, anticipated by historic dandyism, decadent flamboyancy, and camp subculture and its glamorous drag performances and spectacular outfits. "Lavender boys," commonly associated with neatness, stylishness, festivity, indulgence, aestheticism and obsessive interest in opera, classic music, ballet, art and design, were at the forefront of gay scenes around the world for decades, arguably for centuries. Mark Simpson contends that

> The persecution of sissies is a necessary inducement to other boys not to give up their own struggle toward manhood by showing them what happens to those who fail [...] In such a culture, regardless of their actual sexual preference, all sissies are de facto 'faggots'. And all faggots, regardless of their actual level of masculinization, are *de facto* sissies.[1]

Eve Kosofsky Sedgwick pointedly considers the pathologizing and consequent attempts to "cure" or masculinize effeminate boys as an attack against homosexuality. Sedgwick criticizes the psychiatry of the late 20th century for its renaturalization and enforcement of gender assignments and for its incapacity to offer even the slightest resistance to the wish endemic in the culture surrounding and supporting it that gay people *not exist*.[2] Further, most bodies of the state enforce heteronormativity all but unquestioningly, even in the face of violence.

As David Plummer notes, initially young boys are prone to attracting homophobia if they are too close to girls. "Later," he explains, "from puberty onwards, boys who do not associate with girls enough or who do not objectify women are vulnerable to homophobic criticism."[3] Given the omnipresent and unrelenting pressure on gay youth, as Kittiwut Jod Taywaditep notes, it is not surprising that *gender-nonconforming boys* attempt to defeminize and conform to gender-role expectations. "Also unsurprising," he adds, "are the findings that those *who do not or cannot defeminize* appear to pay a price for their persistent gender nonconformity."[4] Richard Dyer notes that the androgyne, or the in-between type, is a prevalent representation of the gays in popular culture. Queens and dykes represent homosexuals based on gender assumptions – that is, queens and dykes are in between the two genders of masculinity and femininity. Thus, dykes are mannish and queens are effeminate. The advancement of the notion of "real men" in particular has led to the unavoidable production of the sissy as an inferior type.[5]

Male adolescents are neglected and persecuted in bigoted environments, particularly if they are effeminate boys who are particularly suspected of being gays because of their overt look, behavior, speech, cultural identification and aforementioned untraditional fields of interest. In my book *Queer Nostalgia in Cinema and Pop Culture*, I suggest that for those boys, *femininostalgia* – nostalgic, recuperating memories of their initial coming to terms with their transgressive masculinity and flamboyant effeminacy – can be highly valuable. Recognizing and respecting one's effeminate nostalgia can be a healing process that reflects a gradual coming to terms with one's early transgression. It is an intimate realization of one's otherness, which retrospectively precedes the subject's (homo)sexuality.[6] Femininostalgia is therapeutic because it reconsiders the gay man's effeminacy and enables him to regard this character not as a stigma, but rather as an inner, integral and intimate part of his personality and self-recognition. Yet staging (and restaging) effeminacy is a complicated, irritating and stunning (counter)cultural assignment with its own perilous risks and pleasures.[7]

If *feminine* expression can be regarded, according to Deborah Tannen, as "genderlect," then I suggest that *effeminate* expression is about "genderialect." Language socialization has a major influence on how males and females use language.[8] Girls for example learn to be more careful in their speech, while boys tend to show their strength and power through language.[9] Tannen[10] and Jennifer Coates[11] support this claim by declaring that language and gender are inextricably linked and both our gender and language are developed through our participation in everyday social practice. Yet I suggest that the distinction between *feminine* and *masculine* is a dichotomous gendered division while *effeminacy* and masculinity are gender traits, qualities, mannerisms and behaviors. Although effeminacy derives from the fundamental gender division, it is a distinct (sub)cultural phenomenon.

Popularity breeds contempt: extravagant homosexuality and its perilous effeminate pleasures

One of the most dominant heterocentric imperatives is an idealization of a strict distinction between ultra-virile manhood and girly womanhood. In contrast, queerness is often perceived by the heteronormative society and its powerful popular culture (and parts of the LGBTQ community itself) as hybridized, somewhat "in-between" androgyny based on interwoven female and male physical and behavioral traits, gaits, gestures and mannerisms.

Richard Dyer considers the "in-between" type as one of the most known and prevalent patterns in the representation of homosexuality in the 20th century (this tendency also exists, to a certain extent, in 21st-century popular culture). The queen and the dyke both represent homosexuality through what is assumed to be a gender correlation – that is, both are represented as if their sexuality means that they are in between the two genders of masculinity and femininity.[12] Thus dykes are mannish and queens are effeminate. The heterosexual notion that a Real Man does exist had led to the unavoidable production of the sissy as an inferior type whose existence proves the superiority of the Real Man.[13] Nevertheless, feminine gays do exist, of course, and concealing or excluding them from the screen is also problematic.

Vito Russo contends in his book *The Celluloid Closet: Homosexuality in the Movies* that stereotypes are based on a grain of truth, and he does not see any reason why there should not be any representations of feminine gays if these are fair representations.[14] Dyer suggests that iconography is a kind of short-hand – it places a character quickly and economically. This is particularly useful for gay characters, for, "short of showing physical gayness or having elaborate dialogue to establish it in the first few minutes, some means of communicating immediately that a character is gay has to be used."[15] Moreover, Dyer notes that by recognizing the gayness of the character during his first emergence, all the character's following actions and words can be understood, explained or explained away, as those of a gay person.

Effeminizing or "in-betweening" gay men is deeply rooted in the history of Western effeminacy. Peter Hennen agrees in his book *Faeries, Bears, and Leathermen: Men in Community Queering the Masculine* that effeminacies currently circulating in the industrialized West reflect a high degree of gender polarity, a minoritizing perspective that nevertheless operates as a nearly universal disciplinary mechanism exacting an impressive level of gender conformity among most men because of effeminacies' strong association with homosexuality.[16]

Notwithstanding, Alan Sinfield emphasizes that the association of effeminacy and homosexuality advanced as necessary and natural by much of our contemporary culture is indeed a relatively new social phenomenon. His research of literature of the 17th, 18th and 19th centuries indicates that the meaning of the word "effeminate" has been radically transformed in the past 400 years. Initially, the word depicts a superfluity of feminine

emotionality and overdramatic sentimentality.[17] The object of the effeminate man's desire could be either male or female; this had no bearing on his
gender status. The critical feature was the fact that he was womanly in his
melodramatic expressive attachment. Certain iconic characters appearing in
the European plays written in this period – the dandy, the beau, and the fop
or the poseur – were mostly perceived by the public as both heterosexual
and effeminate and flamboyantly campy.

Camp is defined in the Oxford Dictionary as "Affected, theatrically exaggerated; effeminate; homosexual."[18] Camp has been categorically defined by
Susan Sontag in "Notes on Camp" as a vision of the world in terms of style –
but a particular kind of style:

> It is the love of the exaggerated, the "off", of things-being-what-they-
> are-not... The androgyne is certainly one of the great images of Camp
> sensibility... What is most beautiful in virile men is something feminine;
> what is most beautiful in feminine women is something masculine.[19]

Jack Babuscio identified camp with queer subculture based on *gay* sensibility:

> As a creative energy reflecting a consciousness that is different from the
> mainstream; a heightened awareness of certain human complications of
> feeling that spring from the fact of social oppression; in short, a percep-
> tion of the world which is colored, shaped, directed, and defined by the
> fact of one's gayness.[20]

According to Daniel Harris, camp subculture is typically identified with
drag shows, worship of fabulous divas, attraction to disco and platform
shoes, emphasized artificiality, kitsch and decadence.[21] Camp subculture,
however, is also political as it criticizes the arbitrariness and non-natural-
ness of heteronormative sexual definitions, and offers freer and more liberated lifestyles. In its theatricality, camp subculture is a mode of productive,
lived experience. It is a journey into the imaginary, a free-spirited way to
reevaluate feelings about mythic urban gay life in metropolitan cities, now
and then. Drag performances, as explicit embodiments of camp subculture,
expose how (artificially) constructed – rather than biological –the gender
identifications are: heavy make-up, flamboyant frocks, inflated wigs and
glittering jewels. Judith Butler suggests that if gender itself *is* drag, and if it
is an imitation that regularly produces the ideal it attempts to approximate,
then gender is a performance that *produces* the illusion of an inner sex or
essence or a psychic gender core.[22]

The gay deceivers enjoying a slice of festive life

Effeminate, festive gayness is flamboyantly performed by *The Gay Deceivers*
(see Figure 1.1),[23] a late 1960s low-budget sex comedy that focuses on two

Figure 1.1 Danny Devlin (Kevin Coughlin) and Larry Casey (Elliot Crane) in *The Gay Deceivers* (USA 1969) (film still).

young men who pretend to be gay when they are required to join the Army. Danny (Kevin Coughlin) and his friend Elliot (Larry Casey) act the part and camp it up in front of Army officer Dixon (Jack Starrett), who doesn't buy it. When the two return to their apartment to celebrate with their girl-friends, they are surveilled by the suspicious Army man.

Danny and Elliot move into an all-gay apartment complex, composed of ornate cottages decorated in lavender, red and all shades of pink and complete with huge rotund beds, mirrored ceilings and plaster Greek statues of naked male athletes. The protagonists try to blend in with the flamboyant residents. At the same time, they try to maintain their straight love affairs and not get caught by the Army. Their pretense is complicated, however, by the reactions of their heteronormative family and straight friends. Danny and Elliot end up losing their romantic relationships with their female sweethearts. But even after the pair is trapped, they are not recruited by the military. The Army investigators who shadow them are revealed as gay men themselves who prefer to keep straight people, like these gay deceivers, out of the Army.

From the beginning of this film, when the deceivers are interviewed by the officer at the recruitment office, Danny and Elliot's pretended homosex-uality is synonymous with theatrical effeminacy. Danny is dressed in elegant gray trousers, a black jacket and a significant feminine scarf, while Elliot's gay outfit includes tight white trousers and a red sweater. They both have stylish men's haircuts and they speak in a coy, childish tone that matches their effeminate appearance.

Later, when they are interviewed by a psychiatrist, they express their flamboyant campiness with Oscar Wilde-esque statements like "Am I homosexual? Perishly thought!", "Do I ever wear women's clothes? I'm no drag queen, doctor," "How much do I prefer young boys or mature men? Do I get a choice?", and "Sex has nothing to do with love; I think it's much more how you feel about the person." When the doctor shows them a photo of a naked woman in a suggestive position wearing necklaces, they respond: "Oh, those are heavenly braids... Her hair is too long." When the expert shows them a photo of a bodybuilder, however, Elliot wonders: "Oh, no. That's nice. Do you mind if I keep it? I don't have this one at home."

Interestingly, Danny's politics of effeminacy is vastly different to Elliot's. Whereas the blond lifeguard Elliot, in his tight red trunks that compliment his muscular and sparsely haired physique, amuses his female admirers by sassy gestures and effeminate speaking, Danny is much more reserved. He rebukes Elliot, "Do you have to pull out your fag routine all around here?!" and Elliot replies: "What's wrong, Danny boy? We're out." Danny says that he realizes it but he just doesn't want anybody to get any ideas. Elliot consents: "OK, don't get spastic over it."

Hence, Danny is afraid that their effeminate gay masquerade will be mistakenly perceived as their authentic gay identity. Elliot, in contrast, discovers the emancipatory yet perilous pleasures of sexual transgression and its undisciplined, joyful theatricality, playfulness and unapologetic festivity. His confidence in *pretending* to be gay derives, however, from his resilient and celebrated heteronormative masculinity, handsomeness and sex appeal that attract his devoted female admirers.

Elliot, who is more sexually attractive than Danny, is less afraid that his gay deception might stigmatize and frame him as homosexual. Although his theatrical effeminate gestures are seemingly contemptuous, it seems that he truly enjoys putting on an act. His flaming behavior, alibied as inauthentic and manipulative, allows him to escape the burden of hetero-masculinity, for a while, and to freely discover the lure of effeminacy without being ridiculed, sanctioned, persecuted or bashed by the straight world for his nonconformity.

Yet their coming to terms with their effeminately gay masquerade and its requirements and challenges is highly dynamic. When they inspect an apartment in a gay neighborhood, for example, Danny finds it suitable for them, telling the real estate agent that they do not need separate bedrooms. Elliot, in contrast, is dissatisfied with the flaming pink bedroom with the huge round pink bed. He rebukes his fellow: "What do you mean this is alright?!... It's bad enough I have to live in here, in Fairyland, now you want me to share the same bed." Danny reminds him that they have to pretend that they are living like lovers, "We got to live like homosexuals."

Their landlord, Malcolm DuJohn, is a flaming queen in a glitzy gray blouse and blond wig, carrying a colorful fruit basket with a red ribbon. Malcolm is swishing and speaking softly, and when he first meets his tenants, he immediately distinguishes Elliot, who harshly shakes his hand: "You are the muscular one, aren't you?" Malcolm's appearance is accompanied by a cheerful tune that mocks his flamboyancy. Elliot, who previously criticized the effeminate setting, instantly adopts an effeminate speaking, in order to please their landlord who is proud of decorating the apartment. When Malcolm criticizes Craig, his "better half," uttering "You know how men are,"

Elliot puts his arm around Danny's shoulder, saying in a flaming tone: "Beasts. All of them."

Near the end of the film, Elliot is invited to a sassy gay party in which the queer participants are dressed in colorful outfits, androgynous clothing, kitschy accessories and garments, clownish masquerades and erotic underpants, and some of them are wearing heavy make-up. Elliot suddenly notices a beautiful blond woman. He approaches her and soon the two move to Malcom's bedroom, where Elliot shockingly finds out that the lady is a handsome drag queen.

Russo criticizes *The Gay Deceivers'* superficiality and shallowness, considering this film as "an 'animated' live-action cartoon version of California gay life" that "offended almost everyone, including homophobic critics who wrote that the film is viciously anti-gay."[24] The publicity material for the film, according to Russo, prepared by Harold Rand & Company, used the words "fag," "queer" and "deviate" to describe the gay characters in the film and advertised the comedy as a "slice of gay life." Interestingly, Michael Greer, who performed as Malcolm the flamboyant landlord, not only wrote his own role as a sassy drama queen but apparently rewrote the screenplay in places, making it "funnier and less homophobic than was intended" wherever he could.

Hence, Russo interprets this flamboyant screen as a good example of gay humor used in an oppressive situation, a stereotype with a sense of pride that could counteract an essentially homophobic film.[25] A closer look at the screening of Malcolm's deceivingly gay tenants, however, uncovers ideological intricacies, contradictions, incongruities and ambivalences in this film's politics of heteronormativity.

The mocking protagonists crudely mediate the often surprisingly ambivalent, multifaceted and multilayered attitude of the late 1960s straight majority toward gay men, sexual authenticity and the perilous yet pleasurable potentialities of wearing gay masks. The adventures of Danny and Elliot, these two Alices in Wonderland (or a "Fairyland" as this film suggests), embody fear, repulsion and confusion interwoven with curiosity and great interest of straight people in the gay community in Los Angeles in the late 1960s and the emergent gay neighborhoods, venues, aesthetics, stylishness, lingo, and notoriously exotic promiscuity and mythic hedonism.

Victorious diva and defeated old queen

Whereas *The Gay Deceivers* shows gay urbanity and its lively sociability, stylish habitus, subcultural communality and countercultural festivity, Blake Edwards' cinematic musical farce *Victor Victoria*[26] (see Figure 1.2) does not explore the gay community and its subaltern communality. Rather, it centers on real and fake gay protagonists who are located in the straight environment, aiming to entertain and amuse straight audiences who enjoy drag shows. *Victor Victoria* focuses on an impoverished soprano, Victoria

Figure 1.2 Victoria Grant (Julie Andrews) pretends to be a gay man who pretends to be a woman in *Victor Victoria* (USA 1982) (film still).

Grant (Julie Andrews) in 1934 Paris, who accepts an offer from a gay man, the drag performer Toddy (Robert Preston), to perform together with him masqueraded as the Polish-born gay count Victor Grazinski. This duo, identified as Victor Victoria, becomes a huge success.

Both performers, however, are infatuated with the handsome Chicago gangster King Marchand (James Garner), who is on a holiday in Paris with his mistress Norma (Lesley Ann Warren). King is initially confused. On one hand, this handsome macho realizes that he might be gay. On the other hand, he intuitively feels that Victor, the person of his dreams, is not really a man. At the same time, his lighthearted mistress is overtly attracted to both Toddy and Victor and pathetically tries to heterosexualize them. The jealous mistress tells her lover's wife that he has an affair with another man. In order to save King's businesses and, particularly, to fulfill her love for him, Victoria finally returns to her genuine female identity, reinstating her and her lover's straightness.

Notably, the heteronormative plotline in *Victor Victoria* never stimulates Victoria to question her gender identity or sexual identification. Victoria is certainly not an F2M transgender person. She never wishes to transgress or challenge her own heterosexual cisgender womanhood. Her pretending to be a gay man is a burden for her, not an inspiring opportunity to question her (and the straight audience's) gendered and sexual premises. Her pretense is presented as merely a profitable gimmick, yet an almost unbearable obstacle in her quest to fulfill and celebrate her love for King Marchand. Her vulnerability is temporary and it derives from a self-enforced masquerade, not an inner and intimate process of exploring and negotiating her sexual and gendered selfhood. *Victor Victoria* is a romantic comedy that clearly demonstrates the Pursuit Plot.

According to Mark D. Rubinfeld's taxonomy of Hollywood romantic comedies, this type involves a "quest of conquest" in which a hero is attracted to a heroine; courts her; encounters resistance from her; and, being a "real man," refuses to take "no" for an answer. Ultimately, the hero woos her, wows her and wins her.[27] This is precisely what happens in *Victor Victoria*. Victoria, who is agonized because of her incapacity to fulfill her love for King Marchand, admits: "Pretending to be a man has its disadvantages." Later, she gives up her glamorous, successful and lucrative career as a-woman-pretending-to-be-a-man-pretending-to-be-a-drag-queen -pretending-to-be-a-diva, confessing that she is nothing more than a fraud, in order to maintain her relationship with the charming gangster and to save his business in the homophobic criminal underworld.

Victoria's hopeless devotion to the gangster fully complies with the notoriously patriarchal and chauvinistic rules of the Pursuit Plot, a type in which the narrative pleasure demands female submission since these are stories of male "ants" and, more important, of males getting what they want.[28] Whereas King Marchand's thinking that he might be gay is presented just as a phase, not a real revelation or coming to terms with his authentic sexual identification, Victoria's and his own straightness is constantly reassured by their "closeted" straight romance. According to *Victor Victoria*'s submissive politics of carnival, Victoria is (mis)represented as a straight woman who pretends to be a gay man who pretends to be a diva who pretends to have a gay romance with a straight macho man.

Arthur Nolletti contends that this film's theatricality by its very nature cautions us not to mistake the comic proceedings for reality or to apply the usual rules of verisimilitude.[29] I agree with Nolletti that one of the principal objections to *Victor Victoria*, however, is that it is never wholly believable because Julie Andrews fails to convince as a man. The romantic convention of a woman in male disguise traditionally dictates that she be convincing only to the characters within the narrative, not to the audience, which is usually privy to the truth in the first place.[30]

Notwithstanding, *Victor Victoria* embodies a particular version of pretending-to-be-gay that consists of a hybridization of femininity *and* effeminacy. In this intricate masquerade, Andrews, a well-known diva, pretends to be a gay man who is masqueraded as a diva. The drag queen's challenge is not to pass as a woman but to pass as a diva, a genuine gendered fiction with its notorious exaggeration, theatricalization and overwhelming mythicizing of ultimate womanhood.

Indeed, as Nolletti suggests, what we see with every glance is Andrews' own irrepressible femininity – her shapely legs, her trim figure, her undeniable décolletage. In fact, "Le Jazz Hot" is nothing but a celebration of Andrews' own sexiness, a quality she has rarely projected before. Indeed, Edwards the filmmaker wants us to see that Andrews (who is Mrs. Blake Edwards) is not only a versatile actress but also a sexy woman. "And what better way to call attention to Andrews' sex than to dress her in the most masculine attire possible – a pin striped suit – then make much ado about her character's obvious and natural discomfort."[31] I agree with Nolletti that Andrews has never been as warm or womanly on the screen, and she is in fine voice. Arguably, Edwards' emphasis on this star's femininity, far from undercutting the plot and theme, actually adds to the satire. "For if Parisian society cannot see through Victoria's disguise when there is obviously so much to see, then it is indeed a society reveling in illusion."[32]

Further, *Victor Victoria* compares this straight woman's pretending to be a man with the gangster's pretending to be a decent businessman. In this way, gayness is problematically, even if humorously, analogized with criminality. King denies that he's a gangster, presenting himself as "Just a businessman with a bodyguard." Victoria replies: "A businessman who does business with gangsters and pretends he's not a gangster sounds like the kind of act I do." These lovers agree that they are both pretenders and that that "is not a very good basis for a relationship."

Significantly, pretending-to-be-gay is not depicted in this film as a precious opportunity to experience new, unexpected homoerotic delights and same-sex romance, but as a perilous device that threatens the partners' happiness. In order to save her beloved gangster's financial empire, Victoria proves to King's carefree, silly girlfriend that she's a "real woman" by exposing her body in front of her (albeit Victoria's nudity is never shown on screen). In this way, *Victor Victoria* conservatively equalizes sexed corporeality and gender identification.

The most grotesque part of this bourgeois fantasy mercilessly mocks Toddy, the aging gay actor. In the final scene he performs as a buffoon in a sassy womanly outfit. He impersonates Victoria in her musical number "The Shady Dame from Seville." Toddy performs bad singing and grimaces. He slides on the stage, missing the choreography and getting wet from the decorative fountain. He also knocks the men next to him and scolds them: "You bitches!" He demonstrates arrogance, aggressiveness, amateurism, gaucheness, ungracefulness and heaviness. This unglamorously ageist musical number ends with Toddy's vulgar French kissing with one of the male dancers. Clearly, the straight audience at the club does not laugh *with* Toddy but *at* him. Victoria's stage partner, in his ridiculous effort to amuse her, her King and the straight viewers, embodies a disgraceful homophobic caricature that concomitantly mocks the flaming queen's effeminacy, faggotry, transgressive masculinity and aging.

Whereas this film pretends to be liberal, open-minded and subversively carnivalesque, it is a rather conservative bourgeois farce that re-stigmatizes homosexuality and, particularly, aging homosexuals, who are grotesquely portrayed as a living circus of eccentricities, a cabinet of curiosities which is disturbingly exposed in front of the vicious and voracious audience. The politics of mockery of this scene is highly exploitive. Instead of mocking homophobia, this musical number caricatures campiness. Toddy's last show does not perceive gay sensibility as a creative energy that reflects a consciousness that is different from the mainstream and its social oppression. Rather, his pathetic show *is* socially oppressive. Toddy's staged foolishness and festive queerness are colored, shaped, directed and defined by this film's heteronormative populism.

Andrew Ross suggests that as make-up and dressing up became a common feature of the flamboyant counterculture, "drag," hitherto the professional conscience of camp, took on the generalized meaning, for straight culture, of all forms of everyday role-playing.[33] Indeed, Toddy's show, in which he sarcastically mimics Victoria the straight female pretender, demonstrates a straight configuration of drag. In straight eyes, Toddy's drag festively mocks the very idea of mockery and reduces drag to the level of ridiculous pretense.[34]

Victor Victoria's false consciousness, and its lack of free-spirited, eman-cipated imagination, disables an identification of the political value of camp subculture/counterculture and its particular gay sensitivities. The result is a scornful spectacle of a symbolic gay bashing that impoverishes the (counter) cultural capital of gay performativity. In this early 1980s film, after the straight woman is redeemed from her *camp* prison, her gay stage partner is doomed to entertain the straight audience with a self-humiliating circus of perversities, festivities, absurdities and stupidities, a pathetic finale to his long career. Whereas Toddy's female straight partner is finally free, he is still confined, surveilled and subdued by *Victor Victoria*'s straight mind.

Perilous heterosexual pleasures and the politics of homeovestism in homo land

More than two decades after the commercial success of *Victor Victoria*, Michael Lembeck tried to double the pleasure of the straight viewers in featuring not one but two female impostors, Connie and Carla,[35] who pre-tend to be gay men and enjoy tremendous popularity as extravagant drag queens. Like Victoria, these musical theatre performers, who sing their own songs, become gay deceivers in order to survive financial difficulties and to save their fading careers, albeit this time, these straight women's pretense is also motivated by the need to camouflage themselves from the Chicago gangsters. The two flee from the criminals, who chase after them, when the women unintentionally witness a mafia hit.[36]

In both *Victor Victoria* and *Connie and Carla* the female protagonists are tormented by their love for straight men, a love that cannot be fulfilled and celebrated as long as they pretend to be gay men. The crucial differ-ence between these films, however, is that Victoria pretends to be a man in drag who is mostly tuxedoed while Connie and Carla pretend to be men in drag who always wear glitzy tiaras, heavy make-up and stilettos. Whereas Victoria mostly pretends to be an effeminate handsome young man, Connie and Carla always pretend to be flamboyant drag queens or excessive, highly theatrical divas in order to camouflage their "natural" womanhood. These camouflaged entertainers perform as "Connie and Carla and the Belles of the Balls" at The Handlebar *gay* club.[37]

In the spirit of *Victor Victoria*, Connie (Nia Vardalos) is soon infatu-ated with good-looking Jeff (David Duchovny), and their secret attraction to each other risks the performers' friendship (like the growing tension between Toddy and Victoria caused by Victoria's infatuation with the charming King Marchand) *and* their profitable (and life-saving) gay mas-querade. The growing popularity of Connie and Carla (Toni Collette) in Los Angeles eventually exposes their real identities. On the opening event of the renovated dinner theatre, they narrowly (and comically) save themselves from being discovered by the Chicago gangsters. Like the heroine in *Victor Victoria*, they finally confess their real womanhood to their fans, who eas-ily forgive their fraud, and Connie finally wins Jeff's love just like Victoria, who ultimately fulfilled her hopeless devotion to King Marchand.

Victoria wears men's clothes in her pretending to be a gay man, in a way that flatters her female body. Connie and Carla's politics of masquerade, however, is more complicated, in that they wear excessive, theatricalized female outfits in order to camouflage their mundane, ordinary womanhood. The tactic employed by *Connie and Carla* in their staging femininity is one best described as *homeovestism*, that is, dressing up as a woman, masquer-ading as "a quintessential feminine type."[38] The term "homeovestism" was originally coined in reference to the work of psychoanalyst Joan Riviere. In the late 1920s, Riviere saw displays of excessive femininity by successful career women as an attempt to compensate for their success in what they viewed as masculine pursuits.[39] Gender roles, and femininity in particular, were seen by Riviere as a form of masquerade.[40]

Butler considers the performance of gender as "the repeated stylization of the body, a set of repeated acts within a highly rigid regulatory framework that congeal over time to produce the appearance of substance, of a natural sort of being."[41] In particular, Butler contends that all identity gains legiti-macy through reiteration, whether it is that of the individual or of gender roles in general. In other words, gender is not a voluntary "performance," but it is *"performative* in the sense that it constitutes as an effect the very subject it appears to express."[42]

Connie and Carla's flamboyant performance is celebrated at the audition scene at the gay club. They attend this venue in sassy outfits that include long brunette and blond wigs, heavy make-up, an orange fake fur coat, mini skirts, pink boots, and expressive gaits and mimics. They demonstrate self-confidence, telling the club owner: "Doll, stop praying. You're looking at the Second Coming."

Connie and Carla's putting themselves on a performative act is decon-structed on screen by a series of close-ups of their dressing up process: pull-ing their pantyhose up, wearing silver bracelets, wearing a corset and pulling its strings. This series of acts which are exposed in a theatrical context are practically not much different to the daily routine of many women in the world who regularly *perform* their womanhood this way. Yet in prepar-ing themselves for a theatrical show, Connie and Carla dramatically turn themselves from *regular women* to *fabulous divas*. In mimicking gay male drag artists, who regularly mimic fabulous divas, Connie and Carla's femininity is transformed into effeminacy – a festive performance of female stardom, powerful stylishness and extravagant superiority that transcends the mundane machismo, sexism and misogyny.

Conspicuously, these women's drag performance is not a burden for them but an opportunity to live a sort of liberated, self-proclaimed womanhood that transcends patriarchal constraints. When Connie and Carla are disguised as gay men, who theatrically pretend to be glorious women, they feel freer than before. They say that they feel like they can finally say what they think. They admit that when they were doing their regular show in Chicago, and when they would say dirty stuff, they could feel the audience going, "Oh, no. Don't do that. Where's my dessert?" But now, when these women are dressed like guys, they can say anything they want. Masking themselves as men-who-pretend-to-be-glorious-women is relieving and self-empowering, uncovering the theatricality of daily life and the mundane reiteration of gendered identities and socially constructed sex roles.

At the same time, *Connie and Carla* re-stigmatizes gay men by portraying them as a bunch of pathetically superstitious wimps who pray before going on stage: "O blessed St. Mary of Drag Queens, please grant your never humble servants... and our new friends Connie and Carla with grace, jewels and support hose. Gay-men." Additionally, the gay drag queens are presented as sexual predators. When one of the guys asks Connie why she wears a bra during the day, the surprised woman replies: "Being in drag helps us practice our moves." The guy touches her breasts but she's afraid to stop him. He says that they are good falsies and asks her what she uses. Connie tells him that it is none of his "beeswax" and her friend Carla encourages the men to have a feel of Connie's body. They touch Connie's breasts and comment: "Supple. Good. Well, they are good. Hmmm." Connie looks furiously at Carla, who gazes back at her with a vicious smile.

The twisted epistemology of this scene legitimizes this harassment: The molesters do not know that Connie is a "real woman"; hence they are eligible to touch their colleague's male body as professionals who inspect his "false" breasts. Even if their harassment of Connie is different from regular abuse, in a way, because they do not know that she's a biological woman, this film problematically presupposes that gay men regularly harass their same-sex colleagues, touching their bodies without permission. Such defamation enhances the stigma of a promiscuous, debauched, uncontrolled, uninhibited and dangerous gay world.

Not only is the gay world sensationalized in *Connie and Carla* as an animalistic, perilous universe, but it also interrupts the amorous heterosexuals' fulfillment of their love. Like in *Victor Victoria*, Connie's pretending to be gay is more agonizing than pleasurable for her. The straight man in love, in both films, never thoroughly contemplates his sexuality and soon realizes that his object of desire is not really of his own sex and, conspicuously, that he is *not* gay.

Both films are mainstream features that primarily aim to satisfy their straight viewers. Thus they never dare to show a straight man who truly doubts his straightness, let alone experiencing erotic delights with another man. Jeff is clearly estranged from the drag queens' camp subculture. He finds it difficult to understand why drag queens like to dress like women. Connie, disguised as a drag queen, explains to him that "it's like dressing how you feel inside." This ambiguous explanation is given by Jeff, who admits that it's strange for him that his gay brother is "getting a manicure right now." He also assures Connie that he never got his back waxed, his body has never been plucked and he doesn't do manicures. According to the heteronormative logics of *Connie and Carla*, Jeff is not an ungroomed man but a fairly masculine guy who celebrates his uncompromising sexy straightness.

Masqueraded Connie, who is infatuated with Jeff, becomes his best male friend and mentor. When she tells Jeff that there are murderers who are after her and that she's hiding out as a drag queen, he isn't easily persuaded: "Really. Really, I'm asking you really. I'd like to know. I wanna figure this whole thing out. Is this the real you, or are you playing dress up?... Connie, you're not a real woman." The woman replies: "Oh, you'd be surprised, baby. I know your type. You like uptight girls." Connie cannot suppress her desire for Jeff anymore, however, and kisses him on his lips. The straight guy, shocked, leaves the bar. Later, agonized Connie bursts into tears, telling Carla: "Oh, my God. I kissed Jeff, and I want to kiss Jeff again without my wig." In response, Carla loses her temper and shouts hysterically at her best friend and business partner: "It was your stupid idea to be drag queens! Now we're in hiding for life as women dressed as men dressed as women so shut up! Shut up! Shut up! You've been weird! Cut it out!"

Whereas pretending to be gay is agonizing for Connie, her friend Carla is afraid to abandon this masquerade, worrying that they might be caught by the Chicago gangsters if their true identities are discovered. In this respect, pretending to be gay is both an invaluable haven and a living hell for these straight women. Even if Connie is basically gay-friendly, her relationship with those of the gay culture is complicated by her masquerade, which keeps her apart from her true love. In her quest for straight happiness, she finds her closet to be a greater obstacle than Jeff's current relationship with another woman.

When Jeff's homophobic girlfriend discovers his frequent visits to the gay club, she suspects that he is a closeted gay man. When she eventually arrives at this venue, she finds out that the reason for his visits there is his complicated relationship with his gay brother Robert, who works as a drag queen. She furiously remarks "They're freaks!" and leaves the venue, paving the way for Jeff and Connie's unification, if and when Connie comes out as a straight woman.

Robert insists that drag performance is not a matter of pretense, falsity or fakery but rather involves truthfulness. He tells the gay deceivers: "Girls, in an art form based on being true to one's real self, welcome to your outing." Connie, motivated by Robert's words, confesses in front of the patrons: "I'm a woman, a female. We were faking it. It's a long story," and Jeff and Connie passionately kiss each other. The sight of this similarly aged heterosexual couple kissing publicly expresses mutual pleasure, affection, love. As a straight kiss, it is a gesture at once of the banal and the iconic, representing metonymically the shared cultural embrace of heteronormative values and behaviors.[43]

If Connie was kissing Jeff while she is still (mis)perceived as a masqueraded gay man, however, it could, in straight eyes, constitute a marked and threatening act, a performance instantly understood as contrary to hegemonic assumptions about public behavior, and the public good, because it invites certain judgments about the men's deviant sexual behavior and its imagined encroachments, violations and contagions – judgments that inevitably exceed the mere fact of their having a mutually affirming encounter.[44] Jeff and Carla's kiss, however, demonstrates a victorious heteronormativity that defeats the horrendous straight closet and the enforced deception that caused great suffering to the "closeted" straight couple who merely yearns to express their authentic feelings for each other. Their straight kissing, in the middle of a gay bar, is idolized in this heteronormative film, as a courageous act that celebrates (hetero)sexual authenticity, earnestness and desired normalcy.

Metrosexual straightness, theatricalized heteronormativity and straight eye for the queer guys

The intricacy of the straight mind and its often peculiar interrelations with the gay community, campiness and particularly effeminate stylishness, is embodied by the satiric TV animation series *South Park*, which celebrates metrosexuality in the episode "South Park Is Gay!"[45] This episode mocks a sudden metrosexual trend endorsed by South Park's men and boys (see Figure 1.3). Kyle, one of the young protagonists, dares to challenge the metrosexual vogue.

Consequently, he is persecuted by his dandy friends. Interestingly, South Park's gay couple, the teacher Mr. Garrison and his submissive partner Mr. Slave, are not at ease with this metrosexual trend since they wish to preserve an authentically gay campiness. Kyle and the gay couple fail to murder the stars of *Queer Eye for the Straight Guy*[46] (a reality show in which five neat gay experts give a makeover to somewhat unrefined straight guys) who inspire and stimulate the town's new fad. Further, the Fab Five of *Queer Eye* are revealed as straight "Crab People," monsters who are merely disguised as gay humans. The dissidents are captivated and are forced to become "Crab People." They are miraculously rescued, however, by the

Figure 1.3 A pedicurist serves Kyle Broflovski and Stan Marsh in the episode "South Park Is Gay!" of *South Park* (TV animation series) (USA 2003) (film still).

furious South Park wives, who are dissatisfied with their husbands' narcissistic metrosexuality.

The metrosexuals in South Park are flamboyantly obsessed with fashion, outfits, grooming, cosmetics, working-out at the gym, and other attributes of contemporary gay culture. They have fashionable hairstyles and haircuts, they speak to each other as if they were girls, not boys, and they use childish nicknames for each other (Kyle's father Gerald, for example, is nicknamed "Jer-Jer"). They speak to each other softly in a coy tone, adopting overdramatic gay slang, e.g., "super-fabulous," "tootaloo," "sweetgum," "I'm freakin' out," "super duper triple-dog," "silly buns," "oh, please, girlfriend," "oh, my God, he's on fire… Put it out, put it out," and "out to the malls and into the streets" (paraphrasing the queer activists' Stonewall slogan "out of the sheets and into the streets").

In contrast, male townspeople who do not adopt the metrosexual dress codes yet, and their female partners, are characterized by untasteful clothing, unfashionable outfits and ungroomed bodies. Another significant trait of the uncultivated straight guys is homophobia. When a TV announcer informs the viewers about the night's schedule that includes *Boy Meets Boy*,[47] *Will & Grace*[48] and "*Love Boat*[49]… with men," Kyle's stereotypically boisterous and hysteric red-haired Jewish mother Sheila is overwhelmed: "My goodness, there certainly are a lot of gay shows on television these days." Her husband Gerald's comment, however, anticipates the town's gay makeover: "I think it's great that gays are finally being so accepted." Yet Gerald is shocked when their son enters in colorful clothes, shouting: "HAAAAA! Kyle! What's happened to you?!" His offspring scorns the traditional father: "I'm just trying to fit in, Daddy. Don't be such a drama queen!" This dialog wittily criticizes the prevalent hypocrisy among liberal Americans who tolerate gayness as long as their own offspring is not gay.

At first, South Park's wives are contented with their husbands' new obsession with grooming and neatness. One of them is thrilled: "My Steven shaved his chest and his balls. Ooooh, I love it!" The only woman who is worried is the (stereo)typical Jewish mother, who smilingly remarks: "I don't know. Sometimes cultural fad takes too far." Her implied worrying is that their husband won't only culturally identify with gay culture but also dare to enjoy homosexual experimentation. Interestingly, the young protagonists perceive their new neatness as a means to attract girls. They traverse the homosexual connotations of male grooming and stylishness by fighting with other boys, who look gayer. In neutralizing the sexual aspects of gayness, they appropriate the obsessive interest in appearance and stylishness and incorporate it into the hegemonic heteronormativity.

When the children quarrel with each other over which one of them is gayer, and who is more metrosexual, they scorn their classmates by calling them "fags." At the same time, they scorn each other "straight!" By using the S word they mock their schoolmates who do not look gay enough. In their ignorance, they also call each other "catamite!" (a pubescent lover of an older man in ancient Greek terminology) and "bisexual!" without knowing the exact meaning of these words. Their gay teacher Mr. Garrison is very upset with his student's trendy gayness, however, telling his partner that it is the craziest thing he's ever seen: "All the children were suddenly acting like being gay was cool. Meaning, maybe we're not the only gay couple in town anymore!" Interestingly, the real gay men in town are worrying that the recent trendiness of being gay may damage their uniqueness. This worrying echoes the British sketch series *Little Britain*[50] in which the chubby gay protagonist Daffyd Thomas (played by the openly gay actor Matt Lucas), who regularly wears tight vinyl outfits in shocking colors, constantly refuses to acknowledge that he is not the only gay man in the village.

Notably, the townspeople's "gay" campiness in this episode is not *homosexual*. Although their visibility apparently challenges heteronormative masculinity, with their overt stylishness, neatness, trendiness and sophisticated dandyism, they are never sexually attracted to other men. Yet this episode is heavily stereotyping gayness. When Gerald wonders if his newly metrosexual mates became gay, they explain:

> Not gay, Gerald, metrosexual. Just because a guy cares about how he looks and is in touch with his *feminine* side doesn't mean he's *gay* anymore. Metrosexual means you're straight, but you *appreciate* the gay *culture*. It's super-fabulous! Would you like some Shiraz?

In their manifesto, the metrosexual townspeople embrace feminine sensibility, and even gay sensibility, but they restrict their new experience to cultural identification that never transgresses the *sexual* boundaries between hetero- and homosexualities.

Mr. Garrison and his slave quickly discover that although gay visibility and mannerisms became hegemonic in South Park, homosexuality is totally avoided and marginalized by the townspeople who strictly refuse Garrison's sexual maneuvers. Furious and frustrated, Mr. Garrison wonders, "Why won't anybody pound Mr. Slave's butt?!" The local men reply that they're straight. When the gay teacher insists, "Those pants and those shoes say you pound butt!," the men reject his association of sassy outfits and all-male sex. Yet one of the guys assures him that they learned that gays are "totally cool, you're just one of us now." Surprisingly, Mr. Garrison is dissatisfied with this festive accepting, yelling: "One of you?! We've spent our whole lives trying NOT to be one of you! You can't do this to us!" In this way, this episode mocks both the townspeople's homophobic heteronormativity *and* gay separatism.

This awkward politics of multiculturalism becomes even more complicated (and traversed), however, in a later scene in which gay (albeit no homosexual) kids are bullying anti-metrosexual Kyle, calling him "butch boy" and "macho man" and claiming that the school's playground is for metrosexuals only. They threaten him, "Take your non-flaming ass to some other school!" before they gather around him and gang up on him. Although this scene criticizes gay bashing by portraying Kyle as a victim of brutal bigotry, it reaffirms dichotomous hetero- and homosexualities and maintains the tension between these two different existentialities.

Later, Kyle explains to his shocked mother: "I've been beaten in school for being different." His parent immediately suspects that his classmates bashed him up for being a Jew, but the child explains that he was attacked because of his refusal to be a metrosexual. This situation becomes even more grotesque when his Orthodox Jewish father Gerald, now a festive, self-absorbed disco dancer, aestheticizes the brutal attack: "We can cover that black eye with some cream base, and we'll bleach with an acid wash for a fun vintage look."

Such an aesthetic, rather than ethical, approach echoes the populist criticism of Oscar Wilde and his aesthetes in the late 19th century, when the aesthetic movement's delicacy, refinement, neatness and artistic sensibilities were mocked by the British press, including the satiric magazine *Punch*. Wilde was regularly caricatured as an oversensitive, effeminate sunflower boy, an image that referred to Wilde's special interest in this particularly impressive flower.

These flamboyant aesthetes were also caricatured in an 1882 "aesthetic" teapot, a clever, two-sided pot that embodies a blond mustached man on one side and a blond woman on the other. This teapot is primarily parodying and emasculating the aesthetic dandy, yet never suggesting that this ultra-effeminate man is not heterosexual.

Sinfield contends that Wilde has adopted the manners and appearance of an effeminate aesthete in 1877; since 1882 he had presented himself as an effeminate dandy.[51] Yet it was in late 1894, only a few months before the trials, that "serious rumors about [Wilde's] private life and habits became more persistent in both London and Paris."[52] And still, not everyone believed them.[53] Sinfield agrees that there was a tendency to perceive same-sex passion as effeminate, but he argues that effeminacy, until the early 20th century, did not necessarily signal same-sex passion.[54]

Furthermore, only gradually did homosexual and heterosexual become the distinction that must precede and inform all others, and even then the change was negotiated by making it important to decide whether a homosexual was "active" or "passive." Hence, Sinfield notes that up until the time of Wilde, effeminacy and same-sex passion might be aligned, but not exclusively, or even particularly; and the masculine/feminine boundary could be deployed for diverse significations.[55]

In parodying contemporary heteronormative culture, however, *South Park* mocks the straight townspeople's flamboyant effeminacy. Whereas *Queer Eye for the Straight Guy*'s Fab Five are admired by the newly metrosexuals, they are challenged by two vastly different opponents: the masculinist child Kyle, who objects to the *Queer Eye*'s bad "effeminizing" influence on the townspeople, and the local gay couple who is anxious about gay authenticity. When Kyle and Mr. Garrison meet each other on the train to New York, holding knives and determined to kill the *Queer Eye* people, the bitter teacher complains: "They took gay culture from real gays and their asses are ours!" Interestingly, this discontent echoes dissident voices inside the gay community that heavily criticized the prevalent gay fandom of *Queer Eye*. Yet Mr. Garrison blames these TV entertainers for marketing a commercialized, mainstreamed and inauthentic version of gay culture to the straight majority while other gay activists challenged the *Queer Eye* for perpetuating the hierarchical myth of the gay servant who obsessively pleases and beautifies his straight master.

Hutton Hayes contends that the underlying message of *Queer Eye* is that unlike their staid, straight brethren, gay men are, as a rule, fashion savvy and therefore useful when it comes to certain aspects of life.[56] Hayes identifies the hierarchical nature of this show, in which the gay man can lend a supporting role to the starring role of the straight man who, though otherwise proficient, can't quite get it right when it comes to the lesser things – the superficial – at which gay men are so good. He insists that as long as gays are seen almost exclusively in campy, servile roles, they can be accepted into mainstream television.[57]

Hayes's criticism resembles, in a way, Mr. Garrison's complaint about the straight townspeople's appropriation of gayness' festivity and confiscation of the gay culture's uniqueness and authenticity. Yet Hayes blames *Queer as Folk*, and other mainstream TV shows that concentrate on gay protagonists, for perpetuating and exoticizing a narrow, hyper-stereotypical sort of an ultra-effeminate gayness.[58] Whereas Mr. Garrison is worried by the popularization of gayness in general, Hayes opposes a particular vocabulary of homosexualities on straight screens which merely includes a ridiculously subordinated, clownish (and inauthentic) gay effeminacy.

Problematically, the *South Park* episode mocks gay activism, including gay prides, and misrepresents them as exhausting countercultural and separatist enterprise. This misperception is at its height in the "metrosexual pride parade" scene, in which the men ride on giant colorful bananas and peacocks, screaming scornful slogans like "We're here! / We're not queer! / But we're close! / Get used to it!" These ridiculous demonstrators, however, are misrepresented as a bunch of wimps who are worried that a real appraisal might damage their perfect hair, their manicured fingernails and their outstandingly pressed uniforms.

Heteronormativity is most extrovertly reaffirmed, however, in a payback scene in which South Park wives break into the *Queer Eye* studio, like a furious mob (or, alternatively, a Lysistrata-like women solidarity front), bashing the Fab Five and screaming: "You turned our husbands into whiny little wusses!" Later, they explain that they didn't have a choice. At first they liked having their men be clean and neat, thinking that having them use products in their hair and wanting facials would make them sexier, "but it doesn't." Then the Fab Five's bodies begin to move, and they are exposed as disguised crab people who systematically make men into wusses "so they could take over the world."

This demonization of a (metro)sexual minority disturbingly echoes some of the most atrocious (mis)representations of gay men in mainstream popular culture. Larry Gross notes that "queers, like the science fiction fantasy body-snatchers, are invisible 'aliens' hidden among normal, God-fearing Americans; apparently like everyone else but, in reality, unnatural, criminal, sinful, or, at best, sick."[59]

Considering the topsy-turvy, carnivalesque attitude of this show, however, it is never truly clear whether this episode viciously (and sophisticatedly) reconfirms the worst anti-gay stereotypes or, alternatively, whether it courageously subverts the prevalent homophobic bigotry. By maintaining this ambivalence, *South Park*, and this show in particular, attracts multiple, often contradicted and rival audiences with "something for everyone."

Unsurprisingly, at the end of this episode, the townspeople turn back to their unrefined sloppiness, and Kyle's friends, now "normal" children, ask this anti-metrosexual to play catch with them. When he complains of their previous shameful attitude toward him, they scorn him in an overtly homophobic tone, "Don't be a whiny little gaywad!... Don't be such a fag, dude!" Kyle stops, thinks for a moment, then turns around and joins his bigoted friends. In this way, this TV show pleases its homophobic clientele, on one hand, and implicitly criticizes the straight majority's notorious homophobia, on the other. In such a sarcastic mixture of gay jokes *and* homophobic humor, however, the "South Park Is Gay!" episode primarily conforms to commodified and populistic politics of identities, theatricalized sexual diversity and liberal heteronormativity.

Masculinist straightness, theatricalized homophobia and campy guilty pleasures

Interestingly, this *South Park* episode was anticipated by "Homer's Phobia," the Emmy Award-winning episode of *The Simpsons*[60] (see Figure 1.4). In this significantly popular episode, the Simpsons make friends with John (resembling the cult filmmaker and gay icon John Waters – the creator of *Mondo Trasho*,[61] *Pink Flamingos*,[62] *Polyester*,[63] *Hairspray*[64] and other cult films – who actually contributed his own voice to this episode), a mustachioed kitsch trader. The fact that he is gay makes Homer afraid of his potential effect on Bart. After a series of ridiculous attempts to turn Bart into a "real man" (and consequent arguments with his wife Marge), Homer assures his son that his love for him is unconditional, whether he is straight or gay.[65]

Ironically, John finds the Simpsons extremely camp. He is thrilled by the corn-printed curtain in their kitchen, the color scheme, the rabbit ears antenna, the Hi-C soft drink and Lisa's necklace ("Pearls on a little girl! It's a fairy tale!"). Homer asks him if his records have camp value, and John flatters him: "You yourself are worth a bundle, Homer! Why I could wrap a bow around you and slap on a price tag." Homer laughs and starts dancing with John to an Alicia Bridges disco hit song "I Love the Nightlife."[66] Marge comments that Homer has "certainly taken a shine to him." The next morning, Homer decides to invite John and his wife over for drinks. But Marge does not think John is married. In fact, she tells Homer that "John is a ho-mo-sexual" (adopting the apparently scientific/medical definition). In response, Homer shouts hysterically.

Notably, *The Simpsons* episode does not perceive gay men as stylish inspiration for the straight men. John doesn't motivate Homer and his bigoted friends to improve their mundane behavior, manners, outfits and grooming. The father remains clumsy, vulgar and often brutal, without any refinement or stylishness. Rather than inspirational, John is misperceived by Homer as a threat to his son's (hetero)normal sexuality, particularly after he sees Bart wearing a Hawaiian shirt, choosing a pink cake over a brown

Figure 1.4 Bart, Homer and Lisa Simpson in the episode "Homer's Phobia" of *The Simpsons* (TV animation series) (USA 1997) (film still).

one and dancing to Cher's "Shoop Shoop Song (It's In His Kiss),"[67] wearing a large black wig with a pink bow in it. Homer's consequent attempts to "normalize" his son are ridiculed by this episode. In contrast, the newly metrosexual townspeople in the *South Park* episode are never afraid that their metrosexuality might be synonymous with homosexuality. They are never afraid that they or their children might become gay because of their newly adopted neatness and dandyism.

Moreover, the metrosexuals in *South Park* live in peace with the local teacher, Mr. Garrison, and his slave partner, whereas the Springfield men do not tolerate homosexuality and they do not respect gay lifestyle, particularly campy lifestyle, especially when they come to terms with the *gay* sensibilities of camp subculture. Even after the gay kitsch dealer saves Homer's and his friends' lives, no friendship or alliance seems to emerge between these men. *South Park* mocks *Queer Eye for the Straight Guy*'s colorful gay flamboyancy, comically portraying the Fab Five as monsters in disguise; *The Simpsons* necessitates unconditional love. Apparently, *The Simpsons* deploys the same masculinist agenda.

Homer decides that if he is to turn the boy into a man, he will need an example of the pinnacle of manhood and virility in his environment. During their visit to the local steel mill, Roscoe, the muscular and mustachioed manager, asks the ultra-virile, highly muscular workers to say hello to the Simpsons. In response, they wave effeminately, "Hello-o." Homer wonders if the whole world has gone insane, watching a slender worker running-in-place while his mate theatrically slaps his back: "Stand still, there's a spark in your hair!" and the worker replies: "Get it! Get it!"

Then a tanned bodybuilder in hot pants walks past Homer holding a vat of hot steel and announcing "Hot stuff, comin' through!," a phrase that echoes gay pornography. As this scene continues, Roscoe states, "We work hard. We play hard." and pulls a chain. Surprisingly, a high-tech disco ball descends and the entire mill turns into a night club called "The Anvil," with flickering spotlights, smoke effects, dance floors, mustachioed body builders and muscular young men at work, proudly exposing their torsos. All the workers dance along to "Gonna Make You Sweat (Everybody Dance Now)," except Homer, who is in shock and leaves this male-only enclave, shading Bart's eyes. Clearly, Homer's phobia is ridiculed here, not the workers' open gayness.

The hit song "Everybody Dance Now"[68] (associated with the disco in the steel mill) forms the sound track for the final scene, however, in which Homer tells Bart that he loves him because he is his own son, whether gay or not. Bart looks quite surprised by his father's statement: "He thinks I'm gay?!" Bart's sexuality remains unclear when John's car drives off and Bart's face is shown in increasing close-ups matching the rhythm and lyrics, "I've got the power." The makers of the "Homer's Phobia" episode dedicated it to the steelworkers of America and wished them, "Keep reaching for that rainbow." By this subversive act *The Simpsons* episode metaphorically liberated an ostensibly hypermasculine, ultra-virile, mega-male yet stylized *and* metrosexual territory – that of the steelworkers – from its prevalent perception by society. The Springfield steel mill laborers work hard, play hard and have got the power (in a camp way). In contrast, the *South Park* episode doesn't support unconditional love or sexual diversification of manhood. Whereas *The Simpsons* episode celebrates camp as particular gay sensitivity and praises sexual multiculturalism, *South Park* mocks effeminacy, dislocating it from its original gay campy sphere and temporarily re-appropriating it before reconstituting the traditional dichotomy between virile straights and flaming gays.

Both episodes, however, do not dare to transgress heteronormativity and never destabilize the protagonists' heterosexuality. Homer is never physically or romantically attracted to the paranoid local bar-owner Moe and the town's notorious drunk Barney. When Bart hears about his dad's plan to go hunting with him and his friends, he whispers: "Something about a bunch of guys alone together in the woods... seems kinda gay." Yet this homoerotic potentiality is never fulfilled. These Springfield men never explore same-sex pleasures and their male bonding is never sexualized. Likewise, Mr. Garrison and his lover's attempts to have sex with the newly metrosexuals fail. Both animation series make sure not to upset their straight audiences, albeit "Homer's Phobia" does challenge the straight father and his friends' homophobia *and* embraces unconditional love, respect and acceptance of sexual minorities.

The power of fantasy: soccer, balls and mirror balls in a pink macho land

Putting gayness on as an act in significantly masculinist and overtly homophobic environments is the main comic device in numerous films. In the straight imagination, which is reflected on mainstream screens, gayness is synonymous with flamboyant effeminacy, and positioning heteronormative machos in flaming campy settings unavoidably creates comic situations. Probably the oldest example of such comedies-of-errors that focus on straight Alices visiting gay Wonderlands is *The Ritz*,[69] a farce that centers on a normative family guy of Italian American origins, who escapes from his gangster brother-in-law and hides in the Ritz, a Manhattan gay bath.

This haven is populated by eccentrically sissified squeaky-voiced detectives, capricious drama queens and wannabe starlets, and countless lustful weirdos. The protagonist, who unwillingly pretends to be gay, struggles to navigate this promiscuous cabinet of curiosities. Less than a decade after the Stonewall riots, the straight protagonist in this film experiences some countercultural delights, including drag performance and diva cult, without losing his privileged status – in the eyes of this heteronormative film – as a gay deceiver who cautiously spies on an unknown exotic land, in a way, without having sex with its queer inhabitants.

Another heterocentric visualization of effeminacy as degenerate gender dysphoria viewed through straight macho eyes is *Happy, Texas*,[70] which comically features the adventures of two tough prisoners who escape to a Southern town in which they are mistakenly perceived as Steven and David, a gay couple invited there to train young girls participating in a local beauty pageant and receive 1,000 dollars for their services. The heteronormativity of this film is maintained by these macho men's unfamiliarity with the effeminate, girly world of show tunes and colorful outfits and by the infatuation of the handsome prisoner Harry (Jeremy Northam) with a local woman.

Happy, Texas, like *The Ritz*, never provides its gay deceivers an opportunity to reexamine and subvert their own heterosexuality or inquire about some intimate and homoerotic aspects of their male bonding. The main comic device in *Happy, Texas* is the dislocation of macho prisoners from the brutal prison life and relocating them in a pinky kingdom of a girly beauty contest. When they realize that they have to pretend to be a *gay* couple, Harry tries to take it easy ("So we're gay, how hard can it be?"), but Wayne (Steve Zahn), an unsophisticated blond mustached prisoner with a heavy Texan accent, responds: "It might not be hard for you, Rock Hudson, but I have got heterosexual, 'not gay' written all over me... I don't wanna be gay." His counterpart, however, persuades him to do it for the money. Their gay deception is spiced with a sort of romantic triangle between handsome Harry, his sweetheart Josephine who thinks he's gay, and the closeted sheriff who is secretly infatuated with straight Harry. Unsurprisingly, this film primarily aims to entertain its straight viewers and is concluded by uncovering Harry's heterosexuality to his beloved Josephine.

Whereas Harry and Wayne are straight pretenders who masquerade themselves in a gay sphere, Shay Kanot's film *Kicking Out Shoshana*[71] concentrates on a gay deceiver who confronts his bigoted straight sphere (see Figure 1.5). *Happy, Texas* features the interrelations between straightness

Figure 1.5 Ami Shushan (Oshri Cohen) is at the center of the homoerotic fantasy of a soccer club's owner in *Kicking Out Shoshana* (aka *Shoshana Halutz Merkazi*) (Israel 2014) (film still).

and a gay environment while *Kicking Out Shoshana* is about an opposite situation in which gayness suddenly emerges in a masculinist straight zone. The latter focuses on Ami Shushan (played by Oshri Cohen), the central striker of the B'nei Yerushalayim ("Jerusalem Sons") soccer team and a local celebrity. At the entrance to a dance club, he encounters Mirit Ben Harush (played by Tal Gadot) and he is instantly infatuated with her. Shushan doesn't know that Mirit is the sweetheart of Kushi ("Blackie") Bukovza (Eli Finish), a notoriously dangerous local gangster. Kushi agrees to spare the soccer player's life only if the latter will organize a press conference in which he will tell the nation, live on air, that he is gay.

After his deceiving coming-out, Shushan is banned by his teammates and scorned by the fans of his own team while he's embraced and glorified by the Israeli gay community. Shushan is represented as arguably the first openly gay soccer player in the world. A British woman reporter arrives in Israel to explore his sensational coming-out but she immediately falls in love with the handsome sportsman. Yet Mirit, who is unhappy with her relationship with Bukovza, is also infatuated with the "irresistibly handsome" gay deceiver.

Shushan's greedy agent (played by Mariano Edelman) organizes a profitable educational lecture tour for Shushan in which he is accompanied by Paz (Einat Weizman), a pathetic and ludicrously coldhearted and paternalistic lesbian activist and academic, an avid fan of the queer scholar Judith Butler. Shushan is constantly harassed and bashed by Bukovza but he finally retaliates against his abuser and defeats him. Then Shushan and Mirit fulfill their love for each other. The final sequence features a somewhat slim version of a Jerusalem pride march.

Interestingly, this film reveals some homoerotic subtleties in the apparently ultra-virile soccer world. The film begins with slow-motioned soccer players moving on the playing field like they were performing a ballet.[72] Later, when the mafia boss humiliates Shushan, after the latter flirted with the gangster's girlfriend, the criminal effeminizes the soccer players: "You players are all pussies. Rubbing cream and shaving your bodies, you fags."[73]

Notably, *Kicking Out Shoshana* echoes the Israeli "bourekas" films, more than 80 populist melodramas and comedies produced in the 1960s and 1970s. These hyper-stereotypical, carnivalesque and patriarchal films center on ethnic folklore and humor. A "bourekas" film that initially focused on an explicitly gay protagonist is *The Ladies' Hairdresser* (aka *Sapar Nashim*),[74] a vulgar comedy-of-errors about twins of Jewish Moroccan origins who exchange social and sexual roles. Michel is a flamboyant gay hairstylist, with a heavy French accent, melodramatic mannerisms, glitzy blouses, tight trousers and effeminately bleached hairstyle, who owns a luxurious hairdressing salon for rich Western Jewish women at the Dizengoff Center Mall in central Tel Aviv. He lives happily with his partner Don in a fancy villa. His twin brother Victor, however, is a lowlife toilet cleaning man with a heavy Moroccan accent and blue-collar outfit who lives with his large family in a poor neighborhood. These twin brothers (both played by the filmmaker Ze'ev Revach himself) exchange identities in order to protect the cleaner, who has stolen some money from his corrupt employers.

Victor's wife tries to seduce Michel as she mistakenly assumes that this is her straight husband Victor. The woman sings a love song to her husband's gay brother, touches his genitals and almost forces herself upon him. Michel is extremely embarrassed, asking her not to breathe near him, and he calls her "Nymphomaniac." The straight woman cannot understand her libidinous husband's unanticipated refusal to make love to her. She whispers, "What have they done to him in jail?!," connoting prison life with enforced homosexual practices.[75]

In contrast, the gay deceiver Victor, dressed as his flaming twin Michel, easily adjusts to the luxuries of the latter's house, including the pleasurable whirlpool bath tub, in which he has sex with one of Michel's devoted clients, the beautiful fashion model Eve, who is aroused by their unexpected sexual encounter. *The Ladies' Hairdresser* was released when homosexuality was illegal in Israel.[76] Correspondingly, this film mocks the effeminate gay protagonist and misrepresents him as a decadent, degenerate, impotent and ludicrous pervert. His twin, the gay deceiver, however, is endorsed in this film as a lowlife yet streetwise and loveable man who successfully uses his gay masquerade as a means of intensifying and diversifying his *straight* sex life. The film stresses that Victor is a "Real Man" whose gayness is merely a masquerade with its own heteronormative sexual benefits.

Although *Kicking Out Shoshana* was produced three decades after *The Ladies' Hairdresser*, when most of the Israeli LGBT community was not closeted anymore and enjoyed annual pride marches, venues, saunas, night clubs, bars and its own role models, including at least one openly gay Knesset member, *Kicking Out Shoshana* is heavily loaded with homophobic and lesbophobic statements.[77]

Shushan is particularly challenged by his teammate Liran (played by the Israeli male fashion model Angel Bonani), who is distressed by Shushan's coming out. The latter scorns him:

> I can imagine you biting on a few things. So you've been playing us all these years, models in nightclubs, threesomes with female flight attendants. They were male flight attendants, huh?!... And what about the training camp in German, where you wanted to take a shower with me 'so we wouldn't waste hot good water'? Are you attracted to me, Shushan? Is that what this is? Am I your type, Shushan? Do you wanna 'do' me, huh?!

Although Shushan is a no less masculine, straight-acting guy than his counterparts, he has been linguistically effeminated by the soccer club's owner Isaac Davidoff (played by Tzvi Shissel), who is in a shiny gray suit, a tight buttoned light-blue polyester shirt, and jewellery. The owner utters mockingly: "Shushan thinks that she's a prima donna. 'She' won't fucking play for the Jerusalem Sons." In Davidoff's fantasy, Shushan holds the Grail, carried in the air by his admiring teammates, whereas the soccer players are shirtless, wearing pink shorts. Then Shushan takes off his shirt and these men dance samba together with tantrums and stimulating pelvic movements while one of them caresses Shushan's hips from behind. Conspicuously, the sportsmen gaze at the camera in an explicit "homosexual gaze" that daringly places all viewers – whether they are straights or gays – in a homosexual position. Such gaze decenters the aesthetic of the heterosexual male gaze.[78]

The soccer club's owner is terrified by this arousing fantasy and whispers in Romanian: "Oh, my God! Oh, mamma!" before he collapses and passes away. Seemingly, the businessman died of shock at the idea that the team would be inspired by Shushan's coming-out and would turn gay, upsetting its narrow-minded fans, who might burn down the stadium in response. It is also possible, however, that the owner died because of his difficulty in coming to terms with his own erotic feelings for Shushan and the other handsome players who are vivaciously starring in his stimulating fantasy. Hence, the owner's fantasy not only fortifies the extant stereotypes but also reveals, in its own way, the intricate incongruities, complexities and interrelations between homophobia and homoeroticism (see Figure 1.5).

Moreover, this scene conspicuously blurs the distinctions made between the homosocial, the homoerotic and the homosexual.[79] Whereas the same-sex bonding in the Jerusalem Sons team is visualized here as homosocial, apparently platonic, this transgressive fantasy is also highly homoerotic. It mostly refers to sexually tinged but not fully sexualized relations in this same-sex group. Notwithstanding, the physical interaction between Shushan and one particular teammate who caresses his hips from behind implies homosexuality, i.e., full sexual relations between these two sportsmen.

Despite the stigmatic, often homophobic tone of significant parts of *Kicking Out Shoshana*, this particular fantasy scene surprisingly challenges what Adrienne Rich[80] defines as "compulsory heterosexuality." The Jerusalem soccer players' heterosexuality is neither natural nor universal but constructed and enforced in conjunction with other relations of power to the detriment of alternative sexual practices and identities. The gay male continuum implies that there aren't simply gays, on one hand, and heterosexual men, on the other, but a broad range of practices and identities in between. In this respect, the old owner's fantasy uncovers a multilayered and diversified sexual reality. Hence, the transformative power of pretending to be gay can be stimulating, risky, perilous and even fatal.

In photographic terms, this fantasy scene manifests sexual fluidity in three stages: (1) *The homosocial yet heteronormative phase* is demonstrated by a close-up shot of Shushan kissing a Grail. Then the camera moves away and exposes the hands of the players who carry their colleague in the air. (2) *The homoerotic phase* begins when the camera moves further to reveal that Shushan is wearing the team shirt whereas his teammates are semi-naked.

(3) *The homosexual phase* starts when the camera moves away, exposing the soccer players in their tight pink pants. Such an effeminate outfit explicitly indicates their gayness. Their transgressive sexuality is enhanced when the camera approaches Shushan, who takes off his shirt and exposes his muscular smooth body, a minute before he dances samba with his co-players who sensually caress his lower torso from behind.

According to the sexual logic of this fantasy, it only takes a few seconds to move from heteronormativity to homonormativity, from straight machismo to homoeroticized brotherhood. Notably, that fantasized soccer players' gayness (or faggotry, in the owner's bigoted eyes) was there from the very beginning. When the camera moves away from the players it reveals their tight pink pants that they have been wearing from the very beginning of the match. The owner is petrified by the idea that his men are men in pink. He is mesmerized, repulsed and possibly (and fatally) aroused by his lively fantasy. Although this grotesque scene is meant not to arouse the straight viewers but to make them laugh *at* the idea that these tough soccer players are gay, it "accidently" colors the playing field pink. Jane Ward notes in her book *Not Gay: Sex between Straight White Men* that in the United States, where "homosexual accidents" make for great comedy, the identitarian context in which homosexuality takes place is of the utmost consequence.[81]

At first glance, this fantasy seems to demonstrate a notoriously abusive attitude toward effeminacy among Israeli machos and to frame gay soccering as paradoxical deviance. Inadvertently, however, this spectacular fantasy uncovers (homo)sexual potentialities, complexes and complexities of young and enthusiastic sportsmen in competitive group sports. This fantasy assumingly entertains homophobes because it caricaturizes the possibility of victorious homosexuality. Yet it features an unapologetic, pleasurable and flamboyant gay effeminacy. The fantasized gay soccer players are the champs, at least in this brief fantasy. In visualizing a gay male continuum with a broad range of practices and transitory identities, the apparently homophobe's fantasy cannot hide its queer potentiality.

Saving straight loves: phallic anxieties, promiscuous gay deceivers and authentic closets

Shushan's sudden gayness immediately involves, in this film's straight mind, the possibility that this sportsman might like to be penetrated by another man, a possibility that shocks and haunts the straight audience. Shushan's mother asks the soccer players, with a heavy French accent, if he's top or bottom. Her son replies that he's neither, and the parent concludes that he's "versatile." Then the mother, who is self-identified as a "modern woman who accepts homosexuality," remarks that she never realized that he is an "okh't'cha" (a common term in modern Hebrew slang for a flaming sissy boy).[82] Interestingly, the mother reproduces the association of a bottom and a sissy. According to her limited understanding of homosexualities, if her son is gay then he might be penetrated; and if his body is permeated then he must be effeminate.

The Jerusalem Sons' avid fans, however, who are deeply disappointed by Shushan's coming out, wave a huge sign, "No Entrance to Homos," that implies their anxiety about same-sex anal intercourse and asserts their fear of being penetrated or "entered" by another man. Yet, when they scornfully effeminize the gay deceiver, they do not condemn the possibility of (symbolically) topping other men, singing: "All the other soccer teams are on our dick! / Not Tel Aviv or Haifa but only Jerusalem is the champion!" Paradoxically, they sing these lyrics to the sounds of the Village People's gay anthem "Go West," demonstrating a peculiar assemblage of brutal masculinity and gay innuendos.[83] Their assumption that gay Shushan is penetrated by other men, however, stimulates them to effeminize the soccer captain: "You're not Shushan! You're Shoshana! Shoshana! Shoshana! Shoshana!"

Whereas Shushan's homosexuality is mocked by these homophobic fans, he inadvertently becomes an inspiring gay icon. Nakhi, a closeted fan (played by the openly gay Israeli actor Yaniv Biton), rescues Shushan from the furious fans, picking him up in his car. When Nachi shares his secret with Shushan, the latter wonders: "How is it you're a soccer fan of the Jerusalem Sons?" The gay fan replies: "You know... A soccer team is like one's sexual orientation. You can't change it." Grotesquely, the closeted gay fan is motivated by a homophobic gay deceiver. This epistemological failure portrays the gay fan as a fool who can be very easily manipulated and deceived. *Kicking Out Shoshana* does not dare to use this relationship for a possible examination of Shushan's queer potentiality. The soccer star never has sex with this avid male fan.

Rather, this film presents the gay deception as a perfect setting for the unfulfilled straight love between Shushan and Mirit, a relationship that motivates this heteronormative romantic comedy. This couple celebrates its love in a Jerusalem gay bar where they can freely dance together to the songs of Israeli drag queens who wear heavy make-up, glitzy dresses and flamboyant hairstyles, and make theatrical gestures. Like the flaming Fab Five in *Queer Eye for the Straight Guy*, the campy drag performers at the Jerusalem gay bar play a servile role in this mainstream film, pleasing and satisfying the discreet straight couple and the straight viewers.

Another cynical use of gayness in this film is Shushan's *ménage à trois* with two young straight women, psychology students who inquire about the local gay male community and yearn for a new challenge: sex with a gay man. Their sex scene with Shushan is primarily meant to arouse the straight male fantasy of having a threesome with two passionate women. Knowing that Shushan is actually gay, the straight male viewers easily identify with this lucky guy who fulfills their fantasy about having sex with two women at the same time *and* cheating their girlfriends. Shushan even calls his agent in the middle of the night to tell him about his rendezvous: "I wasn't aware of the benefits of being a famous fag. Not one female left-winger, but two! I can't believe it. It's the greatest sex I've ever had!" His agent, however, is petrified: "You'd better make sure no one sees you. You gotta be more gay than Elton John, you hear me?!"

In this film's twisted epistemology of the closet, heterosexuality is the forbidden fruit while homosexuality is mockingly depicted as a grotesque perversity, an exotic subcultural phenomenon, *and* an effective means of deceiving women for (hetero)sexual purposes. Eve Kosofsky Sedgwick maintains in her essay "The Epistemology of the Closet"[84] that the heteronormative regime – with its conflicting and restraining rules and regulations of privacy and exposé, knowledge and ignorance – has formulated the way in which many debates on moral issues and epistemology were understood by contemporary Western society. However, *Kicking Out Shoshana* shows that the heteronormative regime not only frames the closet as a powerful means of marginalization and surveillance of sexual minorities.

The closet works for straight people, in this film, as a means of securing their own straightness. Shushan is clearly portrayed as an authentically straight guy whose gayness is nothing but a pitiful masquerade. Shushan, from the very beginning of the pretense that he is gay, does not miss any opportunity to show how much he's disgusted by the homosexual masquerade.

Near the end of the film, Shushan gives a speech at the annual Jerusalem pride march. He first clarifies that he is not gay and satisfies his bigoted fans. In a melodramatic Frank Kapra style, he admits that he lied about being gay because he feared for his life. Even when he compliments the queer audience for its courage, assuring his listeners that they have guts (the synonymous idiom in Hebrew is "you have balls [testicles]"), his apparently progressive statement is immediately followed by a shot of a man in heavy make-up and pathetic blond wig with plaits who cheerfully remarks "Thank God, not anymore!" This transphobic shot is followed by Shushan's commitment to his soccer club:

> My heart is in one place only. Soccer. The Jerusalem Sons. But I was a coward. I let evil people keep me away from my heart. But today, I decided that I'm like you. I, Ami Shushan, no longer afraid. All I want is to get my heart back.

Then he passionately, and publicly, kisses Mirit, his "forbidden" sweetheart.

According to the heteronormative logics of *Kicking Out Shoshana*, pretending to be gay is merely an efficient device for surviving threats from the Jerusalem criminal world *and* fulfilling the protagonist's straight love. This heteronormative happy ending is extremely similar to the closure of *Happy, Texas*, in which the gay deceiver Harry reunites with his sweetheart Josephine. First Josephine suspects that Harry merely manipulated her feelings in order to rob the bank where she works. Harry, who is imprisoned again, promises her: "The difference between what is truth and what is not truth has been a problem for me, Joe. There is nothin' fuzzy about what I feel for you." Josephine remarks, "You know you spoke better when you were gay." The man begs her to open her heart to him, assuring her: "If you give me the chance, I could be very, very good. Perfect."

In both *Kicking Out Shoshana* and *Happy, Texas* the gay deception is not only an essential stage in the development of heterosexual romantic affairs, however, but it also stimulates the coming out of some closeted persons (Shushan's avid fan in Jerusalem Sons and the sheriff in *Happy, Texas*). Thus, the masquerade in these films is necessary for the authenticity of diverse loves and desires, and for the emancipation of people who hide their sexual identities. Through the main characters' gay deception, closeted men in these films gain the courage to live their lives openly and fulfill and authenticate their true selves. Paradoxically, it is the colorful pretense that enables them to show the world (and themselves) their true colors.

Straight drama queens, flamboyant machismo and gay infatuation in a deceptive fashion

Whereas *Kicking Out Shoshana*'s main comic device is pretending to be gay in the heterocentric and chauvinistic Israeli soccer world, the Mexican romantic comedy *Macho*[85] features a straight macho fashion designer who pretends to be gay in order to maintain his "gay reputation" in the colorful, festive and (stereo)typically gay fashion world. If in *Kicking Out Shoshana* gayness is unacceptable because of the notorious machismo of many soccer cultures, in *Macho* the straightness is unacceptable because of the notorious flamboyancy and the notorious gay campiness of the fashion design culture.

Macho centers on Evaristo Jiménez (Miguel Rodarte), a renowned fashion designer, whose dream is to take his clothing brand to international fame but he fears that his empire will be threatened if the world discovers his addiction for women, something that millions of his gay fans would never forgive. In order to maintain his image as a flamboyant yet straight fashion designer, Evaristo reluctantly agrees to date his attractive gay office boy Sandro (nicknamed "Sindy").[86] This romantic comedy portrays their deceptive relationship that (un)expectedly becomes a true love affair between the handsome young employee and the gay deceiver. The protagonist, a grotesquely sassy, eccentric and capricious Mexican macho, is artistically inspired by the young man and gradually comes to terms with his own (homo)sexuality.

This film begins with a citation of Oscar Wilde's epigraph: "Hypocrisy reveals that under the mask there is another mask." According to this film's intricate epistemology, the first mask is the protagonist's straightness, camouflaged by his sassy flamboyancy and effeminate performance. His second mask is his pretending-to-be-gay that camouflages his obsessive womanizing. His third mask is his theatrical machismo that parodies the conventional heteronormative politics of manhood, on one hand, and reconstitutes the stereotype of a capricious, emotionally unstable, vivacious and vicious drama queen, on the other hand. Although machismo and flamboyancy are seemingly contradictory, these grotesquely theatrical phenomena can easily be blended.[87]

When Evaristo is in his private jet, he wears an androgynous flowery suit in dark blue and black, and a feminine black shirt with a gold pin shaped like a flying bird, and gilded gold-rimmed sunglasses that match his stylish mustache. He crosses his feet effeminately while his hand is stretched forward, exposing a huge diamond ring, and his other hand holds a glass of liquor, probably whiskey. Conspicuously, he speaks in a coyly effeminate voice when he complains about the merciless American fashion critics. He is significantly childish and emotionally unstable, and his devoted assistants, together with his servient team of TV documentarists, constantly flatter this bitter and arrogant drama queen. His misogyny *and* effeminacy, machismo *and* flamboyancy, are peculiarly interwoven in this film. Typically, his bitterness is expressed with feminine gestures and mimes when he pathetically cries: "Do you find it easy to fight against a sea of lamé fabrics, chiffon, brocades, tulle, laces, and models who constantly gain and lose weight?!"

Evaristo, who is muscular and tanned, is depicted as a womanizer with an insatiable sexual appetite. In contrast to the fantasized macho in The Village People's notorious hit song "Macho Man,"[88] Evaristo is not a "wannabe" macho man, but a macho already, despite his atypical flaming gestures and playful postures. He is a living hybridization of machismo and effeminacy that do not contradict but complete each other. Evaristo's sarcastic machismo, playful capriciousness and uncontrolled libido are means of caricaturing traditional (Mexican) machismo, the ethics of heteronormativity, the banality of today's celebrity culture and the glamorous yet deceptive aspects of parts of the fashion industry (sexual exploitation, pathologic narcissism, abusive employment, incorrigible jealousy, heartless competitiveness and brutal greediness).

Elizabeth Stephens contends that a theatricalization of macho masculinity problematizes the assumptions about naturalness and authenticity on which its traditional privilege is based.[89] In her analysis of Jean Genet's portrayal of gay machos in his novels, Stephens claims that this criticism is made not by explicitly challenging or subverting the naturalness of heterosexual masculinity, but rather by undermining the distinction between the natural and the theatrical that allow such distinction to be made. Thus, the "natural" becomes another pose, another act, another style of performance.[90] In *Macho*, however, the theatricalization of the passionate Latin macho and his brutal masculinity unexpectedly involves ostentatious effeminacy. Evaristo's androgynous machismo subverts, in its peculiar way, the traditional distinction between macho and drag, natural and theatrical, virility and dandyism. Like Genet's novels, in which "Macho becomes, like drag, a self-conscious and highly stylized enactment of a conventional gender position,"[91] Evaristo's amalgamation of macho aggressions, gaudy attires, melodramatic expressions and festal gaits manifests the absurdity, ludicrousness, futility *and* powerfulness of gender binaries and hierarchies. In other words, Evaristo is funny because of his ruthless androgyny that comically hybridizes lustful virility with festive effeminacy.

Evaristo's colorful theatre of machismo, heterosexuality *and* effeminacy is conspicuously complicated when he decides to pretend to be gay, in order to prove his gay iconicity. Evaristo, who admittedly slept with 322 women in 18 months, pretends to be gay in order to prove to his ultra-effeminate gay colleague Vladimir (Mario Iván Martínez) that he's not an insensitive and predator macho, "an ultra-heterosexual that has taken advantage of the social guilt regarding minorities for his own benefit," and in order to avoid a global boycott of his brand.

Evaristo's devoted female assistant tells him, however, that he doesn't have to become a gay man. "You already look one so it's much simpler," she explains, "You just have to add an accessory to your gay look – a boyfriend." The chosen man for Evaristo's pretense is Sandro, his significantly handsome young employee. Notably, his gay deception doesn't affect his relentless machismo. He blatantly ignores Sandro's heartbreaking confession about his beloved partner who died of cancer, for example, and he cruelly manipulates Sandro's feelings when the latter is hopelessly infatuated with him. Evaristo remains a *homophobic* drama queen. When the young lover passionately kisses him in front of the paparazzi, the shocked designer starts running and screaming hysterically that he might lose his maleness.

According to the conventions of a romantic comedy based on a Coldhearted Redemption Plot,[92] the bitter hero is incapable of love, too heartless to know that he is heartsick. What he most needs, in this gay film, is a redemptive hero, a "nurse and nurturer" who is synonymous with the "good wife" who is quite masochistic. Evaristo is knowingly cruel. Like the beast in *Beauty and the Beast*,[93] he is consumed by hate until he is touched by the young man's pure love. Sandro's love transforms the hero into a complete man who is capable of loving. In so doing, the young employee "softens" both the male and cultural signifiers of heteronormative masculinity and its infamous machismo and homophobia. But at the same time, the young, delicate lover is also trapped in a narrative that, while downplaying the brutal macho, nevertheless manages to reinforce macho domination. *Macho*'s Coldhearted Redemption Plot is basically a warmhearted fairytale that manages to suggest equality while typically en/gendering inequality.

As I suggest elsewhere, the young protagonists in gay adolescence melodramas are often considered sissies by their hostile environment because they are gentle, delicate, stylish, dislike sport activities and invest no time or energy in working-out. Significantly, they all admire, fall in love and have sex with highly masculine boys who are straight-acting, well-shaped, athletic, strong and characterized by a spectacular physique that contradicts anti-gay stereotypes of the effeminate, sissy drama queen. The bodies of these masculine objects of desire (and love) do not "frame" their own (homo)sexuality but function as a sort of corporeal "alibi" for their real desires. In contrast, the young protagonists *are* perceived by the straight society as "less masculine" and are suspected to be gay.[94]

Likewise, Sandro in *Macho* is a sensitive young man with a smooth, light-skinned body, whose masculinity is stylized, refined and sophisticated. His older partner Evaristo, a relentless, aggressive macho with a hairy tanned body, finds it difficult to come to terms with his real gayness, and, consequently, he mistreats and constantly humiliates the young man Sandro. Unlike typical queer youth melodramas, however, the younger and more sensitive partner *is* more mature, more emotionally stable, more sensible and cleverer than his older counterpart. Although Evaristo's physique is more mature than Sandro's adolescent body, the older man is significantly childish, capricious, unstable, hysterical and dramatically disturbed. In this way, *Macho* complicates and often traverses the relationship between the juvenile and the mature, the "twink" and the "stud," the seducer and the seduced, the mentor and the learner.

Such intricacy derives from three particularities of Evaristo, who is a flamboyant drama queen, a gay deceiver and a heartless macho. Unlike conventional gay coming-of-age romantic comedies and melodramas, not only are there intergenerational, physical and cognitive differences between Evaristo and Sandro, but there is also an immense epistemological gap. Whereas Sandro is at ease with his gayness, from the very beginning of this film, Evaristo is merely pretending to be gay, using the young employee as his "homosexual alibi," and it takes him a long time to come to terms with his romantic and sexual attraction to the boy that he torments.

Sandro apparently manages to traverse the power relations between him and Evaristo – the boss and the employee, the straight and the gay, the authentic and the fraud, the worldly known persona and the junior assistant – when he orders him to get on his knees and beg for Sandro's assistance in creating a new artistic installation. Their power relations are resettled, however, when Evaristo refuses Sandro's kisses, beating him and crying: "Faggot! Queer! Fancy! You faggot!" After bashing his gay lover, the fashion designer immediately apologizes and whispers: "I'm bipolar!" In the realm of Evaristo's bipolarity, his macho brutality and his gay tenderness negotiate, mediate, struggle, construct, deconstruct, masquerade and authenticate each other.

These opposites, however, become symbiotic and perilously interwoven. Evaristo's conspicuous emotional and behavioral instability, beyond its comic aspects, reveals the complex psychology of each one of these partners and their dynamic interrelations. The tension between Sandro's authentic gayness and Evaristo's fabricated homosexuality is interwoven here with a tension between Evaristo's masquerade and the truth he discovers about himself through his pretending-to-be-gay *and* the tension between Evaristo's machismo and spectacular flamboyancy, or non-homosexual faggotry (a compulsive womanizer who is a flaming drama queen). These interrelated tensions yield a grotesque carnival of theatrical authenticities, melodramatic sincerities, inconsistent masculinities and queer eccentricities.

The fabricator's heart belongs to fabric in a queer fashion

The somewhat surrealistic plotline of *Macho* posits Sandro as the saver of the fashion designer who is almost kidnapped by a gang of men in black. The gentle, angelic boy suddenly turns into a brave warrior who uses a submachine gun like he was a queer Rambo. After a series of quarrels between these men, the fashion designer confesses: "I'm not gay. I don't have the gay gene. It's nothing personal. I've been using you all this time and I owe you a sincere apology." Evaristo's dichotomous essentialism is immediately challenged, however, by Sandro, who reminds him that last night they made love three times. When Evaristo insists that it's impossible, Sandro insists: "Three times, asshole! Three times is possible when there is love!" A soft melody accompanies Sandro's tears and Evaristo's persistent denial of his same-sex attraction: "Today I like bananas, tomorrow I love papayas... Last night you were as gay as it gets." In refusing to acknowledge his queerness, Evaristo primarily reconstitutes his coldhearted machismo, telling his younger lover: "Stop crying! You're crying like a girl. You're crying rivers of tears."

Paradoxically, Evaristo admits his queerness only when his deception is mocked by the press. A headline in a gossip magazine determines "Evaristo Isn't Gay!" and illustrates this exposure by a series of photos of the fashion designer's sexual encounter with Vivi, the top female model. Consequently, Evaristo is criticized by the magazine as "a disgrace to all straight and gay people." He is condemned as a pretender who relentlessly exploits both men and women, gays and straights, for his own benefit, "an impostor, psychopath, and *closet heterosexual*." Consequently, the LGBT community attacks and burns down his stores, and, paradoxically, scorns him: "Faggot!"

Evaristo finds refuge in his mother's home, where they are watching family films together and the fashion designer's mother analyzes his queerness: "You got stuck in the anal stage because of too much pleasure. You spent hours in your potty, dressing and undressing dolls. Just like you do now." Yet the parent does not show her unconditional love to her queer son, but reconfirms her son's *heterosexual* effeminacy. Evaristo confesses: "I wanted to give my heart to fabric, beads, flounces. Since I was a little boy, people said I was gay." His mother rebukes him: "You took advantage of the privileges of looking gay and fluttered around... Everything was going well until you fell in love with Sidney." The son initially refuses to realize that his mother knows him better than he knows himself, and he denies his infatuation with Sandro. Yet he asks his mother if he can live with her, demonstrating another homophobic stereotype about (closeted) gay men and their quasi incestuous, oedipal relationships with their powerful mothers.[95]

Nevertheless, Evaristo is gradually liberated from his own theatrical, golden cage of his public image as an extravagant persona and from his eccentric narcissism and pathetic festivity. His pretending-to-be-gay anticipates his emancipatory journey to authentic selfhood and manhood, toward a better understanding of his strengths and weaknesses. Through his romantic relationship with Sandro, Evaristo gradually grasps a new kind of sincerity while the fashion world is criticized in this film as a kingdom of mockery and deception. The emotional climax of this film is in Evaristo's grand fashion show. Evaristo's wicked competitor, Vladimir, deceives the audience against his rival: "That's a set up! It's a lie! Don't applaud a phony!" Paradoxically, in this flamboyant topsy-turvy fashion world, Evaristo's gayness is a shield, and when it is undermined, the fashion designer is undefended. At the end of the show, however, Evaristo goes on stage in an eccentric outfit, holding hands with Sandro. Eventually, reluctant Sandro merges with the "new" Evaristo.

Unexpectedly, however, the happy ending of *Macho* is not this unification of the two men but a polyamorous wedding ceremony in which Evaristo, Sandro *and* Vivian are announced "husband, husband, and wife." Queerly, this ending proves that Evaristo *is* queer, although he is *not* gay but probably bisexual. In gay eyes, however, this populist closure primarily aims to satisfy the straight majority by refuting the possibility that Evaristo is exclusively gay, on one hand, and pleasing the gay viewers by assuring them that the same-sex romance *is* fulfilled, on the other hand. By embracing the macho's bisexuality, though, this populistic ending stimulates a wider array of hetero-, homo- and bisexual identifications, thus appealing to a greater variety of audiences and, in a way, avoiding a classification of *Macho* as a "gay film." The politics of transgression in *Macho* is substantially designed and restricted by its commercial heteronormative framework. This film's apparently free-spirited parody of masculinities, and particularly machismo, shows its own limits.

Toward effeminate authenticity

Although all these films are targeted at mainstream audiences, and definitely do not reflect a transgressive, radical queer politics, they do uncover some authenticities. If to be authentic is to know oneself and act accordingly, the discussed films' sort of reversal epistemology comprises a dramatic revelation of hidden effeminate liberties. In this manner, the effeminate masks provide a pleasurable experimentation of the theatricality of machismo *and* effeminacy. These phenomena are based on powerful systems of signs that are not always rivalrous and contradicted but sometimes can be liquidized and hybridized as *Macho* proves.

In focusing on the possibility of crossing the boundaries between sexualities, masculinities, visibilities and normalcies, these films concomitantly reproduce heteronormative dichotomies and theatrically subvert them.

Although these films are primarily set to please their mostly straight clientele, they inadvertently explore the joys of effeminacy redundancy. While the effeminacy in these films is conventionally staged in a heteronormative manner, the sissified protagonists occasionally enjoy the disruptive pleasures of sassiness as nonconforming masculinity *and* femininity, experiencing an unfamiliar freedom of effeminate speech and unruly performativity that evade heterocentric frameworks. Although the discussed films typically, and problematically, caricaturize campiness and male festivity, they comprise multiple scenes of joyful musical numbers, spectacular outfits, outstanding choreographies, and comic dialogs and situations of spectacular effeminacies. These films, with their diverse heteronormative attitudes, are haunted by male flamboyancy and its undisciplined perilous pleasures.

Notes

1 Simpson 2001: ix.
2 Sedgwick 1994: 160–161.
3 Plummer 2003: 313.
4 Tawaditep 2002: 6 (emphasis added).
5 Dyer 1977.
6 Padva 2014.
7 Padva 2014.
8 Tannen 1990.
9 Hamdan 2011: 61.
10 Tannen 1993.
11 Coates 1993.
12 Dyer 1993.
13 Dyer 1993.
14 Russo 1987 (1981).
15 Dyer 1977: 300.
16 Hennen 2008.
17 Sinfield 1994.
18 *Oxford Dictionary* 1996: 206.
19 Sontag 1999 (1964): 56.
20 Babuscio 1999 (1978): 117–118.
21 Harris 1997.
22 Butler 1993.
23 *The Gay Deceivers* 1969.
24 Russo 1987 (1981): 186.
25 Russo 1987 (1981): 186.
26 *Victor Victoria* 1982.
27 Rubinfeld 2001.
28 Rubinfeld 2001: 4.
29 Nolletti 1982.
30 Nolletti 1982: 49.
31 Nolletti 1982: 50.
32 Nolletti 1982: 50.
33 Ross 1999 (1988): 325.
34 In queer eyes, however, this scene misrecognizes the political subversion of camp subculture. In turning the campy into ridicule, this scene fails to acknowledge – and certainly to celebrate – camp's gay sensitivity, or what Ross defines as "the

other side of camp" which is characterized by creamy wit, wicked fantasies and *gaité de coer*, the heart's cheerfulness *and* gayness, "all that was, and still is, priceless" (Ross 1999 [1988]: 327).

35 *Connie and Carla* 2004.
36 This situation is also the one that motivated Jack Lemon and Tony Curtis' pretending to be the straight women Daphne and Josephine in Billy Wilder's classic 1959 comedy *Some Like It Hot*.
37 In contrast, Victoria and Toddy perform their variety show in mostly *straight* night clubs.
38 Gamman and Makinen 1994: 70.
39 Gamman and Makinen 1994: 70–71.
40 Riviere 1929.
41 Butler 1990: 33.
42 Butler 1990: 315.
43 Morris and Sloop 2006: 2.
44 Morris and Sloop 2006: 2.
45 "South Park Is Gay!" (7th season, 8th episode of *South Park*): 2003.
46 *Queer Eye for the Straight Guy*: 2003–2007.
47 *Boy Meets Boy* 2003.
48 *Will & Grace* 1998–2006; 2017–present.
49 *Love Boat* 1977–1986; 1990.
50 *Little Britain* 2003–2006.
51 Sinfield 1994: 2.
52 Holbrook Jackson, cited in Beckson 1970: 331.
53 Sinfield 1994: 2.
54 Sinfield 1994: 45.
55 Sinfield 1994: 46.
56 Hayes 2003.
57 Hayes 2003.
58 Hayes 2003.
59 Gross 1988: 194.
60 "Homer's Phobia" (8th season, 15th episode of *The Simpsons*): 1997.
61 *Mondo Trasho* 1969.
62 *Pink Flamingos* 1972.
63 *Polyester* 1981.
64 *Hairspray* 1988.
65 See Padva 2008.
66 "I Love the Nightlife" 1978.
67 "Shoop Shoop Song (It's In His Kiss)" 1990.
68 "Gonna Make You Sweat (Everybody Dance Now)" 1990.
69 *The Ritz* 1976.
70 *Happy, Texas* 1999.
71 *Kicking Out Shoshana* 2014.
72 This scene vaguely echoes the beginning of the film *The Raging Bull*, in which a slow-motioned boxing scene is poetically transformed into a ballet dancing.
73 Notably, the imaginary team Jerusalem Sons is loosely based on one of Israel's most successful albeit controversial soccer clubs, Beitar Jerusalem, whose fans are (stereo)typically depicted by the Israeli media as fanatic, racist, Islamophobic, homophobic, chauvinist, nationalist, traditional low-life Israelis of Jewish oriental origins who are devoted to Benjamin Netanyahu's nationalist Likkud party. Some of these fans are extremists who were involved with particularly violent acts of the racist organization "La Familia." Eight members of "La Familia" were jailed in 2018.
74 *The Ladies' Hairdresser* 1984.

75 Padva and Talmon 2001.
76 The law was rescinded by the Israeli Knesset in 1988.
77 For example, Shushan, who is horrified by the gangster's ultimatum, tells his agent that he's going to lose his career and move to another team, "Jerusalem Tigresses" of the women's league, "And even there I'm going to be the only one who is not attracted to women. 'Not attracted to girls'... I start speaking like a fag." Later, a TV sport analyst criticizes Shushan's coming-out and recalls another coming out of a soccerer, "a goalkeeper in the Japanese league who, right after his coming-out, performed hara-kiri on live TV."
78 Wallace 1994.
79 Fortier 2002: 123.
80 Rich 1980.
81 Ward 2015: 27.
82 "Okh't'cha" is probably derived from the word "akhot," meaning "a sister."
83 Probably, these fans do not realize that "going west" means going westbound to gay San Francisco.
84 Sedgwick 1990.
85 *Macho* 2016.
86 The role is played by the angelic-faced, blue-eyed actor Renato López, who was murdered at the age of 33.
87 The collapse of the distinction between ruthless chauvinism and flaming campiness is graphically demonstrated when the logo of the film, *Macho*, first appears in blue letters that imitate a rough fabric, probably denim. Then the logo turns into a flowery logo in brown, orange, pink and red. In this way, the macho is colorfully subverted and symbolically effeminized.
88 "Macho Man" 1978.
89 Stephens 1990.
90 Stephens 1990: 55.
91 Stephens 1990: 57.
92 Rubinfeld 2001.
93 *Beauty and the Beast* 1946.
94 See Padva 2004.
95 This stigma is visually metaphorized by the body-colored labyrinth at his mother's house that comprises channels and corridors, and significantly resembles a giant womb.

2 Take it like a man

Cruising machismo in Leatherland

Both flamboyant effeminacy *and* ruthless machismo in pretending-to-be-gay films are grotesque theatricalities that ironize the dominant gendered observations of reality and expectations of others. Exaggerated flamboyancy *and* machismo are sorts of drag performances that playfully negotiate the sign of gender, a sign that is not the same as the body that it figures, but that cannot be read without it. The theatrical subordination to the gendered imperative can reveal the social status of the gendered norm itself. In Judith Butler's perspective, it can become the cultural sign by which that cultural imperative might become legible. Heterosexuality, in particular, can be said to operate through the regulated production of hyperbolic versions of "man" and "woman," and these are for the most part compulsory performances, ones that none of us choose but that each of us is forced to negotiate.[1]

The hegemonic masculinity, in particular, by defensively separating butch men into "gay" (drag) and "straight" (real), perceived the macho ideal as an object not only of gay desire but also of gay identification. And once straight men suspect that their own masculinity is an act, this problematizes the authenticity of their own image as "real men looking like real men," leading perhaps to the realization that no man can be "real."[2] Indeed, the vociferous machismo in pretending-to-be-gay films like *Macho*[3] is shown as a grotesque spectacle, ostentatious mask, lively masquerade and showy charade. The protagonist Evaristo's masculinity, a grotesque amalgamation of sassy machismo and flamboyant effeminacy, is merely an act, certainly not an authenticity.

Yet machismo is not always amusing like the fashion designer's mannerisms in *Macho*. In certain cases, machismo can also be a lethal masquerade, even a murderous camouflage. As William Friedkin's controversial Hollywood thriller *Cruising*[4] shows, the mainstream is acutely sensitive to subcultural codes, and the signs of an underground scene very quickly become exposed and exploitatively exoticized and sensationalized. *Cruising* dredged up from the underground the sadomasochist demimonde of a gay leather scene that had not been seen in mainstream cinema before.

This film centers on a pretender who is an undercover straight policeman in New York who tries to track down a serial killer in gay leather bars.

The young officer, Steve Burns (Al Pacino), goes undercover and tries to attract the murderer. He pretends to be Tom Ford, a gay resident in the Greenwich Village. He begins to integrate himself into New York's leather bars, while the murderer continues to pick up his victims in cruising areas of Central Park and the West Village sex clubs. Steve oscillates between his gay masquerade and his private straight life. He frequently visits gay clubs, in which he witnesses numerous men engaging in oral and anal intercourse and brutal sadomasochistic sex acts.

The undercover policeman often admits that his gay masquerade affects him, however, and whenever he needs to revalidate his straightness, he passionately makes love to his devoted girlfriend Nancy (Karen Allen). Despite his requests, his bosses refuse to let him resign from the case. Steve becomes more tense and puzzled until he physically attacks his gay neighbor Gregory (James Remar), which in a way implies that the undercover policeman might be jealous of him because of his romantic relationship with Steve's friend Ted Bailey (Don Scardino). The police mistakenly blame a violent gay guy, Stuart Richards (Richard Cox), for being the serial killer, while the real killer continues to murder gay men. In the last part of the film, a man who looks like the killer from behind walks into a gay sex club. Steve shaves at Nancy's apartment with a mixture of shaving cream and blood, while his girlfriend tries on the policeman's sunglasses and his leather outfit. The final scene replicates the first scene of the film in which a tugboat moves across the Hudson River.

This film presents the hypermasculine performance of gay sadomasochist practitioners in a way that connotes gayness with ruthless machismo, perverted brutality, monstrous sadism, delirious masochism and uninhibited phallic instincts. *Cruising*'s deployment of such blatant signifiers of masculinity, however, produces an intricate and contradicted "drag macho," who is theatrically demonized and demonically theatricalized. Significantly, this film notoriously introduces mainstream audiences to gayness as a horrendous lifestyle that significantly disturbs their comfortable heterosexual lives. *Cruising* makes gayness a spectacular nightmare.[5]

Cruising introduced mainstream audiences to gayness as an aberrant lifestyle that in no way could be tolerated or respected by the straight majority. This film sensationally reinscribes a perverting pedagogy that includes merciless stereotyping, homophobia and pathologization of homosexuality. This film markets otherness for its intimidating exoticism and it misrepresents queerness as one of the biggest and most terrifying threats to American Christian values. *Cruising*, in its heterosexist manner, essentializes "authentic" gayness, and it recovers the power of patriarchy from the threats of post-Stonewall gay rights movements.

Consequently, the New York ghetto community was effectively polarized by this film. Both extras and protesters claimed greater numbers, and accusations were flung between the groups throughout the location while filming.[6] The film's producers issued a cattle-call to local leathermen willing to play themselves as extras in the film, and many were happy to turn up and shake their money-makers for the cameras. From the perspective of some of those men, who often proclaimed themselves "Proud to be Hot Sex Pigs!" there was no reason not to let the rest of the nation rubberneck over the door of the sty.[7]

The *Village Voice* columnist Arthur Bell, however, led an attack on this defamatory film. Twenty thousand pamphlets were distributed, branding the movie "a rip-off" – *Cruising* used numerous gay locations and extras, including gay centerfolds as nude murder victims. "This is not a film about how we live," said the literature. "It is a film about why we should be killed." At Bell's urging, committees formed and the production was widely picketed, causing expensive delays and debate over Hollywood's social responsibility. "The *Cruising* problem," wrote Bell, has united all gay factions for the first time since the [Anita] Bryant campaign. What's different is that this time homosexuals are taking the aggressive role. Instead of "poor us," it's "poor them" (cited in Hadleigh 2001 [1993], p. 89). Arthur Bell added: "If the First Amendment applied to me, I'd be willing to give it to others, but we don't have any civil rights in this country."[8] Bell stressed that *Cruising* would be the "most oppressive, ugly, bigoted look at homosexuality ever presented on the screen."[9]

Not unlike the anti-Briggs action, the organized protests against *Cruising* revealed a progressive and militant strategy of confronting bigotry.[10] On the evening of July 26, 1979, over 8,000 people gathered in Sheridan Square, Greenwich Village, to protest the film. Charles Brydon, Co-Executive Director of the National Gay Task Force, was booed off the speaker's platform when he "deplored violence" as a tactic for stopping the film. In the march that followed, the "non-violent" marshals sought to mediate between cops and crowd, and, arguably, in so doing not only threatened to defuse the anger of the marchers but led them into situations in which they were surrounded by club-wielding cops and were unable to defend themselves. The marshals were later accused of taking directions from the cops in the ensuing riot.[11] During the week that followed, however, the riots continued throughout the village: Windows were smashed, cars overturned, technical equipment on Friedkin's set damaged.

Subsequently, *Cruising* carried a controversial disclaimer at its beginning: "This film is not intended as an indictment of the homosexual world. It is set in one small segment of that world, which is not meant to be representative of the whole."[12] A few decades after the film was released, however, Friedkin admits that the disclaimer is ludicrous. He contends that "that disclaimer was put there by the studio because they panicked. I knew it was a foolish response."[13]

Cruising the controversy

Over the four decades since the release of *Cruising*, this film has been critically condemned. Shortly after it was released, *The New York Times* critic

Vincent Canby defined it as "a homosexual horror film."[14] Vito Russo argues, "The monster in Friedkin's horror film is homosexuality itself. Everything accompanying the homosexual scenes is loud, intimidating rock, while the score when Pacino is with his girlfriend is a Boccherini violin suite."[15] Russo explains that the fact that Burns' girlfriend ends up in the last shot trying on his leather gear "says that this lifestyle is seductive and contagious, threatening to what's good in the world."[16] In the same spirit, Simon Watney suggests that Burns is sent out into this "gay world" in much the same way that the US marines are sent out to face the aliens at the end of *Close Encounters of the Third Kind*.[17]

Raymond Murray considers *Cruising* to be the most notorious film from the late 1970s–early 1980s' assault of Hollywood-inflamed homophobia. Yet he agrees that "the film is now part of queer film history and a testament to how a frightened Hollywood treated a disenfranchised minority."[18] Kylo-Patrick R. Hart criticizes *Cruising* for "simultaneously communicating the outdated notion that gay men are psychologically ill individuals, reinforcing historically influential perceptions of homosexuality as an illness, a pathologized way of being."[19] Hart notes that *Cruising* features the typical gay man who lives an extreme, wild and out-of-control lifestyle. Further, it includes sexually charged images involving poppers, fisting and sadomasochistic activity, and recurring shots of horny gay men hanging out in packs, just waiting to engage in presumably anonymous sex in back alleys or bushes with other passersby.[20]

Yet not all critics agree about the defamatory qualities of *Cruising*. In retrospect, this film is frequently advocated and embraced as a daring cult film that provides a nonconventional, even campy and theatrical interpretation of queerness, performativity and countercultural masculinities. *Cruising* has been recuperated in the late 1990s and early 2000s for cultdom, mainly by a younger gay audience, for which the film's allegedly lurid depiction of Manhattan's gay sadomasochist underworld is a compelling and historically valuable envisioning of the libidinal intensities of the 1970s New York leather scene that is scarcely available elsewhere on celluloid.[21]

Mark Kermode, for example, notes that "*Cruising* broke all the existing taboos of mainstream cinematic sex with its frank, tactile portrait of an exotic, erotic underworld" and reconsiders this film as "some kind of dark triumph" praised for "its bold depiction of a world unseen elsewhere in modern cinema."[22] Paul Burston argues that *Cruising* is not really a film "about homosexuality" at all, any more than *Halloween*[23] is a film "about heterosexuality."[24] He explains that "in both films the killer is driven by a mixture of sexual revulsion and the need literally to kill his own desire."[25] Burston stresses: "I simply think its reputation as one of the most homophobic films ever to come out of Hollywood is undeserved. And yes, I do get a kick out of it."[26]

Thomas D. Clagett compliments *Cruising* for a certain kind of authenticity, asserting that "the reality that the sex-filled bar scenes were shot using actual patrons (approximately 1,600 of them, who were paid as extras) offers a refreshing neorealist documentary-style touch."[27] Steven Paul Davies also praises *Cruising* and suggests that, a few decades after its original release, *Cruising* has transformed from a political issue into an intriguing cultural document that can be seen as "a glimpse of a pre-AIDS gay subculture" and as "an opportunity to see Al Pacino's naked butt on screen," and even "can be viewed as a piece of filmmaking, one of the most original thrillers of the 1980s."[28] Davies admits that *Cruising* is a lurid, twisted film, yet he considers it as a film that draws the viewers into its world and completely works them over.[29] Watney, in his reevaluation of *Cruising*, perceives the leather subculture shown in this film as both a response to the historical association of homosexuality with "effeminacy" and a subversion of the original connotations of the style which it takes over, "on approval" as it were, from the world of heterosexual masculinity.[30]

Yet, as Alexander Wilson points out, the victims in the film are all gay. They all cruise for casual sex. The one murderer we're sure of is also gay. Rather a "deranged" gay, according to the film's clichéd psychologizing: He grew up deprived of his father's love and respect, and is infertile.[31] Wilson contends that the presentation of the killer's character is so incoherent, however, that an analysis of his place in the film is difficult. Friedkin has further complicated the matter by claiming that neither the known killer nor Burns (the other likely killer) is gay.[32] Wilson explicates that this sexual and psychological ambiguity would be a healthy one if it was developed further and if, indeed, it was extended to the gay characters themselves.[33]

But it is precisely here, with the overtly gay characters, that the overall structure of *Cruising* becomes for a moment visible. All of the gay relations in the film (most of which have something to do with sadomasochism) are violent, and at least one of the locations Friedkin uses for general *Cruising* scenes as well as a murder (The Rambles in Central Park) has in recent years increasingly been the scene of brutal attacks on gay men by straight men. I agree with Wilson that the one thing that does seem clear about all of this is that Friedkin is confused about the links between sadomasochism, violence, promiscuity and homosexuality. "Simply put, his perspective is that of the *voyeur*."[34]

A voyeuristic disguise and a voracious gaze of cannibalistic culture industry

The voyeur's voracious eyes passionately consume the gay sadomasochist subculture, hopelessly attracted and disgusted by its perilous pleasures. Friedkin's insatiable appetite for the sadomasochistic gay cabinets of curiosities demonstrates the mainstream media's *cannibalization of subcultures*, a structural feature of the culture industry. Chuck Kleinhans contends that the culture industry is populated by people who are dominantly petty bourgeois professionals whose very occupation implies a distance from and an irony toward the personalities, programs and products they produce – a true dissociation of sensibility. "Unable to believe in what they make, to have a naïve acceptance of it, mass-culture makers are often drawn to subcultures precisely for the difference, their newness, their not-as-yet-commercialized qualities," Kleinhans argues. "All of which, not so incidentally, can be turned back into one's work; a weekend in the subculture inspires Monday morning's new ad campaign."[35]

An irresistible curiosity impels Steve Burns as he is increasingly attracted to the sadomasochistic scene's repulsive and shocking theatricality, in his heteronormative eyes, until he feels that he is not in control of his own actions. Rather, he feels forebodings of evil, haunted by an uncontrollable desire to penetrate the secrets so jealously guarded by this subaltern subculture. His discovery of a predatory sadomasochistic subculture is prompted by a curiosity he cannot repress. *Cruising* describes the policeman's curiosity as something alien to himself, an uncontrollable desire which is much like an "invisible power" that impels him. This double bind of attraction and repulsion almost paralyzes him during the devastating investigation of the promiscuous dungeons. These venues provoke the policeman's horror and forbidden attraction. He is properly horrified by these places. He feels a terrible revulsion, yet he is mysteriously alive to a dreadful feeling. He can hardly bring himself to leave.

One of the most intriguing images in Burns' visits to the promiscuous gay sadomasochistic venues is the gimp mask, a controversial part of leather subcultures that is used in *Cruising* for enhancement of horror and disgust. The gimp, arguably the most intimidating part of straight and gay sadomasochistic outfits, is a leather or rubber mask that covers the face of a submissive person.[36] The gimp mask is expressly connotative of extreme bondage, suffering, torment and sexual slavery, deprivation and debasement – even terrorists and serial killers are invoked by the gimp mask.[37]

Cruising's emotional double bind – of horror and fascination, of attraction and revulsion, of delicious shudders – unmasks "homosexual panic," a term that Eve Kosofsky Sedgwick borrows from the Freudian terminology. According to Sedgwick, homophobia is not just hatred directed toward gay men. Systematic fear and distrust of male-male intimacy in Western Europe predate the identification of the homosexual as a deviant "species" by more than a century.[38] Homophobia, according to Sedgwick, is social blackmail. It is an ideology that controls affections and relations between men – of any orientation – by obliging them to eternal vigilance lest they be labeled effeminate, inverted or (later) gay. Homosexual panic is "the most private, psychologized form" of this blackmail.[39] When a man becomes aware, however liminally, of attraction to another man, he resorts to paranoia. It is a desperate defense. The attraction becomes revulsion, horror and even violence.[40]

Metaphorically, *Cruising* is even cannibalistic in its compulsive consuming of gay men who are serially killed, actually scarified for satisfying the straight viewers who eagerly explore *Cruising*'s Leatherland. What is

disturbing about gay sadomasochistic practitioners in *Cruising* is not a matter of reason, but a matter of feeling. Once revulsion at the particular act
of same-sex anal intercourse is overcome, it is screened as a different, and
no worse, social organization of an eroticized powerful violence. Similarly,
once revulsion at the particular act of homosexuality is transcended, or
at least compromised, it can be seen by the straight mind as an alluringly
exotic structure of affection. The sticky bit is always the peculiar act. This
leads to a provisional explanation for the congruence of symbolic cannibal
voyeurism and sensational mediation of homosexuality.

The peculiar act of voracious consumption of a subaltern community by
the overwhelmed heteronormative gaze merges in *Cruising* with multiple
spectacles of voluptuous consumption of male bodies. Both acts offer the
straight policeman *and* his straight viewers' ecstatic unions; they offer to
relieve the self of the burden of selfhood; they offer a chance to surrender
the lustful male body, to consume or be consumed by it. The policeman,
a solitary and self-reliant straight man of the late 1970s New York, desperately yearns to lose his self. Playing intimacy with another man would
threaten this policeman with collapsed boundaries between play and real,
resulting in mutilation or killing. It would compromise both his cognitive
and bodily integrity. He would not be his own man. He would no longer
be free. He would be emasculated, and he would therefore no longer be fit
for the role of a sovereign straight man who is socially, heteronormatively
expected to police the city, his desire and straight viewers' polymorphous
lustfulness.

Cruising's symbolic cannibalism and its ecstatic consumption of spectacular homosexual acts violate the distinctions between identity and desire.
In particular, Burns' fear is that the sadomasochistic gay patrons mean to
consume him from behind. But it is strange that he never considers the alternative: Maybe he is anxiously devoted to the idea of being penetrated by
another man. Devotion, in this case, can be as possessive and as irrational
as avoiding it.

The policeman's impatience and wistfulness also suggest that he takes
erotic pleasure in the murderous sadomasochistic underworld. Before he
goes to the subcultural venues he is carefully dressing up, meticulously wearing the sadomasochistic gay subculture's accoutrements and regalia. His
somewhat neurotically meticulous preparation is an intimidating version
of a lover's disrobing. It draws morbid attention to Burns' attractive young
male body, and to the deceiver's preparation for stimulating interaction
with the licentious men. The atmosphere at the perilous clubs is exciting and
mysterious. The pleasure is too important to be surrendered or repressed.

Burns – serving as an agent of the viewers' straight eyes that colonialisti-
cally explore these unknown nativities – becomes a somewhat too refined
connoisseur to allow this intermingling to be evaded. In *Cruising*'s sensational perspective, the eager explorer finds an (un)expected fetishistic pleasure in the filth he finds. Indeed, Burns is afraid of consuming other men's

bodies, as much as he's afraid of being consumed by the perverted men. These dangers, however, could also be seen as a kind of affection, but not a personal, one-on-one affection: Here, man-on-man (anal) action threatens Burns with the affection of the group or community. The stimulating same-sex debauchery threatens to consume Burns by inviting him to join the all-male ecstasy that would be voluptuously corrupt and gay. In his eyes, by immersing his body in perilous pleasures, he would join in the ferocious love that unites the people in these exoticized, demonized and estranged clubs.

Undisguised demonization of gay sadomasochistic pleasures

In a significant scene, the detectives secretly listen to a sexual encounter between Burns and Skip and realize that Skip is about to tie up their colleague. They dramatically break into the room and untie Steve's hands while he lies naked on the bed, exposing his shapely smooth buttocks. Steve, who doesn't look upset by the sadomasochistic ritual, is angry at his counterparts who invaded the room at the wrong moment. Steve's reaction indicates that he is more than disappointed that the cops disrupted his intimacy with Skip. His anger does not necessarily derive from the policemen's breaking in before he could prove that Skip is the serial killer. Rather, he seems upset because he *liked* what he did with Skip.

In *Cruising*'s heteronormative eyes, to get from "heteronormative inquiry of the sodomites" to "sodomy" itself, you have to cross several lines. You cross from legitimate to perverted. You cross from spirit to body. You cross from civilization to barbarity. And you cross from policing observation to licentious participation. In *Cruising*'s voracious eyes, the act of sodomy implies coercion and submission; it is alluringly and dauntingly uncivilized. Notably, the word "homosexuality" means different things to *Cruising* and to most gay men. *Cruising* twistedly refers to the gay sadomasochistic sub-culture as ruthless brutality, communal bullying and violent sexual practice. *Cruising* powerfully mediates a defamatory generalization about gay lifestyle.

In *Cruising*'s dark world of sadomasochistic venues, physical intimacy between men is inextricable from power. It almost always implies a loss of control over the body and consequent compromise of the self and a disintegration of autonomous identity. In *Cruising*'s eyes, even when a gay sadomasochistic practitioner takes care of his partner's pleasures and his corporeal needs, by virtue of that, he controls him. *Cruising* reads the homosexual through a cannibalistic exoticization of the gay sadomasochistic scene. The nightmarish portrayal of this subculture in *Cruising* enthusiastically favors the spectacular over the natural, real, true, reliable or sincere.

Daniel Harris insists that for most homosexuals, sadomasochism has never been the psychological fetish of the lone pervert guiltily salivating over whips and groveling on the cold dungeon floor while eagerly awaiting the crack of his master's riding crop or the stomp of his hobnailed boot.

Instead, in the case of the vast majority of homosexuals who engage in sado-masochistic sex, "leather is a *social* fetish, an 'acquired' or 'learned' fetish that has little to do with an inherently kinky predisposition for alternative erotic practices."[41] Harris suggests that while the leather fetish helped some homosexuals solve the problem of effeminacy, it nevertheless unleashed a wave of criticism from both the psychiatric establishment and from members of mainstream America who interpreted sadomasochism as further evidence of the homosexual's innate perversion. Harris notes that in an effort to achieve a new kind of legitimacy as a macho clan of menacing hoodlums, gay men only succeeded in reinforcing the prevailing belief in the homosexual's unsavory status as "an unbalanced psychopath who slaked his bloodlust on innocent victims while prowling through a seamy underworld of rapists and child molesters."[42]

In contrast to the prevalent fear of the stigmatizing power of the gay sadomasochistic subculture, however, Michel Foucault praises BDSM (bondage, discipline and sadomasochism) as a practice that allows participants to "take control of the erotic charge factored into domination and subordination," thus "turn[ing] those binary power differences against themselves"[43] even when the roles taken within BDSM appear gender normative (i.e. man as dominant and woman as submissive).[44] Whereas some practitioners identify with particular BDSM role identities and engage in certain dominant/submissive activities more frequently than others, a significant portion of the participants celebrate BDSM role fluidity, willing to change roles based on partner characteristics.[45] Such a dynamic, anti-essentialist approach celebrates the creative theatricality of sadomasochism and subverts this subculture's predatory image.

Yet *Cruising* explicitly adopts a demonizing approach against gay male sadomasochism in portraying this subculture as a bacchanalia of unbearable cruelty, brutal promiscuity and murderous perversity. Even when this film implies that the undercover policeman Burns might be gay, it does not regard this possibility as a daring experimentation and exploration of his sexual authenticity. Rather, *Cruising* posits him as a straight man crossing the line between blissful normativity and abhorrent perversity.

Disguising sexual authenticities and subversions

Burns' on- and off-duty same-sex sadomasochistic playing does not necessarily generate a sense of self-renewal with cathartic qualities. Even if Burns does experience intense sensation and psychological and emotional stimulations, at times, *Cruising* does not perceive this straight policeman's gratifications as emancipatory delights but rather condemns them as risky perversions of his straight masculinity. Burns apparently loses control and becomes a part of the hopelessly distorted community that he investigates. According to these homophobic logics of *Cruising*, the protagonist's perilous gay masquerade possibly corrupts his heterosexual soul and pollutes his heteronormative authenticity *and* morality. In this way, however, *Cruising* not only warns its straight viewers to stay away from voracious gay subcultures. It also admits the irresistibly enticing appeal of playing homosexuality, sadomasochism and ultravirility in steaming all-male venues, bedrooms and cruising grounds.

In the book that *Cruising* is based on, the killer never has sex with his victims. In contrast, the film claims that while the victims show evidence of anal intercourse, with traces of "seminal fluid," there was no actual sperm to be found. Watney notes that in this way another ideological slippage concerning homosexuality is constructed, between repression and violence on the one hand, and between physical disorder and psychopathy on the other.[46] Watney suggests that not surprisingly *Cruising* relies heavily on the contagion theory of homosexuality, for Burns is revealed, in a highly scissored and ambiguous denouement, to have been taken over by the by-now dead killer's personality, or "instinct" or sexuality, or whatever, having slaughtered the only gay man with whom he had hitherto enjoyed any kind of pleasurable social relationship. "The negative implications here for what homosexuality 'does' to a man are legion," he adds, "especially since it is stressed that this last victim, unlike the others, contained (horror of horrors!) sperm."[47]

D. A. Miller states that Steve's Dream of the Fist, in particular, replicates the film's own expedient fantasy, already in place, of an unidentified Homo Killer, a gay who murders gays in the very impetus of gay desire.[48] Conspicuously, in this fantasy there is no gay sex unaccompanied by gay violence, as its intrinsic punitive counteraction: "No butt-fucking without back-stabbing, no blow job without spurts of blood in place of cum; no polymorphous perversity without the body literally in pieces and floating in the Hudson."[49]

However, Davies suggests that *Cruising* is a unique thriller in that the main source of interest isn't in the cop-and-killer angle, however, but in the hero's psychological state. Burns is himself sexually frustrated, perhaps even more so than the killer he is chasing.[50] Notably, he uses his girlfriend Nancy as little more than relief. After a night undercover in the gay district he returns to her for a night of hard sex and angrily warns her, "Don't let me lose you." These words open up the possibility that Burns was gay, possibly even the killer. Boze Hadleigh agrees that Burns uses Nancy as little more than relief from his frustration.[51] Hadleigh assumes that Burns is impotent, or requires heavy stimulation. The murderer – whose semen contains no sperm – is likewise sexually frustrated. Hadleigh contends that as a sexually explicit film, *Cruising* is really about emotional repression and perversion. After the first atrocious mutilation-murder, the villain childishly murmurs, "You made me do it." In fact, he murders out of personality-driven and societally nurtured hatred.[52]

Whether Burns is impotent or not, Nancy plays a significant phallic role in her notorious pretending-to-be-a-gay leatherman – possibly the "gay"

serial killer – near the end of the film. At the beginning of Nancy's masquerade, Steve shaves in the bathroom while his girlfriend looks with great
interest at a leather biker cap decorated by a sort of quasi-Nazi silver hawk.
The young woman puts on the sunglasses and wears the leather hat. There is
a cut to Burns finishing shaving; he nicks himself with the razor and flinches.
Cheerful, playful music sounds as the woman wears the leather jacket that
hides the upper part of her white dress. This scene ends with a close-up of
Steve's face gazing into the camera, a shot that possibly indicates his fear
that Nancy the straight woman might be the serial "gay" male killer.

The close-up of Burns' face dissolves to a shot of a river trawler crossing
the screen, recalling the discovery of the arm in the opening scene. Davidson
suggests that with this edit, *Cruising* concludes that there *is* a possibility that
Burns has become "infected" with both homosexual desire and a desire to
kill through his interactions with the gay world – the aspect of the film that
most outraged the anti-*Cruising* activists.[53] Davidson stresses that Nancy's
dressing herself in the outfit and watching herself in the mirror might also be
read as an indication that identity in postmodernity is premised on simula-
tive processes, as well as that "identity under this cultural regime is provisional and fluid."[54]

Whether *Cruising* highlights the indeterminacy and invisibility of sexual identity, or rather emphasizes a dichotomous sexual regime, this film
claims that not only sexual masquerade but also the "authentic" sexual
identity comprises perilous uncertainties about the totality and purity of
one's sexuality. In this respect, sexual identity is not rigidly determined but
rather dynamic, shaped and reshaped, designed and redesigned, under multiple, exuberant circumstances, pulses, drives, curiosities, experimentations,
potentialities, taboos and transgressions. Thus (homo)sexual masquerade is
never one-dimensional or strictly limited to external features and theatrical
mannerisms. Living a condition of straight skin, behind a gay mask, requires
constant reexamination of the borders between mainstream and countercultural domains. Pretense requires dynamic reevaluation of the power relations and the symbiosis between the visible and the obscured in order not to
be exposed. Such intimate reexamination and reevaluation, however, often
involves blurred boundaries between masquerade and authenticity, as well
as possible diffusion of the staged identity into one's reality.

Cruising the interrelations between disguise and disgust

The film *Cruising* can be easily regarded as a disgusting film, with its multiple unbearable sights: from atrocious killings to ostentatious spectacles
of helpless victims crying for help when the coldhearted murderer rapes
them and stabs their backs; from mutilated bodies and floating body parts
to bleeding beds, walls and floors; and *Cruising*'s notorious portrayal of
gay sadomasochist practitioners as animalistic, obsessive, repulsive and
possessed perverts who cannot change their deadly habits. The inevitable

consequence of the essentially horrendous gay sadomasochism, according to *Cruising*'s logic, is the serial killing of dozens of these sadomasochists by a mysterious murderer who merely radicalizes the inherent brutality of the hellish sexual practices.

After the first murder scene, for example, a police pathologist inspects the victim's body and detects that the anus was dilated at the time of death, in addition to slight rupture above the anus, indicating intercourse. When Burns enters such an aberrant demimonde, disguised as one of its compulsive creatures, he dives into this inferno, in order to provide the straight viewers some voyeuristic pleasures that combine exotic fascination with alluring disgust. The audience is assumed to be entertained by repulsion, to be vividly loathed, to be tremendously satisfied by multiple images of tortures and deaths, and to identify with the protagonist who is risking and scarifying himself, committed to uncovering a realm of incorrigibly disgusting sadomasochists.

Amos Zeichner and Dennis E. Reidy, in their research of prevalent homophobia, elaborate an evolutionary perspective that conceptualizes fear, anger and disgust as representing emotional defenses against risk, danger and morbidity.[55] Disgust, in particular, is explicated as a response to the perceived risk of contamination, and it might motivate protective defenses.[56] Hence, it would seem that an individual who espouses negative attitudes about homosexual behavior might not only respond with fear and anger to such acts, but might also experience other negative emotions such as disgust.[57] Zeichner and Reidy identified that feelings of anger and fear are coupled with low levels of disgust after homophobes are exposed to homoerotic material.[58]

Cruising, with its notorious abundance of homoerotic spectacles and sex scenes, including excerpts from a gay porn film that depict anal penetration, however, aims to provoke significant anger, fear *and* disgust among its straight clientele. The heteronormative spectators are expected to be repulsed by the specters of consensual anal and oral sex between men, not only by conspicuously brutal sadomasochistic scenes *and* sex crimes. Interestingly, *Cruising*, primarily made for straight eyes, paradoxically recognizes how alluring this disgust is. The particular sort of disgust manufactured by *Cruising* stimulates curiosity and delight among the straight voyeurs who are sensationally introduced to the apparently savage, uninhibited life of the gay sadomasochists in their horror cabinets of curiosities.

The straight establishment of brutal response to this phenomenon is powerfully manifested in an interrogation scene, in which the policemen brutalize the gay suspect Skip. They brutally hit him until he is bleeding, calling him "faggot" and "a lying son of a bitch" before ordering him to take his pants down and jerk off in order to get a sample of his sperm (the latter acts are not shown on screen). Friedkin makes sure that the audience will not identify with the interrogated gay man. He shows Skip at long distance, avoiding close-ups of the tortured man and his wounded face. In this way, the abusive behavior of the homophobes is legitimized. According to the heterocentric logic of this scene, the normal give the pervert what he deserves. The police brutality is perceived as cathartic and purifying, rather than disgusting. Even when the policemen realize that he's the wrong guy, they are not ashamed but only disappointed. Predominantly, beating the queer is represented in this film as an almost glorified act of fighting *disgust* in both its mild and extreme versions.

R. W. Connell explains that although not many men are able to embody hegemonic masculinity, all are positioned in relation to it, occupying less valued, culturally subordinated masculinities.[59] Gay masculinities are subordinated because same-sex sexual relations between men negate the hegemonic ideal of male domination over women, and because to derive sexual pleasure from another man is elided with femininity, the antithesis of hegemonic masculinity. The tortured queer in the interrogation scene seems to be weaker, gentler and more civilized and educated than his abusers, on one hand, but he is viciously portrayed as a sickening individual who is involved in aberrantly kinky, pitiless and often fatal sadomasochistic activities, on the other hand. Hence, the cops' brutality is affiliated by *Cruising* with heteronormative hegemony that aggressively, albeit blissfully, purifies a perverted sin city. At the same time, the gay sadomasochists' brutality depicted in this film is associated with a horrendously perverted cult that aggressively deteriorates the normal American society.

Burns, whose gay sadomasochistic masquerade leads him into a somewhat liminal position, tells Captain Edelson that the brutalized Skip is innocent:

> You worked him over like he shot the president or something. You destroyed that kid. You didn't even have a case against him... I didn't think anybody was gonna go that far with him... He didn't have a knife. I didn't come on this job to shitcan some guy just because he's gay, captain.

The officer's response, however, indicates the predominant ideological perspective of *Cruising*: "You're gonna come into days where you have to collar a dozen guys like that. Scared, weird little guys who don't know why they have to do what they do. It isn't their fault. It isn't your fault. It's the job." The captain's homophobic explanation amalgamates disgust, righteousness, paternalism, ignorance and neoliberal loyalty of the worker to his employer, no matter how unjust, sadistic (and disgusting) they both are.

Steve's advocacy of the investigated subaltern community, however, reflects his ambivalent attitude toward the subaltern community that he investigates. In one of his visits to the leather world, he passionately dances with another guy while they sniff a blue handkerchief presumably dipped in poppers. Steve looks stoned, ecstatic, vibrant, overjoyed. The soundtrack comprises male singing integrated with wild screaming of happiness. For a minute, self-indulgent Steve seems to be fully integrated into this "disgust-ing" queer habitus. His body "flickers" as if it were excitingly duplicated or endlessly reproduced, surrounded by perilously intriguing visions, smells, sounds and physical sensations.

Yet *Cruising* deviates the gay sadomasochists in order to strengthen and necessitate the heterosexual order. When Nancy gives Steve a blow job, for example, he sighs with delight but, at the same time, he tears up, and the soundtrack is filled with the voices of sighing and groaning men that he reg-ularly hears in his on- and off-duty visits to the sadomasochistic clubs. Does Steve imagine that he is getting a blow job from another man? Has his het-erosexuality been "polluted" by his uncontrollable, stimulating homosexual fantasy? Or is it that his latent homosexuality surprisingly arises through this heterosexual sexual act? Whether Burns is "damaged" or "inspired" by his mission, *Cruising* admits, a decade after the Stonewall uprising, that homosexuality plays a significant, invaluable part in the construction of het-erosexuality as its exciting eternal Other.

Cruising, in its nightmarish gothic atmosphere, demonstrated by dark spaces, mysterious cruelty, erupted passions and uncanny perversities, sensationalizes the gay sadomasochistic dress codes, behaviors, practices and uncertainties as well as enhances the spectators' fears of the ruthlessly unknown, exotic, threatening, intimidating and demonically disgusting "Other." Disgusting the audience involves unbearable events and senti-ments that are theatrically overwritten and overblown. *Cruising*'s narrative is linear; each brutal confrontation, surprising discovery or dreadful event is exaggerated and overplayed for its own sake, for the immediate thrill. The form of disgusting is episodic, building up to local abhorrent climaxes, rather than a final catastrophe involving all the dramatis personae.

Burns *and* the viewers, who narcissistically identify with him, are dis-gusted by their own wayward, unadmitted attraction to the multiple per-verse pleasures shown on screen. Yet they cannot take their disgusted eyes off the deviant spectacles that uncover some of their own forbidden desires. They are astonishingly disgusted by Burns' perverted disguise but they are tremendously attracted to such bizarre disgust. Their horror is increased, heightened and elevated by Burns' cruising of straight men's greatest fears and unadmitted desires.

The gay dungeon as stimulating cabinet of curiosities

Cruising, as a cinematic cabinet of curiosities, contributes a certain concep-tion of the sexual universe to the scale of heteronormative people, assuming that Friedkin's ambition is primarily to assemble a shocking microcosm of an unknown scary world. The content of cabinets of curiosities, in general, came to form a *theatrum mundi* governed by conspicuously commercial principles that organize and map the gay sadomasochistic spaces, labyrinths of desperate depravity and horrendously dangerous same-sex bacchanalia.

Indifferent to his detractors, Friedkin's practice of collecting visceral curiosities is central to the straight world's post-Stonewall episteme. In this respect, *Cruising* provides an almost didactic approach to the homophobic disciplining of gayness, which, like the most ambitious defamatory cabinets, endeavors to reconstitute a dichotomous and hierarchical heteronormative order of the sexual universe. It is a heteronormative order based on privileged heterosexuals whose normalcy is reconstituted as the opposite of perverted sadomasochistic homosexuals and their fatally attractive demimonde.

This film's practice of collecting and the ordering of sexual knowledge aspires to reconstructing and understanding the sexual universe, both psychic and corporeal. *Cruising*'s collection of deviant behaviors appears both as a repository of digressed urban decadence's creation and as a way to address the issue of sexual transgression and the straight hegemony's post-Stonewall fear of a queer planet. Michael Warner suggests that the dawning realization that themes of homophobia and heterosexism may be read in almost any document of our culture means that "we are only beginning to have an idea of how widespread those institutions and accounts are."[60] *Cruising*'s sensational portrayal of gay sadomasochism, in particular, demonstrates the deepest anxieties of the late 1970s Hollywood film industry in regard to the gay liberation movement. The result is the creation of Burns, the heteronormal agent who meticulously investigates an immensely twisted, perverted and apocalyptic kind of Noah's vessel, a voluptuous ark which is turned on its head in the middle of the flood of serial killings (see Figure 2.1).

A few generations after the rise and fall of the 16th and 17th centuries' cabinets of curiosities, with their notorious natural and artificial *mirabilia* objects, the contemporary culture industry sensationally manufactures its own ostentatious Others. Instead of collecting rare botanical specimens, peculiar animals, and dwarves and giants, however, *Cruising* establishes its own cabinet of curiosities that centers on strange, fantastic and exotic gay sadomasochists. The gay sadomasochistic lifestyle is misrepresented as

Figure 2.1 Steve Burns (Al Pacino) inspects the gay leather scene's cabinets of curiosities in *Cruising* (USA 1980) (film still).

hybridization of the virtuosity of decadent *artificialia* (the leather regalia and this subculture's sexual scripts) and perverted *naturalia* (deviant, promiscuous and permeated male bodies that are obsessively involved in brutal sex acts, having no skill to master their forbidden desires).

Even though the extras in Friedkin's film were authentic gay sadomasochists, this is certainly not a documentary. Rather, these men were staged by the filmmaker in order to satisfy his commercial and ideological needs. In its desire to supply the audience a shocking entertainment, *Cruising* is a product of an enthusiastically disgusted bourgeoisie such that its discriminatory sexual structure refigures a modern cabinet of curiosity in which the (sadomasochistic) homosexual is the ultimate freak.

Reclaiming authentic disguise in *Interior. Leather Bar*

Friedkin, in an interview he gave to *Sight and Sound* that promoted the William Friedkin Season at the National Film Theatre in London in 1998, admits that he was forced to make changes in the film, and especially to cut out many scenes, in his negotiation with the American censors. After watching the genuine version of *Cruising*, Richard Heffner from the rating board told him: "It's the worst film I've seen in my life. It's terrible... Rating?! Are you crazy?! This thing would need 5 billion Xs!"[61] Friedkin claims that subsequently, the producers asked Aaron Stern, Heffner's predecessor at the board, and the guy who got Friedkin's classic horror film *The Exorcist* through, to look at particularly difficult pictures in *Cruising*. "And at the cost of 1,000 dollars a day," Friedkin recalls, "he worked for about 40 days suggesting cuts, sending it back to the board, having them go through the roof again, taking it back and looking at it again, until finally we arrived at a version they would approve."[62]

In his interview with *Sight and Sound*, Friedkin verifies the myth of the 40 minutes. He confesses:

> It was butchery... We must have lost about 40 minutes of material. A lot of it had to do with the Pacino character's genuine fascination with what was going on in the clubs – you get a sense of it now, but what you've lost are the real excess.

Friedkin reveals that they had a graphic fist-fucking scene that comprises an image of a fist visible in somebody's stomach, and golden showers. "But what's important," he recalls, "is that you saw Pacino starting to participate."[63]

When Friedkin was asked by the *Sight and Sound* reporter if he had any plans to restore that material, he said that he hopes someday it will be possible to restore the lost footage, but only if it can be integrated into the picture. He discovers that they did consider including it on a laser disk that has been prepared, but he wouldn't want to do it as an addendum the way they did with the outtakes from *The Exorcist*. "I don't think anything I cut from *The Exorcist* detracts from the movie," he added, "but I think the cutting of *Cruising* detracted from the overall effect."[64]

The myth of *Cruising*'s censored 40 minutes captured the imagination of filmmakers James Franco and Travis Matthews who have collaborated since 2012 in imagining their own lost footage. Matthews explains at the beginning of *Interior. Leather Bar* that he was motivated by a fear that the assimilation of the gay culture is erasing all the radicalness and the queerness of that sort of world. He praises their project: "I think what we're creating here helps to form choices." For better or worse, these filmmakers are not obliged to produce an accurate reconstruction of the lost 40 minutes. "It's beyond our grasp, for a lot of reasons, like time and money, and all of that, trying diligently and honestly to recreate these real 30 or 40 minute cuts," he tells the actor Val Lauren when he prepares himself for playing the role of Al Pacino, who played Burns. Matthews continues to apologize:

> I think even trying to do that is just like a long way to go. So this is more like our reimagined idea of it. There's room to be fluid with your interpretation of your character. But I do think that it's important, on some level, to show that you have some struggle with your acceptance of this.

Indeed, straight Lauren's endless dilemmas, during his preparation, rehearsal and shooting of the reconstructed 40 minutes, occupy most of Matthew and Franco's semi-documentary film. Considering the awkward situation, in which gay-friendly-albeit-straight megastar Franco intrudes one of the most radical queer subcultures with its voyeuristic camera, there's no wonder that *Interior. Leather Bar* provoked mixed feelings that oscillated between adoration of this film's sophistication and originality, and condemnation of *Interior. Leather Bar*'s sensational voyeurism and paternalistic curiosity toward the demimonde of gay leather.

Manohla Dargis from *The New York Times*, for example, praises this film as "a sly conceptual *coup d'art* and a deeply sincere exploration of masculinity and its discontents, with a little hot sex thrown in."[65] Dargis agrees with Franco that *Interior. Leather Bar* functions as a response – "searching and serious, playful and teasing" – to the mainstreaming of homosexuality in the United States. Adam Feldman from *Out*, however, is more skeptical. In gay perspective, he contends that James Franco's been winking at gay audiences for years, and it's sometimes hard to tell if he's flirting or kidding. "Both are possibilities in his latest project, *Interior. Leather Bar*, a 'docufiction'," Feldman suggests, but he guarantees to *Out*'s gay readers: "Francophiles should find plenty here to keep them looking."[66]

Nathan Lee (2014) from *Film Comment*, though, is more reluctant about Franco's project. Lee reminds his readers that *Cruising*, an "amyl nitrate fever dream of leering subterranean perverts, delirious fisting orgies, and lurid montages of sodomy and stabbing,"[67] has been recuperated in some quarters as a singular archive of pre-AIDS sexual abandon, yet for others it remains a touchstone of Bad For The Gays cinema. Lee insists that *Interior. Leather Bar*, however, positions itself squarely in the former camp, "emphasis on square." He stresses that *Interior. Leather Bar* might have been called "*Gay. For Pay*," *and* he contends that as for the unabashed homosexuals on set, notably the "real-life" couple willing to fuck on camera, the pleasure they take in each other's bodies "is the least affected thing on view, a rebuke to the flaccid identity games being mobilized by a movie star with a boner for queer theory."[68]

Whether this film cynically exercises an accepted, formulaic radicalism or truly expresses a progressive and daring (straight) endeavor to save queer radicalism in the age of assimilation, *Interior. Leather Bar* is predominantly a reflexive portrayal of staging, directing, manipulating and designing the pretending-to-be-gay phenomenon. *Interior. Leather Bar* uncovers intense situations between actors and directors, including auditions, guidance and interviews with actors who mostly confess their sympathy for *Cruising*.

When a mustached sadomasochistic practitioner asks Val if he's gay, however, the latter responds: "No. This is the thing. But as an actor I can act whatever I feel like... As an actor, you don't want to kiss a guy 'cause you're limited? I don't understand." Notwithstanding, Val admits, in a later scene, that he feels "a little uncomfortable" and explains that he doesn't know exactly what he's doing "but it's cool" when he "figures it out." Val wonders: "You know, what exactly am *I*?!" Franco instantly replies, "Sounds like Al Pacino is uncomfortable. And he did it."

On set, Val's uneasiness with his role doesn't seem to disappear. Like Pacino, in his first visit to a gay sadomasochistic venue on screen, Val looks uncomfortable when he initially inspects the anal and oral sex at the club. He looks puzzled when erections are touched and sucked and butts are spanked by wooden paddles. Later, Val complains to a straight friend in a phone call: "Dicks are out, balls are out, people are paddling each other in the ass, there's bruisers, there's fuckin' welts. Sucking, fucking, armpits, balls, assholes, everything's out, dude." The shocked friend tries to persuade him to quit this job. He asks Val whether he would agree to butt fuck another guy if Franco asked him to do so for artistic reasons.

Val, however, advocates Franco, who sincerely expresses what he feels about sexual freedom. The friend insists that there's a reason "why this stuff doesn't play in mainstream theatres." Val contends that it *is* a pornography set by his own standards. Yet the friend warns him that he's the one who is "at the center of all this thing." Val insists that he trusts Franco. When this phone call ends, however, Val looks upset and distressed, almost crying. Afterward, Val is overtly horrified and disgusted by an "off-screen" gay sadomasochistic session that involves spanking, groaning and moaning.

In a way, his angst alludes to Franco's own intricate relationship with straightness, heteronormativity, gay iconicity and unpracticed pansexuality.

Franco frivolously glorifies Val's pretending-to-be-gay, perceiving it as a sort of a holy mission motivated by vigorous artistic desire for egalitarian and emancipatory experimentation. He first asks Val if it would feel different if a guy and a girl are in a sadomasochistic session. Val agrees: "Yah. It won't make it ok, but why would it feel different for me? I guess I'm a little bit more used to it." Then Franco confesses:

> I don't like the fact that I feel like I've been brought up to think that certain way. I don't like thinking that. I don't like realizing that my mind is been twisted by the way that this whole world has been set all around me. And what that is, is straight normative kind of behavior. It's fucking instilled in my brain. And it's... Yah, I would say that was little shocking to me at first, when I watched that, but [...] Only, I believe [that] only because of the world around me. Because every fucking toilet paper commercial has a guy, a man and a woman living in a house together. And every fuckin' love story is [about] dude that wants to be with a girl. And it only gets up happy is if they walk up in the sunset together. I'm fuckin' sick of that shit. So if there's a way for me to just break that up in my own mind, I'm all for it. And that's I think why you want to be an actor and be an artist.[69]

In this monologue, Franco reflects the same sort of massive self-revelation and public exposure in which Frank Capra used to revel in the 1930s and 1940s. Franco unrepentantly idolizes the device of pretending-to-be-gay that he perceives as a hilarious performance, an especially superior level of acting that encapsulates the essence of an acting career: endless yearning to undermine conventionalities, to question (hetero)normative axioms, to subvert heterocentric imperatives and to set new frontiers that remarkably expand the (straight?) imagination.

In order to ease Val's anxiety about homosexual sex, however, Franco claims that "sex should be a tool, a storytelling tool." He attacks filmmakers who do not dare to put transgressive sex scenes in their movies, "or you are like to talk about it in certain ways, like fuckin' locker room humor or frat house kind of humor but you say 'Oh, don't show gay sex. Don't do that. That's so fuckin' devil'." Franco encourages Val to free his mind: "You're playing a guy who's going undercover. But he's not going into dark, evil place. He's going into actually a place that I think beautiful and attractive." Val cynically remarks: "That's beautiful and attractive?!" and Franco confirms: "I think so."

Interestingly, Franco doesn't perceive pretending-to-be-gay as fraud or deceit but rather as positing himself and his actor "out there," devoting themselves to uninhibited artistic exploration that forcefully transcends the straight world's and their own fixity and mundanity. For better or worse, gay cruising and leather subculture are (mis)perceived by these devoted straight voyeurs as an unknown, seductive, attractive and perilous yet spicy

New World to be eagerly colonized and voraciously experimented by the brave explorers. In this respect, traveling the "beautiful and attractive" dungeons is a courage test, like a *straight* eye for the *queer* guy and his magnificent bizarreness in "Franco's fagots project" (as Val's homophobic phone pal calls this enterprise).

Interior. Leather Bar meticulously attempts to reimagine the sort of identity crisis that Burns experiences in *Cruising* when the maliciously seductive gay sadomasochistic demimonde "corrupts" the straight's soul. Franco and Matthews are conspicuously interested, for their own reasons, in the moments in which Burns' heterosexuality seems to be "polluted" by the atrocious realm that he thoroughly investigates. In Friedkin's film the straight protagonist admits that his research of the homosexual leather world affects him. He begs his girlfriend Nancy not to let him lose her. Likewise, Val in *Interior. Leather Bar* is asked by one of his fellow actors what his wife thinks of his participation in this venture. Val replies:

> She's cool, man. She's a really cool girl. You know, she knows that I'm not taking part in any sexual things but... She says, "I don't understand," and I find myself getting frustrated trying to explain it to her, really frustrating, and it became apparent that I don't fuckin' understand either. But she's cool. She wants me to make time to go to dinner tonight.

Yet, like Burns in *Cruising*, Val admits that he somewhat enjoys the same-sex dynamics, and he even compliments his counterparts, "We are a sexy bunch."

Notably, viewers who expect to find a real reconstruction of the mythically lost 40-minute segment might be highly disappointed. The scenes of this "reconstructed reconstruction" comprise no more than a few minutes sporadically. The rare moments of the loosely reconstructed censored footage comprise same-sex sexual interactions in a dark claustrophobic space with blue shades and alienated techno music. Conspicuously, *Interior. Leather Bar*'s main concern is not about the reconstruction itself but about straight Val's (and Franco's?) dilemmas, anxieties, frustrations and despairs regarding this project. The straight actor is increasingly, and somewhat uncannily, merging with Burns, *Cruising*'s straight protagonist, and his difficulties in coming to terms with the heavy emotional price of his pretending-to-be-a-gay leather guy.

In a reconstruction sequence, however, Val seems to be more adjusted to the perilous, stimulating atmosphere of the gay leather bar. He dances freely with the cruising men, gets into the groove and even seems to enjoy his undercover mission in the sexually charged venue (see Figure 2.2). At a certain point, he gets excited and dances faster and more expressively, getting into the rhythm and waving his arms in the air. Flickering shots of his body resemble a specific scene in *Cruising* in which Burns seems to be really into

Figure 2.2 Val Lauren (on the right) gets into the groove in *Interior. Leather Bar* (USA 2013) (film still).

it, in a crucial point in which his sexual masquerade and sexual authenticity are blurred, merged, conflated, interplayed and subversively interwoven. This fusion of fakeries and authenticities is enhanced when delirious Val is joyfully patted and stroked by a handsome man in a leather outfit.

Jon Braddy and Billy Huff suggest that *Cruising* and *Interior. Leather Bar*, "with their accurate portrayals of 'deep, dark, evil places'," become "necessarily shitty movies to the stigmaphobe."[70] This is because "the films themselves become something to be feared, shamed or simply disavowed. Yet to the stigmaphile, these films are resplendent in the anxiety they provoke."[71] However, I find *Cruising* extremely stigmaphobic, whereas *Interior. Leather Bar* oscillates between the stigmaphobic and the stigmatophilic, particularly its last sequence in which cruising men gaze at the camera or, possibly, at Val, or maybe at the straight and gay viewers, or at filmmaker Franco. These cruising faces look back at those who vividly explore this wonderland and its perilous homosexual delights. Notably, this ending is vastly different from the last scene in *Cruising*, which shows a boat sailing the Hudson River and recognizes an amputated rotten hand floating in the water (a scene which is almost identical to the opening scene of *Cruising*). In contrast, *Interior. Leather Bar*'s ending undermines the rigid boundaries between fakery and sincerity, pretense and authenticity, masquerade and originality.

Both the presumably straight filmmakers, their straight actor who plays for Pacino the straight-actor-who-pretends-to-be-gay, the real gay sadomasochists on set, the straight actors who are acting as gay sadomasochists and the authentic or stage's cruising men, however, are all taking a part in a passionate, voracious theatrical spectacle. All those subjects can be regarded as figures in masquerade.

Jean Baudrillard suggests in *Carnival and Cannibal, or the Play of Global Antagonism* that western hegemony "is accompanied by an extraordinary process of reversion, in which power is slowly undermined, devoured or 'cannibalized' by the very people it 'carnivalizes'."[72] Baudrillard contends that it is this dual – *carnivalesque* and *cannibalistic* – which is a form that we see reflected in every corner of the world, with the exportation of our moral values (human rights, democracy), our principles of economic growth, *performance* and *spectacle*.[73]

Although both *Cruising* and *Interior. Leather Bar* are produced by the voracious mainstream culture industry, they reflect different ideological premises. Friedkin's film is a populist, often merciless sensationalizing of a subaltern group, while Franco and Matthews' semi-documentary aspires to provide an independent, alternative perspective on the power relations between the sexual hegemony and subaltern sexual subcultures *and* to problematize and occasionally subvert the distinction between hetero- and homosexualities. Whereas *Cruising* demonically carnivalizes *and* cannibalizes the gay sadomasochists, *Interior. Leather Bar* glorifies *and* ironizes Friedkin's insatiable exploitation of the gay sadomasochistic demimonde. In a way, the semi-documentary is an exploitation of exploitation, or a metaphoric cannibalizing of *Cruising*'s cannibalizing of the gay leather subculture. In contrast to *Cruising*'s symbolic cannibalism, however, *Interior. Leather Bar* celebrates a carnival of juxtaposed, contested, interchangeable *and* amalgamated sexual identifications, authentic masquerades and masqueraded authenticities that both affirm and subvert the power of disguise.

Notes

1 Butler 1993: 237.
2 Healey 1994: 90.
3 *Macho* 2016.
4 *Cruising* 1980.
5 *Cruising* began life in 1970 as a novel by Gerald Walker, a script of Philip D'Antoni, the producer of Friedkin's thriller *The French Connection*, and finally the title was acquired by Jerry Weintraub, who had been told Friedkin was interested in filming the novel. In an eerie echo of a 1960s case that inspired Walker's novel, a string of horrific murders was taking place in which the gay victim's body parts had started to wash up along the Hudson River, earning the killings the press moniker "the Bag Murders" (Kermode 1998: 22).

Reports of these crimes were of particular interest to Friedkin, however, because while filming *The French Connection* he had developed a close relationship with Detective Randy Jurgenson, who had worked undercover in this area of Manhattan in the mid-1960s. Jurgenson had been instructed to investigate a scam in which gay men were being arrested, detained and then blackmailed by two men posing as cops – thus creating a tense situation in which the roles of cop, criminal and victim were bizarrely blurred. Bringing together all these elements, Friedkin resolved to develop his own screenplay of *Cruising*, focusing on the central theme of Walker's book (Kermode 1998: 22).
6 Wilson 1981: 100.
7 Young 1995: 97.
8 Cited in Hadleigh 2001 (1993): 90.
9 Cited in Kermode 1998: 22.
10 Wilson 1981: 103.

11 Wilson 1981: 103.
12 Cited in Hadleigh 2001 (1993): 90.
13 Cited in Kermode 1998: 24.
14 Cited in Russo 1987 (1981): 261.
15 Russo 1987 (1981): 261.
16 Russo 1987 (1981): 261.
17 Watney 1982: 110.
18 Murray 1996: 393.
19 Hart 2013: 52.
20 Hart 2013: 53–54.
21 Davidson 2005: 25.
22 Kermode 1998: 22.
23 *Halloween* 1978.
24 Burston 1998: 24.
25 Burston 1998: 24.
26 Burston 1998: 24.
27 Clagett 2003: 249.
28 Davies 2008: 102.
29 Davies 2008: 102.
30 Watney 1982: 111.
31 Wilson 1981.
32 Wilson 1981.
33 Wilson 1981.
34 Wilson 1981: 101 (emphasis added).
35 Kleinhans 1994: 187–188.
36 This mask possibly echoes a hood that an executioner attaches to the convict's face before killing him. It is a *tout ensemble* of black leather, buckles, zips and lacing that assumes sexual expression of terror and submission to torture (Needham 2014: 151).
37 Needham 2014: 153.
38 Sedgwick 1985.
39 Sedgwick 1985: 89.
40 Craine 1994: 33.
41 Harris 1997: 184.
42 Harris 1997: 185–186.
43 Cited in Bristow 1997: 188.
44 Martinez 2018: 1302.
45 Martinez 2018: 1316.
46 Watney 1982.
47 Watney 1982: 110.
48 Miller 2007.
49 Miller 2007: 73.
50 Davies 2008.
51 Hadleigh 2001 (1993).
52 Hadleigh 2001 (1993): 90.
53 Davidson 2005: 31–32.
54 Davidson 2005: 50–51.
55 Zeichner and Reidy 2009.
56 Curtis, Aunger and Rabie 2004.
57 Zeichner and Reidy 2009: 231.
58 Zeichner and Reidy 2009: 235.
59 Connell 2005.
60 Warner 1991: 6.

61 Cited in Kermode 1998: 22–23.
62 Cited in Kermode 1998: 23.
63 Cited in Kermode 1998: 23.
64 Cited in Kermode 1998: 23.
65 Dargis 2014.
66 Feldman 2014.
67 Lee 2014.
68 Lee 2014.
69 *Interior. Leather Bar* 2013.
70 Braddy and Huff 2016: 119.
71 Braddy and Huff 2016: 119.
72 Baudrillard 2010: 4.
73 Baudrillard 2010: 5 (emphasis added).

3   Pretending to be allies?

Straight women, their pretending-to-be-gay admirers and sexual authentication

Relationships between gay guys and their best straight female friends or "fag hags" have been extensively theorized as complicated, multilayered and multifaceted friendships that often involve mixed feelings, mutual commitments, caring, empathy, infatuations, frustrations and creative, often unanticipated, interactions between those members of subaltern groups. When the gays involved in these relationships are deceivers, straight men who pretend to be gay for various reasons, however, their relationships with the fag hags become more complicated, contradicted and transgressive, thus appealing to filmmakers who are anxious to surprise and stimulate their viewers. This chapter focuses on diverse films that center on pretenders who develop seemingly platonic friendships with straight women in order to win their hearts. This chapter aims to unmask the particularities and peculiarities of screening straight women's friendship, alliance and unanticipated attraction to gay deceivers.

The term "fag hag" dates back to the late 1960s in the United States, dismissively directed at women who were considered not attractive enough to hang around with "real men." But like so many other derogatory terms, it was reclaimed in the 1990s as a stereotypic term to be worn with pride. Gay men introduced their female friends to a world free from sexual harassment by men, where the emphasis was on fun and where more often than not they would find themselves the center of flattering and unthreatening attention. Hence, "fag haggery was in fashion."[1]

Stephen Maddison explains that since straight women and gay men share a common sexual interest in men, and since women's desire is ascribed to cultural legitimation and widespread representation, desiring men through an identification with similar desires in women would provide gay men with not only a much wider range of places to locate themselves culturally, but also "a potentially greater diversity of narratives with which to make sense of that desire."[2] Moreover, Button notes that a *frisson* of sexual flirtation, or some kind of sexual dynamics, does in fact often occur between gay men and straight women when they first meet.[3]

Sincerity and reliance may be the basis for close friendships made between straight women and gay men. Maddison suggests that if hags and fags are "sisters," however, then they indeed are queer ones. The sisterhood we have the potential to share by virtue of our mutual oppression within hetero-patriarchal regimes "is 'queered' as a function of the way our identities are circumscribed by the homosocial narratives that uphold those regimes."[4] In other words, the sisterhood between gay men and fag hags is stimulated by the oppression of these two groups by the masculinistic heteronormative society. Although fag hags are women, not men, they are regarded by gay men as allies, supporters and advocates, and, in many senses, a significant part of the gay community.

In the same spirit, Nicola Evans contends that fag hags by their very existence challenge the substance and stability of our sexual orientations, an issue that is especially fraught for gay men, for whom the endorsement of more flexible accounts of sexual identity may play into the hands of those demanding that gay men "cure" themselves. "Alternatively," she adds,

> can we read fag hags in a more positive light as less a threat than as an invitation to open up spaces for relationships that are closed down by the reductive alignment of sexual practice, sexual object choice and gender?[5]

The discussion of fag hags and their multilayered relationships with gay men has been significantly popularized by the romantic TV sitcom *Will & Grace*[6] that celebrated the particularities and peculiarities of platonic love between the straight woman Grace and her handsome gay flatmate Will. This sitcom's significant popularity was anticipated by the successful film *My Best Friend's Wedding*,[7] starring Julia Roberts and Rupert Everett, about a woman who asks her best gay male friend to pose as her fiancé to help her break up her straight male best friend's wedding. *Will & Grace* stimulated a wave of feature films that romanticize woman–gay relationships, e.g. *The Object of My Affection*,[8] starring Jennifer Aniston and Paul Rudd, focusing on a social worker in New York who is pregnant and prefers her beloved gay male friend, over her straight boyfriend, as a partner for raising her child; *The Next Best Thing*,[9] starring Madonna and Rupert Everett, a film that focuses on a woman who becomes pregnant by her best gay male friend, after a drunken night of sex, and their efforts to raise the child together; *Bend It Like Beckham*,[10] starring Parminder Nagra and Ameet Chana, about a female footballer and her closeted gay male friend, who are both of Indian-British origins; and *A Home at the End of the World*,[11] starring Robin White and Harris Allan, about a straight woman and her best gay male friend who develop a romantic relationship with the same man.

Fag-hagging (and hugging) Sedgwick's angst

A significant academic controversy over the term "fag hag" and its percep-tions and implications in queer theory sprang up in 1989 with the ideological debate between Eve Kosofsky Sedgwick, a straight woman who was one of the most influential queer scholars, and David Van Leer, a gay man who was a prominent queer cultural studies scholar. Apparently, at an important moment in fag hags' theoretical history, one "difficult nomination" of the term was speciously so difficult that it – and she – could not even be so overtly termed. Such was the charge leveled at Sedgwick by Van Leer in the first of a series of quarrelsome interactions on the pages of *Critical Inquiry*. Their debate relates to Sedgwick's dynamic theorization of the role of straight women in intimate relationships between men.

Notably, Sedgwick explored in her book *Between Men* the representational convention wherein erotic relations between men are mediated by a woman, who, as the supposed object of the two men's desires, stands surely for their heterosexuality.[12] In her later essay "The Beast in the Closet," however, Sedgwick suggested that ways of expressing sexual relations between men have developed in the 20th century, which do not require routing through a heterosexual matrix – that is, through a pretense of affections for a woman.[13]

Van Leer wrote, in part, in response to Sedgwick's characterization of May Bartram in "The Beast in the Closet," her now-famous essay on Henry James' "The Beast in the Jungle." He criticized Sedgwick's (in his view) unpersuasive reading that the kind of woman discussed in the essay is stigmatized in gay slang with the unpleasant term "fag hag." Although Sedgwick never explicitly used the term "fag hag," Van Leer presupposed that she had it in mind, and has purposely suppressed it, a self-censorship to which he imputes, as it happens, a positive motivation: "It is possible," he claims, "that having sexualized [the character John] Marcher's situation, Sedgwick needs to defend May from what she feels is the attendant sexual cliché."[14]

In her response, however, Sedgwick stressed that the introduction of fag hag into the critical discourse was wholly Van Leer's doing, and her objection suggests implicitly that she has been personally interpellated, hurt and offended by the term: "Having had, perhaps, some occasion to perceive that use of the ugly disyllable is not exclusively confined to contexts of affectionate respect, I would be unlikely to use it anywhere."[15]

Later, however, Sedgwick confessed her uneasiness with the term "fag hag." She stressed that she doesn't understand what the term "fag hag" means. Anyway she doesn't understand what it could mean nowadays. She explained that "fag hag" conjures up for her a scene at a bar in the 1950s where a lot of self-hating people are getting very drunk. Sedgwick speculated that maybe it does the same work that, say, "nigger lover" did in the 1950s and 1960s: to punish anyone who just doesn't feel some form of contempt that their society says they ought to feel. "So I don't have any sense whether or not the term describes me."[16]

Sedgwick, who is one of the gay-friendliest influential queer theorists, can honorably be awarded as the ultimate fag hag, albeit in a positive sense, away from the pejorative and demeaning articulations of "fag haggery." I agree with Maddison that women contesting patriarchal ideas of woman-hood create Hag-ography or Hag-ology, and this seems to be an appropriate use of the word in this context. Maddison goes on to argue that "women who bond with gay men do so as a form of political resistance."[17] In the same spirit, Dawne Moon stresses that the term "fag hag" parodies the patriarchal order, "at times subverting and at times reproducing it."[18]

The sexual pleasures of the fag hag and her gay partner

The complicated, always dynamic and often surprising relationships between male gayness and female straightness are exhaustively discussed in the Canadian documentary film *Fag Hag*.[19] The most intriguing couple in this documentary is the 60-something Dodie and Kevin, who are poets and novelists in San Francisco. Dodie admits that Kevin was "on the far end of the gay continuum," and she never believed that anything was going to really happen between them. Yet she hasn't experienced that type of intimacy with a man where she could just tell him anything. They were occasionally kiss-ing but still denying their romantic feelings for each other. Dodie started sleeping with Kevin though, but they wouldn't have sex. Kevin confesses: "I wasn't interested in having sex with her, not for some time. Many months, months and months, years, before we began. When our minds met, then we began to be interested in each other physically." Kevin insisted that they get married. Conspicuously, he uncovers a sort of initiation story:

> I came to her a shivering novice. I mean it's hard enough to get a guy off without having the complicated "unknown territory," *terra incognita*, the anatomy of a woman… And I said, I'm not gonna be good at that, you know, I'm going to give a 100, a 110 percent. And I guess I got pretty good pretty-good.

Still, Dodie admits that people often ask her to explain Kevin's sexuality. "It's not something I really understand," she admits. "Yah, he doesn't see himself as bisexual because the heart of his desire is toward men and he just seems to think that this is just some kind of accident that has happened." Dodie adds that Kevin is different to the man she dated before in that he was very supportive of her and she doesn't have to negotiate equal status. "I don't feel like a gay man in my heart," she explains, "but I feel that often I have the relationship of gay men. I'm treated as if I were a gay man. So that's really empowering." Interestingly, the female partner here considers their somewhat unorthodox straight relationship as a type of stimulating same-sex relationship in the sense of a dynamic, non-hierarchical and more equal and open-minded intimate interaction.

Kevin, on his side, stresses in this documentary that if he'd come to the end of his life and never had a relationship with a woman, he would feel –

although he might not even know it – that he had wasted his life because he wouldn't have tasted "the other side of life." Realizing that such a statement might sound heterocentric to some viewers, he instantly explicates that he supposes it's also true about people who are just heterosexuals and never had any gay experience: "They're probably missing out on something. They would have been better off by trying." Being a self-identified gay man who fell in love with a woman, he felt all of a sudden that there wasn't really a place for him anymore. "I still thought that I was gay, I knew I was gay," he realizes melodramatically, "but the collectivity of gay male society took me out and placed me in another place. So in a way, our experience parallels that of Adam and Eve being thrust from Paradise."

Whereas platonic relationships seem to be one of the main characteristics of friendships between gay men and straight women, however, the possibility that the platonic condition will be challenged and even undermined, under certain circumstances, fuels numerous documentary and fictional representations of these relationships. The sexual *and* cultural gap between the gay and his straight female friend often implicitly involves the possibility that this gap will be reshaped, redesigned, redirected and even deconstructed over time. This tension between existent platonic man–woman relationship and its imaginable overturn stimulates filmmakers and their clientele, whether they yearn to eroticize these relationships and reconstitute heteronormativity or, rather, to challenge the prevalent sexual categorizations and to unveil the human sexuality's unpredicted subtleties, multidirectional playfulness and interchangeable role playing.

From fag hag to fag fuck: unmasking authentic desires

The romantic comedy-of-errors *Boat Trip*[20] grotesquely portrays a relationship between a straight man, who pretends to be gay, and his devoted fag hag. The film focuses on straight buddies, Jerry (Cuba Gooding Jr.) and Nick (Horatio Sanz), who mistakenly join a gay cruise populated by mostly swishy, theatrical drama queens. During their trip, they gradually realize that gay men are less objectionable than they first supposed. Soon, Jerry is infatuated with the cruise's beautiful dance teacher Gabriella (Roselyn Sanchez), and in order to win her over, he masquerades himself as gay so he can become her close friend and sophisticatedly woo her. Meanwhile, dumb Nick develops a romantic relationship with Inga the Swedish bikini model. After an inadvertent sexual liaison with her wicked aging coach Sonya, Nick fails to get Inga, and instead falls in love with her sister. But in the end, he is trapped by the voracious coach. Jerry, however, has been outed as a straight guy by his ex-girlfriend, who is determined to win him back, but finally, according to the rules of romantic comedies, he manages to win his real love, Gabriella.

Jerry is immediately infatuated with the beautiful dance instructor who thinks he's gay like the rest of the passengers. She tells him that she prefers to teach dancing on a gay cruise, rather than on a straight cruise, because on a gay boat she doesn't have to confront "horny creeps." Jerry, wearing tight white sport trousers, leans forward while his back is directed at Gabriella. Conspicuously, the straight woman gazes erotically at Jerry's shaped behind and says: "I bet men are hitting on you all the time." Then she looks closer at his fit body and announces: "You've got a hot ass!" Jerry is surprised and Gabriella repeats in a sexy voice: "Your ass. It's hot." Moreover, Gabriella looks straight into the pretender's eyes and teases him: "You know what else? Let's say I do get horny one day. Maybe I can even find a gay guy and he can do me the favor," and she details her erotic fantasy about gay men: "He can make me scream, make me moan!" Then she raises her leg so that her crotch touches Jerry's face and adds "Screw my brains out!"

The blurred boundaries between a platonic relationship and potential sexual attraction, in this scene, uncover the complexity of sexual identifications. The fag hag is re-formed, trans-formed and de-formed, in a way, when she turns into what I initially define here as *fag fuck*. Her desire to have sex with a gay man fucks the dichotomous division between hetero- and homosexuality. Her transgressive desire voluptuously subverts the traditional formation of the relationship between fag hags and gay men.[21] In a way, the fag hag's desire to have sex with a gay man celebrates the women's right to assert and satisfy their sexual needs regardless of conventional sexual taxonomies. Her transgressive fantasy radically contaminates or vividly fucks the oppressively purified sexual classifications and allows members of diverse sexual communities to free their minds and have consensual sex with each other.

Notwithstanding, in a queer perspective, the "fuck fag" fag hag is connoted with the bigoted heterocentric belief that a gay man can get rid of his homosexuality and be normal if only he finds the right woman. Such a belief perceives homosexuals as inverts and considers gayness as an aberrant lifestyle sinfully adopted by sexual perverts. According to the heterocentric logic of *Boat Trip*, Jerry courageously maintains his heterosexual normalcy in a seductively bizarre gay cruise while Gabriella courageously yearns to cure the freak or uncover his normalcy.

Hereby, there's not only one pretender in here, but two. Although Gabriella assumes that Jerry is gay like the rest of the passengers, she admits that her fag-hagness masquerades her persistent woman–man desire that transcends and subverts the male addressee's homosexuality. In this sense, the platonic not only camouflages but also stimulates the voluptuous. Although this is basically a heterocentric scene in a highly heterocentric film that primarily aims to arouse the straight viewers who identify with the agonized straight guy "trapped" in a gay disguise, it is also a rather queer situation. If queerness predominantly supports liquidized sex roles, deconstructed sexual binaries and disrupted sexual dichotomies,[22] then Gabriella's straight confession is somewhat queer. Instead of obeying patriarchal imperatives that constrain women's sexual expressions, and instead of enforcing dichotomized perceptions of straightness and gayness, Gabriella sensually interrupts the sexual order.

The queer hypersexualization of the pomosexual Latina

Pamela Robertson notes that the fag hag stereotype often seems to presume a failed object of choice on the part of the woman, the "hag" – that is, the fag hag chooses gay men because she "can't get a man" (she is stereotypically unattractive) and/or "because she desires a man who doesn't want her (she is stereotypically secretly, desperately attracted to gay men)."[23] Yet Gabriella's hot fantasy about sex with a gay man does not necessarily mean that she is desperate. Rather, her fantasy could reflect sexual creativity and open-mindedness, and as a new mass-media fag hag who is smart, sexy, sassy and *happy*, she is definitely not a "hag."[24]

Conspicuously, as Deborah Thompson suggests, what defines the fag hag most is not *what* she *is*, but *whom* she allies *with*. That is, what makes a fag hag a fag hag is not – or not only – *what* she identifies *as* (usually, but not always, a straight woman of sorts), but more importantly *whom* she identifies *with* (primarily gay men, and secondarily the queer community at large).[25] Further, the fag hag "embodies the possibility and pleasures of a radical disjunction between identifying *as* and identifying *with*, or perhaps between identity and identification."[26] If identification precedes and enables identity, and if identification always exceeds identity – then fag hag identification is not aberrant, but normal, "not identification gone wrong, but a very clear example of the proper relations between all identities and identifications."[27]

Maddison suggests that such identifications are gradually becoming re-conceptualized. Once thought of as aberrant and unhealthy, gay men's identifications with and through women are increasingly seen as "affiliations which resist heterosexualised manhood."[28] In aligning themselves with gay culture, women apparently undertaking acts of gender dissent, and their bonding with gay men, is a form of political resistance.[29] Thompson considers such alignment as an "ideological breakthrough" although it is never guaranteed – "but it is," she notes, "implicitly *desired* and, at least, *potential* in fag hag identification."[30] Thompson insists that fag hag identifications need to be felt as innate, natural and pre-conscious in order to be effective politically. She assumes that such felt essentialism is what keeps fag hags accountable to and rooted in the queer community, rather than politically correct cultural tourists. "But that felt essentialism occurs as such in a specific cultural context, one of sexism and heterosexism," she adds, "which hails its subjects into positions of both obedience and dissent."[31]

In the case of Gabriella the temptress in *Boat Trip*, however, sexy gay men appeal to her not as political comrades in a struggle for gender and sexual equality, but as sexual objects that she's powerful enough to "redeem" from their sordid gay lifestyle, even momentarily, by showing them what the assumed clientele of this film considers as the only sexual normalcy. As a conversion fantasy, the fag hag's yearning for a hot gay man does not trouble but reconfirms the borders of "queerness." Gabriella's craving

for *sex* with a gay man is situated in a mainstream straight film that constantly avoids gay sex scenes while showing numerous heterosexual sex
acts. Hence, Gabriella's fantasy does not posit her as a pomosexual but
underlines the fact that she is heterosexual. Coined by Carol Queen and
Lawrence Schimel, the term "pomosexual" "references homosexuality even
as it described the community's outsiders, the queer queers who can't seem
to stay put within a nice simple identity."[32] In contrast, Gabriella's relationship with the gay community is never presented as political solidarity or
identification with the gay men's daily hardships, discriminations, persecutions and harassments. She primarily yearns for attractive gay men for her
personal sexual pleasure.

Moreover, this woman is designed and objectified as the one who can
turn even a gay man into straight by redeployment of signs of "the sexy
Latina." Isabel Molina Guzmán and Angharad N. Valdivia suggest that
US Latina/o identity is a complex and contradictory postcolonial paneth-
nic construction. Under the trope of tropicalism, in particular, attributes
such as bright colors, rhythmic music and brown or olive skin comprise
some of the most enduring stereotypes about Latina/os, a stereotype best
embodied by the excesses of Carmen Miranda and the hypersexualization
of Ricky Martin.[33] "Gendered aspects of the trope of tropicalism include the
male Latin lover, macho, dark-haired, mustachioed," Guzmán and Valdivia
add, "and the spitfire female Latina characterized by red-colored lips, bright
seductive clothing, curvaceous hips and breasts, long brunette hair, and
extravagant jewelry."[34]

The latter pattern is explicitly demonstrated by Gabriella's physique,
hairstyle, heavy make-up, erotic outfit, slutty gestures and explicit sexual
talk, including the vulgar way in which she simulates oral sex with a big
banana (see Figure 3.1). Notably, Jerry is one of the very few people of color

Figure 3.1 The phallic joy of Gabriella (Roselyn Sanchez), the fag hag, and Jerry
(Cuba Gooding Jr.), who pretends to be gay in *Boat Trip* (USA 2002)
(film still).

among the gay passengers and his relationship with Gabriella establishes a sort of "extended tropicalism" that comprises straight Latinas and black gays. Yet Jerry, who hardly conceals his desire for Gabriella, represents the yearning of both white and black straight viewers to hetero-normalize the queer and, particularly, to see Gabriella in erotic contexts.

Lessons in effeminacy, faggotry and fag-haggery

Significantly, both Jerry and Gabriella are presented in this scene as pretenders. Although she introduces herself to him, in this intimate scene, as a straight woman who adores gay men, she confesses about her wish to transform a gay man into her sexual partner. In this manner, Gabriella's fag-hagness can be perceived as a means of deception; her gay-friendliness seems to masquerade her voluptuous heterosexual intentions. This situation, in which both participants are pretenders, is not only a comic device but also fuels new sexual possibilities, aspirations and stimulating transgressions. The apparent *improbability* of fulfilling their love encompasses the *probability* that their true sexual identifications will be uncovered, authenticated and celebrated. For example, when Jerry dances behind Gabriella in a sensual way that simulates sexual intercourse, Gabriella wonders: "You know... it's strange... The way you stare at me sometimes. The way you touch me like that, you know? It's exactly the way a straight guy would." Jerry tries to look surprised: "Me? Straight?! Girlfriend, please! Huuuuu! (making a flamboyant gesture above his head) Nobody's gotta teach me how to be gay!"

In the next scene, however, Hector – a flaming gay man with a heavy Spanish accent, golden coat, effeminate hairstyle and expressive mimics – teaches the protagonist about gay culture. In a seeming effeminacy lesson, sissified Jerry learns that Bette Midler is also known as "The Divine Miss M," and how to sound theatrically flamboyant ("Don't say 'refreshing cocktail' but 'to die for'! Also acceptable 'divine!'"). The lesson ends with their joint piano playing (and grotesque singing) of Gloria Gaynor's gay anthem "I Will Survive." Hence, the pretender, like any other actor, needs to thoroughly research the character that he plays and to rehearse it intensively; he studies how to be gay. In order to play his role properly, he has to learn the logic of subaltern, countercultural identification and the particularities of gay culture. In order to pass as gay, straight Jerry needs to acknowledge and immerse into a flamboyant gay folklore with its own language, expressions, gestures, iconography and role models.

The gay culture mediated by Hector the sassy instructor and learned by his voyeuristic student *is* joyful, vital, happy and unapologetic. Hereby, Jerry's pretending-to-be-gay is multifaceted and highly contradictory: ridiculing and emancipating, disgraceful and graceful, heterocentric and multicultural, shameful and respectful. Unlike the demonization of gay existentiality in William Friedkin's *Cruising*, the gay subculture exposed in *Boat Trip* is certainly not atrocious and murderous, and gay men are not portrayed as hopeless compulsive sadomasochists. Yet, in *Boat Trip*, in order to satisfy the straight audience, the sissification and stereotyping of modern gay culture and its identification with flamboyancy, emasculation and androgyny are overtly perverted and estranged.

Notably, the majority's sexuality produces the illusion that sexuality is fixed and unchanging and not highly organized and regulated.[35] Although Jerry is a devoted student who quickly learns the subtleties of a flaming gay culture, *Boat Trip* erects the boundaries between fixed and unchanging hetero- and homosexualities. This film denies any possibility that Jerry might cross the borderline between straightness and gayness and experience the joy of gay sex. Conventionally, this romantic comedy poses obstacles that the heterosexual couple has to overcome in order to fulfill its love.[36] In this respect, Jerry's pretending-to-be-gay functions as a playful *obstacle*, definitely not as a life-changing experience that exposes Jerry to new, unanticipated sexual delights.

When Gabriella and Jerry finally kiss on a tropical island, she apologizes: "I'm sorry, I'm sorry, I'm sorry. I don't want to feel like I am pressuring you into doing something you don't want to do." Jerry replies: "I want to do this very badly." Gabriella volunteers to be his guide. She deploys an initiation framework, in which she promises him that she's going to be "gentle and patient" and that she's going "to take it very, very slowly." The viewers obviously know that Jerry is straight, and yearn for erotic unification between the man and the woman. The film fulfills the viewers' expectations. Jerry and Gabriella kiss and make love intensively until the tree they are underneath is shaken. The oranges fall out of it and surround the naked, sweaty couple. Gabriella remarks "You're a really quick stud" and exhausted Jerry replies "That's enough foreplay."

Their straight love is interrupted, however, by a sudden visit of Jerry's ex-girlfriend Felicia to the boat. Felicia is devastated with Jerry's drag performance on board, in which he masquerades as a female Brazilian carnival dancer with a golden hat, sexy golden jacket, white thong and heavy make-up, singing with the other gay performers the diva Diana Ross' hit song "I'm comin' out." This grotesque situation includes some homophobic statements that might satisfy the more bigoted spectators. At the end of the musical number, Felicia shouts: "Cocksucker!" Later, in their unavoidable confrontation, the frustrated woman cries,

> What were you thinking about when we were making love, Jerry, Cabana Boys?! And to think I wanted to be your wife... I really missed you, Jerry. All the special times we had. We complemented each other. We could've built a life together.

Jerry, wearing effeminate jewelry and heavy make-up, is astonished: "What?! You think I'm Gay?!"

Jerry finally convinces his ex-girlfriend that he is straight, however, and even marries her. In the middle of their wedding, however, he runs away. Surrealistically, Jerry parachutes down from a plane and lands at the swimming pool of the boat that now hosts a lesbian cruise. Gabriella, who is now a dance instructor of the "Daughters of Sappho," is furious but eventually forgives him. This romantic comedy conventionally terminates with the reunited couple's passionate kiss. In this respect, *Boat Trip* is primarily a gay-sploitation film that manipulatively reconfirms a privileged heterosexuality by reestablishing a hierarchical distinction between renormalized and re-authenticated straightness that is dramatically contrasted with flamboyantly fabricated and ridiculed gayness. According to this film's heteronormative route, Jerry's gay masquerade is just an adventurous *trip* while fulfilling his love for Gabriella as his *destiny*.

The real man and his (un)masked heteronormative desire

A young straight guy pretending to be gay in order to fulfill his love for his fag hag is also at the center of the low-budget college comedy *Freshman Orientation*.[37] The film centers on Clay (Sam Huntington), a typical Midwestern 18-year-old freshman at a large state university, who hopes to improve his social status by joining a fraternity. Amanda (Kaitlin Doubleday), another new student, also hopes to join a sorority, and as part of her initiation she and the other candidates are each required to pick up "loser" guys for a party where the boys will be voluptuously humiliated.

Amanda is supposed to find a guy who is obviously gay and mistakenly thinks Clay is homosexual. Clay exposes Amanda's scheme but he decides to play the role in order to go out with the beautiful woman. He learns how to put gayness on as an act and he hopes to win her love with some help from friendly queer bartender Rodney (John Goodman). Meanwhile, his roommate Matt (Mike Erwin) falls in love with the pretender. Expectedly, this romantic college comedy terminates with the sought-after unification of Clay and Amanda, who realize how precious they really are to each other, despite, and in a certain way because of, their mutual charades.

As a rampageous college comedy, *Freshman Orientation* typically relates to student culture which involves beer drinking, multiple and often pansexual erotic encounters, infatuations, debauchery, promiscuity, vulgarity, wildness, transgressive behaviors and complicated relationships between students and their lecturers, and the young adults' existential concern about their professional, familial, personal and social future in the highly stratified American society (both Clay and Amanda are of lower-class origins and deal with problematic family backgrounds).

Freshman Orientation does not ignore the homoerotic subtleties of college life, including the dynamics between same-sex roomies, the emergent brotherhood in a beer-driven male student culture and peculiar rituals in fraternities that involve male nudity, physical contacts and even same-sex sexual activities. At a hazing ritual, which is a part of their fraternity ini-tiation of new members, the young candidates are instructed by the older students to undress, expose their buttocks and spread hot porridge on each other's testicles and lick them. The young people also deliver egg yolk from mouth to mouth. Apparently, these mischievous tasks are playfully carni-valesque rather than abusive. Mikhail Bakhtin notes that in carnival, the material bodily principle, that is, images of the human body with its food, drink, defecation and sexual life, plays a predominant role. Images of the body are offered in an exaggerated way that Bakhtin initially defines as "grotesque realism."[38] The essential principle of grotesque realism is deg-radation, that is, "the lowering of all that is high, spiritual, ideal, abstract; it is a transfer to the material level, to the sphere of earth and body in their indissoluble unity."[39]

The realistically grotesque cinematic portrayal of the derogative fra-ternity rituals in *Freshman Orientation*, however, encapsulates a particu-larly intriguing sexual complexity. In her book *Not Gay: Sex between Straight White Men*, Jane Ward discusses such sexually charged practices in American college fraternities. She disagrees that these are scenes of power and humiliation, not sex. Ward notes that these encounters can be read as humiliating or disgusting precisely because they involve normal, hetero-sexual young men behaving like fags, or being subjected, ostensibly against their will, to homosexual contact.[40] And yet, despite the homophobia of the participants, Ward is also captivated and excited by the existence of this kind of contact between straight men. "The budding queer critic (and pervert) in me was impressed by the imagination required to manufacture these scenarios, the complex rules that structured them," she admits, "and the performative and ritualistic way that straight men touched one another's bodies or ordered others to do so… They believed they were doing some-thing *productive* – something fundamentally *heterosexual, masculine,* and *white.*"[41] The popularity of such hazing rituals, or at least their persistent existence in the college culture's imagination, stimulated by numerous col-lege comedies and Internet websites by and for young men in fraternities, enables *Freshman Orientation* to posit the protagonist Clay and his room-mate Matt. The explicitly homoerotic character of these rituals implies that Clay is soon going to pretend to be gay and, consequently, revises his own sexuality, while Matt will soon come to terms with his homosexuality and come out.

In the morning, however, naked Clay and Matt wake up on a lawn, in the middle of the campus, cuddling each other under a blanket. Clay cries: "Please tell me that you're not spooning me… Dude, you've got morning wood!" The students who arrive at the campus are gathering around this couple and Clay, who finds himself wearing a blue thong, whispers: "I wanna die." Later, in the atrium, someone scolds them: "Hey, faggots!" Matt asks Clay to forget about this morning but Clay is still disturbed by this incidence: "I felt your boner against my thigh, man!" Although these young men probably did not have sex with each other but only slept under the same blanket, they experienced physical intimacy that anticipated their concern about their sexual identification and their mutual interest in each other.

The erotic tension between these friends and rivals derives from their different masculinities. Whereas Clay the manipulator wears a blue T shirt and jeans, the moralist Matt is designed as a nerdy young man who wears a buttoned shirt over a white T shirt, glasses and a conservative hairstyle. Clay arrogantly rationalizes his pretending-to-be-gay: "We all know chicks love gay guys. I mean, they are all so sensitive. I guarantee in no time this girl will be saying, 'Why don't all guys be like you, Clay? Why can't you be straight?' And then, one night, when we're wasted, I'll say, 'I told myself that I cannot love a woman but you changed all that. You make me feel like a real man. Maybe my total life has been a total lie and I'm not gay. I think I'm in love with you," he gently caresses Matt's face and whispers: "Make love to me, please!" Matt, who is closeted, murmurs: "I'm gonna puke!" This dialogue reflects a dichotomous heterocentric perspective that connotes gayness with gentleness, sensitivity *and* perversion, whereas straightness is associated with horniness, roughness, unsophisticatedness, straightforward-ness *and* normalcy. Hence, Clay is willing to be perverted, according to his logic, in order to conquer his female object of desire and reaffirm his hetero-masculinity.

Interestingly, Clay's monologue embodies an ambivalent attitude toward *faggotry*, i.e. flamingly theatrical effeminacy that the straight mind ste-reotypically connotes with gayness. On one hand, Clay misperceives the delicacy and sensitivity of gay men as part of their perverted, twisted and abnormal masculinity. On the other hand, he regards their sensitivity as a valuable playground for unthreatening interaction with women. In Clay's heteronormative eyes, a platonic relationship between a gay man and a straight woman can easily be sexualized and hetero-normalized if a woman drinks enough alcohol and a man's gayness is deceptive. Clay's paradoxical "corrective" strategy is based on peculiar logics of the "inside out," of the turnabout, of a supervention shifting from perversion to normalcy, from rear to front, of a heterocentric travesty – a strategy which is conspicuously the opposite of a free-spirited and emancipatory carnival.

The joy of gayness and the fear of homosexuality

Significantly, *Freshman Orientation* parodies LGBT activism and heavily caricatures political queer assemblies, meetings and demonstrations. This film clearly portrays LGBT activists as fanatic, dogmatic and self-absorbed commissars. Clay's pretending-to-be-gay allows the straight viewers to have a glimpse at the allegedly strange world of queerdom in a heterocentric way that mockingly confirms vicious anti-gay stereotypes. Notwithstanding, Clay's pretending reveals that the straight majority perceives gays as a distinct community with its own culture, heritage, history, folklore, bars and venues.

An interesting intercultural interaction occurs between Clay and the effeminate middle-aged bartender Rodney (John Goodman) at the local gay bar Dorothy's Shoes, when the straight boy asks Rodney to teach him how to be gay: "I'm a bad gay," Clay complains, "Look at me, I dress like shit, I can't dance, your language confuses me." Rodney promises the gay guy that all he needs is "confidence and experience." Interestingly, Rodney assures him: "*Anything gay is learned*. It's not just about..." He makes an expressive effeminate gesture, and an elderly gay patron completes his sentence: "Take it up the pooper." Rodney silences the vulgar customer and comforts Clay: "You don't just pop up and suddenly know everything. Think of it as your *second birth*." Rodney instantly becomes Clay's mentor and he instructs him how to dress and dance fabulously. As part of this initiation, Rodney shows the boy photos of gay icons and subcultural phenomena, including Melissa Etheridge, Tom of Finland, poppers, mega-condoms, Alexander the Great, *Queer as Folk*, bareback sex and even a provocative drawing of an "intergenerational orgy."

Notably, *Freshman Orientation* never tells its viewers that straightness is also learned and practiced. On one hand, straight culture is re-naturalized in this film and standardized as emblematic normalcy while gay culture is significantly estranged, exoticized and parodied. On the other hand, the idea that "anything gay is learned" and coming-out is a sort of "second birth" is not entirely baseless. Whereas most straight adolescents have many straight icons and role models to identify with since birth, many youths and young adults who come to terms with their gayness do not have knowledge about what it means, beside same-sex sexual desire. Indeed, they have to learn what gay history, legacy, heritage, folklore, subcultures and lifestyles are, and they might feel that their coming-out *and* socialization into the gay community is indeed their "second birth" – a stimulating exploration of an alluring unknown territory, a *terra incognita* they ought to experience.

Clay's name connotes a material that can be shaped and reshaped before its form is solidified and determined; it alludes to this young man's coming of age and the ethical and sexual dilemmas he experiences through the love triangle that develops between him, Matt and Amanda. The romantic complications of this love triangle affect and shape this adolescent's personality and (hetero)sexual identification. Yet *Freshman Orientation* is more a conventional, heteronormative romantic comedy than an unruly college comedy. This film conservatively glorifies man–woman unification while representing Clay's attraction to Matt as nothing but a phase that doesn't really challenge his heterosexuality.

Clay merely goes through a visual, not an innate transformation. His makeover comprises a new gay look that includes trendy spikey haircut, stylish eyewear, red sandals, fashionable retro corduroy trousers in beige, red lipstick, effeminate red belt and an orange T shirt with a slogan: "Take a photo, It'll Last Longer!" Notably, Clay goes through gayification but he is not homosexualized. In other words, this young man adopts a gay visibility and subcultural outfits, gestures, speech and jargon, but he only desires women. He claims that "being gay is much cooler than being straight," but he never states that *sex* with men is cooler than *sex* with women. This ideological structure is enhanced by Matt's unfulfilled (gay) love to him. When Clay catches his roommate Matt reading *Advocate* gay magazine and jerking off, the latter confesses: "I want you, Clay" and the boys passionately kiss. This transgression, however, is immediately erased when this situation repeats with a corrective twist: Clay asks Matt what he is doing and the latter replies, "Ah, nothing" and confesses about his loneliness. In this way, *Freshman Orientation* "saves" its freshman's (heterosexual) orientation, and populistically re-distances itself from the label "gay film."

Pretending-to-be-gay inside and outside the patriarchal order

The fear of being labeled as a "gay movie," a fear shared by *Freshman Orientation* and *Boat Trip*, motivates the sexualization of the fag hag in these films. In *Freshman Orientation* Amanda clarifies that she is not satisfied with the title "fag hag." Clay's plan to conquer the sexy woman by pretending-to-be-gay seems to succeed in a scene in which Amanda puts her beautiful head in Clay's lap and wonders: "Why can't all guys be like you?... What am I doing here?! I really like you." Clay answers that he likes her too and assures her, "You're the most amazing person that I've ever met." They kiss but Amanda stops him: "This is… not right. It's *unfair* to you and it's *dishonest*." Clay almost admits his own dishonesty, but Amanda hinders his sensational confession.

Amanda embraces an allegedly gay-friendly attitude, at this point, while explicit homophobic messages are asserted by another character, the sorority leader Serena (Jud Taylor), who hates men and criticizes Amanda for her infatuation with a gay man. She rebukes her: "Wake up, Amanda! *Gays manipulate women to fall in love with them* all the time." (Emphasis added.) Serena's claim manifests this film's ideological frameworks. Unsurprisingly, Amanda replies that Clay is not like that, but Serena insists:

> Fine, then let's say he's giving up gay life for you. You really think he can tow himself out of it? He likes a dick in his mouth and he's gonna want it again because fags, Amanda, are still men!

Interestingly, Serena fantasizes an all-male sexual spectacle in which Clay plays a receptive "feminine" role which is synonymous, in her straight mind, with faggotry. Yet she thinks that this boy is "still a man," a young male adult whose presumed lustfulness and compulsive voluptuousness demonstrate his masculinity, even if it is a damaged or perverted masculinity.[42]

In Serena's eyes, Clay is a member of a sexual community that is both deviant and discriminatory. Her description of a man taking a penis in his mouth demonstrates many straight men's (and some straight women's?) nightmare, on one hand, and emphasizes gay Clay's involvement in a sexual subculture that totally excludes women, on the other hand. Hence, *Freshman Orientation* caricaturizes both gay sexual practices and radical feminism which is misrepresented in this film as fascist misandry, a relentlessly dogmatic hatred of all men.

According to the ideological framework of this heteronormative romantic comedy, Clay and Amanda can fulfill their love, only if Clay's gayness is refuted. Clay, a young adult who is devastated by his unfulfilled love for Amanda *and* affected by his roommate's feelings toward him, re-negotiates his place in the dichotomous sexual structure. When Matt drunkenly kisses him, Clay first tells him that this is "freaky," calls him a "shitface" and asks him "not to make that weirder." In a crucial moment, however, Clay apologizes and seems to be attracted to his roommate. *Freshman Orientation*, however, doesn't allow such a same-sex romance. Matt refuses Clay's homosexual offer.

The sought-after unification between Clay and Amanda, however, is not easily achieved. In a secondary plot, Clay is attacked by another gay student who tries to kiss him and brutally pushes him against a traffic sign and wounds him in the head. The LGBT community at the campus is angry at Clay when he refuses to press charges against the attacker. Although Clay was not bashed by homophobes but attacked by another gay man, the LGBT students use him as a poster boy for their campaign against gay bashing despite his protest.

The furious LGBT protesters march into a straight party and start a mass brawl. Clay tries to stop the riots and publicly confesses that he wasn't gay bashed, and he points at the gay guy who attacked him. Clay admits, in a Frank Capra style, that he is a deceiver:

> I'm just this jerk who pretended to be gay to get this girl to notice me. I'm in love with her. That's right. I love her. I'm not even gay! I thought about it. It isn't really my thing... Let's stop this... This is really my fault.

He begs his audience: "Look around you, you guys, there aren't much differences between you. OK, you see the person next to you? Give him a big hug! I'm serious. Big brute hug!" Nobody hugs, however, and the black lesbian leader of the local LGBT community cries "Fuck that shit!" and a homophobic student shouts "Shut up, you dyke!" before the mass brawl restarts.

Clay's failed peace initiative, however, has crucial implications on his relationship with Amanda. She is expectedly angry at him: "You have lied to me so you could fuck me?! I get it." Their melodramatic confrontation, however, cannot stop the desired resolution. At the final scene, Clay meets Amanda at the bus stop and she admits how much she misses hanging out with him. Clay assures her that he's "the same guy, just another idiot guy." He tells his sweetheart, in a somewhat flamboyant manner, that she's "totally fabulous" and they expectedly kiss to the sounds of Britney Spears' hit song "I did it again." This resolution reconstitutes the privileged heterosexual love while glorifying straightness and representing it as the real thing.

Gay performativity and mimetic desire

The Argentinian film *Plan B*[43] focuses on Bruno (Manuel Vignau), a young working-class man who is dumped by his girlfriend Laura (Mercedes Quinteros). Bruno plots to come between the new lovers by pretending to be gay and seducing her handsome, apparently bisexual boyfriend Pablo (Lucas Ferraro). Bruno discusses his plan and his progress with his macho friend Victor (Damián Canduci). Bruno and Pablo share interests and youth memories and use alcohol and soft drugs together. Their mutual exercises in pretending to be gay for theatrical experimentations increasingly make them consider their own sexualities in a new light. Although they continue to have occasional sex with women, their intimate relationship is strengthened and they eventually come to terms with love for each other. Unlike the flamboyant masqueraders in *Boat Trip* and *Freshman Orientation*, Bruno in *Plan B* is a straight-acting, masculine guy. He is a thin, hairy, green-eyed guy with bristles on his face and curly brown hair in a ponytail. When he tries to seduce Pablo, he still looks like an ordinary guy without any campy mannerisms, gestures, mimics, high pitched voice or theatrical capriciousness.

In their first meeting at the locker room – a notoriously homoerotic site – they get dressed and start talking about Bruno's favorite television series. Pablo tells him that he tapes the episodes of this show, and Bruno asks if he can borrow the recordings. Then Pablo invites him to watch *Blind* together with him. They watch television together, sitting on Pablo's twin bed, and Bruno's shirt is unbuttoned, exposing his young hairy torso. Intriguingly, the intimacy between these young men is mediated by Bruno's stories about the nice experiences he had with his girlfriend. Pablo doesn't know, of course, that the woman that his new friend talks about is Laura. In this way, the straight woman unknowingly functions as a moderator between these two men, who are gradually coming to terms with their attraction to each other.

Bruno's straightness is initially questioned in his comic homoerotic dialogue with Victor (Damián Canduci), Bruno's straight friend, however, who knows about the latter's scheme. Victor, who is convinced that Bruno is totally straight, asks if he ever touched Pablo's penis, and Bruno replies: "No, but I saw it at the gym, and it's a good size." Victor says, "Really, yah? Aren't you a lucky faggot?! You're such a faggot!" and they both laugh. Interestingly, this scene uncovers the homoerotic dimension of these straight men's friendship and their persistent curiosities and desires. Although the heteronormative framework is stabilized, as these men's interest in each other's genitals is represented as nothing but a harmless joke, this scene does anticipate their sexual attraction to each other.

When they meet Ana, a straight woman who is undeniably attracted to these boys, Bruno tells her that he met Pablo at the gym's showers. She teases them: "How big can it get if it's so small? Your sister showed me a naked picture of you." Pablo plays the game and compliments his mate's genitalia: "I don't know what it does otherwise, but with me it gets pretty big. Have you seen it?" Ana says that she never had the pleasure. Bruno caresses Pablo's hair and puts his arm on his shoulder. Ana suspects that they only pretend to be gay and she dares Bruno to kiss his boyfriend. He tries to avoid it and tells her that Pablo is still embarrassed about doing it. He finally kisses Pablo briefly. In this awkward situation, two allegedly straight men masquerade themselves as gays while their gayness is both questioned *and* eroticized by a straight woman who is explicitly attracted to them, despite and maybe because of their gay identification.

Clearly, Ana derives erotic pleasure from her friendship with the allegedly gay couple. She speaks with them freely and vividly about her sex life, men and phalluses. When Bruno and Pablo drink together with Ana and her boyfriend at Pablo's home, she tells the boys that her boyfriend's penis "when alive is really huge," and she admits: "He's all dick and no brain, but I'm happy anyway." Bruno reveals to them that Ana's partner used to be his sister's boyfriend, and he scorns them: "Yes! Whores! You're both whores." She dares the young men to free their mind and they kiss. Their insincere kiss, however, doesn't ease Ana's mind. She says "Kissing a guy doesn't make you gay. Sometimes I kiss girls. Yes. It drives the boys crazy." After she passionately kisses Pablo, however, Bruno intends to kiss her too, but she dares him to kiss his handsome friend. Ana's desire is only accessible indirectly through the desire of others because it is mimetic or imitative.[44] In a short while, however, they all fall asleep while Bruno hugs Pablo spontaneously and voluntarily, not as part of their pretending-to-be-gay. Their sentimental same-sex interaction conspicuously demonstrates the power of "staged" kisses and "false" all-male intimacy in stimulating a process of authentication or coming to terms with the pretenders' forbidden desires, repressed feelings and transgressive arousals.

Working like a Proustian homosexual in the fields of heteroflexibility, intercorporeality and inter-pretense

Although Bruno and Pablo do not have sex with each other, these young men derive pleasure from a total range of homoerotic sensations, emotions and experiences of their multifaceted all-male intimacy.[45] Guillermo Abel Severiche argues that the eroticism in *Plan B* strongly depends on the camera's homoerotic gaze that captures the protagonists' bodies.[46] He notes that Berger homoeroticizes the cinematic gaze by meticulously shooting parts of the male body – usually parts of his protagonists' bodies within the same frame – to create eroticism between film and audience, and to suggest eroticism between his characters on screen.[47]

Moreover, Pablo and Bruno seem to have grown up in the same sociocultural context and they share similar memories about Peter Pan, about toys such as *Rastis* (similar to *Lego*) and about some experiences like sleepovers at a friend's house. In this way, according to Severiche, "Berger's film pays special attention to the growing homoeroticization of the spaces of friendship socially assigned to heterosexual masculinity."[48] In a scene that significantly blurs the boundaries between falsity and authenticity, Bruno tells Pablo that he is going to be auditioned for a commercial that obliges him to kiss another guy. He tells Pablo that he doesn't know what to do. Pablo reminds Bruno that the other day he was drunk and he kissed him. Bruno confirms that he was drunk. Pablo is clearly embarrassed. He laughs: "Are you kidding? You're kidding me! It's one thing giving a little kiss or fooling around drunk." Bruno asks him not to mistake it for the little kiss and Pablo confirms that he doesn't mistake it. Pablo is clearly reluctant. "It's weird kissing each other so you can practice," he contends, but he finally agrees. "I'll do it because you're my friend. I even agree to try it without being drunk," he explicates, "It's easier to go over there and just do it." Bruno dares him: "But you would do it!"

This situation complicates this film's epistemology of the closet and politics of intimacy. Pablo's responsiveness might reflect his coming to terms with his transgressive, non-straight sexuality. His willingness to practice same-sex kissing with his best (platonic) friend is not only a comfortable tactic for Bruno for exploring and initially fulfilling his growing sexual attraction to Pablo. Yet this "kissing maneuver" is a precious opportunity for Pablo to exercise his unspoken *desire* for Bruno. The theatric exercise is a fascinatingly manipulative and dynamic amalgamation of authenticities and masquerades.

At this stage, Bruno and Pablo's (homo)sexual desire is still Proustian. Anna Fahraeus notes that Proustian homosexual desire is hidden desire, "from others certainly but sometimes even from the self."[49] Notwithstanding, these men's pretending-to-be-gay *while* pretending-to-be-straight oscillates between meticulous *work* and lively *play*. Hannah Arendt identifies labor and play as distinct categories of human experience. She notes that all serious activities, irrespective of their fruits, are called labor, and every activity which is not necessary either for the life of the individual or for the life process of the society is subsumed under playfulness.[50] In this case, Bruno invests a lot of *work* in pretending to be gay, in taking revenge on his former girlfriend by seducing her current boyfriend. At the same time, his work is blurred with emergent sexual *playfulness*. He gradually realizes that he not only is fooling Pablo but also *plays* with his heart. Concomitantly, Pablo's "work" at fending off Bruno's gay initiative gradually becomes a *playful* courting charged with mutual sexual *and* romantic attraction.

Plan B is clearly set against the backdrop of working-class Buenos Aires and the modest domestic installations these two *pibes de barrio* ("boys in the 'hood") inhabit.[51] The protagonists are clearly not privileged glamour boys, in contrast to typical closeted protagonists in American and British gay adolescence films of the 1990s and 2000s.[52] Bruno and Pablo are typical machos who negotiate their intense feelings toward each other in a cultural environment that glorifies heteronormativity. Blond Bruno, however, is tougher, hairier and apparently more masculine and bearded than handsome, dark-haired Pablo. Yet each one of them is more sensitive, fragile and emotional than the other, at different stages of the plotline, as they both struggle with their transgressive desire and are not at ease with coming to terms with their "forbidden love" (see Figure 3.2).

Pablo's sexuality, in particular, is conspicuously liminal, though, and he is not necessarily willing to cross the line between heterosexuality and homosexuality. He remains somewhat in-between in these allegedly dichotomous tropes. Pablo demonstrates a sort of hetero*flexibility*. Ward suggests that part of what is said to distinguish heteroflexibility from gayness is that it involves engaging in same-sex sexuality while distancing oneself from the lesbian and gay movement.[53] People who identify as heterosexual, unlike gay men and lesbians, are generally content with *straight culture*, or heteronormativity; they enjoy heterosexual sex and, particularly, they enjoy heterosexual culture. Simply put, "being sexually 'normal' suits them. It feels good; it feels like home."[54]

Yet these "culturally straight" boys are frustratingly self-constrained and oppressed by the hegemonic masculinity's restrictive laws of desire. Thus, their attempts to fulfill their love for each other repeatedly fail. In a scene in which Pablo initially tries to have sex with Bruno, he hesitantly unbuttons Bruno's red shirt and takes it off. He then takes off his own T Shirt. Pablo almost kisses his friend, but he suddenly tells him that he has to piss.

Figure 3.2 The relationship between Pablo (Lucas Ferraro) and Bruno (Manuel Vignau) oscillates between heteroflexibility and homosexuality in *Plan B* (Argentina 2009) (film still).

Meanwhile, Bruno takes off his shoes. Pablo comes back with his shirt on, smoking a cigarette and telling Bruno, in a reversal of their power relations:

> I love you too but I can't... We're going crazy. I don't like guys. I'm not gonna change, even if I try once. I'm sorry. Really, I am. I'm a bit shocked about everything, but I know I don't. We're not 12 years old. This is beyond my control. I *pretend* to be modern but I'm old fashioned and I have a girlfriend. Everything's... I don't know... fine, though. In the future we can be friends.

In response, Bruno puts on his shoes and buttons his shirt. He sits on the stairs and looks angsty, contemplating their mutual emotional manipulations. He intends to go back to Pablo's room but then he leaves.

Notably, this sequence reflects a painful failure. But it can be perceived not as one of the typical heteronormative failures, in which a boy initially fails to have "proper" sex with his sweetheart because of diverse psychological reasons, interpersonal dynamics and sexual dysfunctions, but rather as connoting the queer art of failure. Jack Halberstam theorizes the particularities of *queer failure* and suggests that in a queer perspective, "we can recognize failure as a way of refusing to acquiesce to dominant logics of power and discipline and as a form of critique."[55] In this respect, the young adults in *Plan B* are critically presented, at this stance, as martyred young men, who fail to fulfill their mutual desire for each other because of an omnipresent oppressive dominant logics of power and (hetero)sexual discipline in proletarian Buenos Aires. Yet, Pablo's initiation, even if it fails, uncovers an existent sexual *possibility*.

Bruno and Pablo overcome their initial sexual *and* romantic failure, however, by their growing intercorporeality. This process is at the center of a scene in which they stand (semi)naked and silent at the communal showers where a low wall separates between them, physically and metaphorically. In this conspicuous one-shot scene, each one of these young adults is erotically appropriated *and* Othered by his friend's glance. Pablo's body yearns for Bruno's body and vice versa. Each one's corporality *and* same-sex attraction are reflected, represented and stimulated by the other's presence. The notion of "intercorporeality," originally coined by Maurice Merleau-Ponty, stimulates a reconsideration of Others' bodies as constitutive for one's own sense of embodiment.[56] In this case, each boy's nakedness embodies his friend's same-sex desire.[57] Thomas Fuchs realizes intercorporeality as a "pre-reflective intertwining of lived and living bodies, in which my own is affected by the other's body as much as his by mine, leading to an embodied communication."[58]

David William Foster suggests, however, that it is not that these individuals "discover" that they "actually" are gay. Rather, they end up discovering a wider field of erotic potential for their bodies than they ever, up to that point, imagined.[59] Whether Bruno and Pablo's physical and romantic attraction to each other is identified as gay, bi-curious, pansexual, omni-sexual or "sexually extended," I initially consider their intercorporeality as a sort of *inter-pretense*, a multilayered interrelationship in which these two young men concomitantly cover and uncover their masqueraded hetero- *and* homosexualities. Each of these pretenses is liquidized, metamorphosed, subverted and traversed by its inter*playing* with the other.

These two young men embody two symbiotic settings of masquerade that playfully, vividly and sometimes devastatingly affect and stimulate each other. The inner tension inside each masquerade and the tension between them fuel a lively interaction between sexual authenticities and potentiali-ties, forbidden fantasies and transgressive experimentations. The unadmit-ted truths behind these pretenses are complicated and intensified by perilous instabilities, indeterminacies and uncertainties. These two deceivers manip-ulate each other's politics of the closet and negotiate contested feelings, desires and identifications. They concomitantly experience compulsive het-erosexuality, erotic same-sex intimacy and transgressive identifications and their consequent emotional crisis.

The fag hag as director and moderator of sexual authentication

The young protagonists live in a sphere in which homosexuality is consid-ered a derogatory term and a despicable lifestyle which is regularly connoted with repulsive, emasculating sexual practices. Their emotional difficulties in coming to terms with their sexual transgression are visualized by a series of poetic long shots of gloomy old buildings and slums in proletarian Buenos Aires, as much as sights of a deserted seashore in grey shades. The poetic, melancholic images authenticate Bruno and Pablo's inner struggle when they are torn between their machismo and their newly discovered sexual authenticity.

At some point, they cut off their connections, and when they meet again, Pablo tells Bruno that he broke up with Laura. Bruno asks him why he didn't come back with her, and Pablo replies that he "got confused" with him. Bruno confesses that he's in love with him. In response, Pablo gazes at him silently. This is not a happy love, though. Bruno apologizes for his infatuation: "I'm completely sick. I don't know how it happened. I couldn't handle it." Then the boys kiss passionately. Then they vividly rush into Pablo's bedroom to fulfill their love for each other.

Conspicuously, *Plan B*'s ethical framework is totally different from *Boat Trip* and *Freshman Orientation*'s ideological premises. In the American comedies discussed, the connection between the fag hag and the man who pretends to be gay reminds him and his viewers that his gayness is merely a comic masquerade on his way to fulfilling his love for his woman. In other words, the gay is not really gay, the fag hag is not really a fag hag, and the only real thing is the man–woman romance. In the Argentine film, however, the connection between the fag hag and the gay men helps them to understand that they are *not* straight. Each of these young men continues to sleep with women, as long as he is in denial.

The fag hag Ana, however, doubts the gayness of the "impostors," but, paradoxically, her reluctant attitude, and her consequent instructions to the boys to perform their same-sex attraction, stimulates their realization that they truly enjoy hugging and kissing each other. The staged gay expressions, gestures, connections and interactions, instructed by the manipulative fag hag, cross the line between theatricality and actuality, falsification and authentication.

Notably, the protagonists in *Plan B*, despite their homosexual desire, find it difficult to identify themselves as gays. These machos never visit gay bars, gay dance clubs, gay saunas, gay cruises or gay cruising grounds, *and* they never have sex with other men beside each other. Whereas the gayness in *Boat Trip* and *Freshman Orientation* is associated with stereotypical campiness, effeminacy, festive theatricality, sassy eccentricity, subcultural obsessions and fanatic activism, the gayness in *Plan B* is not associated with any countercultural role models, iconographies, festivities, mannerisms, political struggles or folklores. Bruno and Pablo do not know any other gay men; they are not supported by the Buenos Aires gay community, and they are not interested at all in gay history and politics. They know only each other. The only countercultural phenomenon they share with gay folklore is their friendship with a fag hag.

Throughout most of the film, the protagonists experience the "social impossibility of gay love,"[60] while avoiding a sexual relationship with voluptuous Ana. Bruno and Pablo feel comfortable when they meet Ana and can put gayness on as an act. Only in front of this platonic female friend do they allow themselves to experience physical contact with each other, in a way that theatrically acts out against the compulsory heterosexuality.

At the end of this bitter comedy, however, the amorous couple finally overcome the traumas of heteronormativity and joyfully rush into Bruno's bedroom to have sex. Yet it is not necessarily their final destination. Rather, it is possibly only a beginning of these *fresh* men's unmasking and emancipatory journey toward acknowledging and embracing their *orientation*.

Notes

1 Button 2000: 46.
2 Maddison 2000: 6.
3 Button 2000: 46.
4 Maddison 2000: 194.
5 Evans 1999: 22.
6 *Will & Grace* 1998–2006; 2017–present.
7 *My Best Friend's Wedding* 1997.
8 *The Object of My Affection* 1998.
9 *The Next Best Thing* 2000.

10 *Bend It Like Beckham* 2002.
11 *A Home at the End of the World* 2004.
12 Sedgwick 1985.
13 Evans 1999: 35–36.
14 Van Leer 1989: 595.
15 See Sedgwick 1989: 749. A year later, however, Sedgwick confessed that "the vicarious investments most visible to me have had to do with my experiences as a woman; as a fat woman; as a non-procreative adult; as someone who is, under several different discursive regimes, a sexual pervert; and, under some, a Jew." She explained that "living in the stigma-impregnated space of refused recognition is sometimes also a stimulating either of the unnamed, the lived experiment" (Sedgwick 1993 [1990]: 267–268).
16 Sedgwick 1998: 625.
17 Maddison 2000: 10.
18 Moon 1995: 489.
19 *Fag Hag* 2005.
20 *Boat Trip* 2002.
21 This fag hag doesn't wish to heterosexualize all gay men, however, or even to change one specific gay man's orientation. She only yearns to erotically unite with a member of different, apparently contrasted sexual community. In this respect, she aspires to deconstruct the psychoanalytic concept of difference without subscribing to any sexual truths about the relations of gayness or straightness to sexual practice.
22 Bartle 2015.
23 Robertson 1996: 8.
24 Further, Deborah Thompson stresses that the fag hag was hailed into the queer community early on, and that is her home. Hence, "she does not just go there to visit; she lives there" (Thompson 2004: 42).
25 Thompson 2004.
26 Thompson 2004: 43.
27 Thompson 2004: 43.
28 Maddison 2000: 12.
29 Maddison 2000: 10.
30 Thompson confesses, however, that she did not choose the fag hag identity. Rather, it chose her – and chose her "long before I had the cognitive ability to recognize fag hag identity, much less homophobia or heterosexism" (Thompson 2004: 44).
31 Thompson 2004: 44–45.
32 Queen 1997: 20.
33 Guzmán and Valdivia 2004.
34 Guzmán and Valdivia 2004: 211.
35 Ingraham 2005: 2.
36 See Rubinfeld 2001.
37 *Freshman Orientation* 2004.
38 Bakhtin 2004 (1968): 220.
39 Bakhtin 2004 (1968): 220.
40 Ward 2015.
41 Ward 2015: 3–4.
42 Earl Jackson, Jr. notes that gay men as men live dually within the systems of meaning of the dominant order and within their own constitutive transgressions and betrayals of that order (Jackson 1995: 17).
43 *Plan B* 2009.
44 Girard 1976: 26.
45 Korn 2016: 328.

46 Severiche 2019.
47 Severiche 2019.
48 Severiche 2019: 283.
49 Fahraeus 2014: 30.
50 Arendt 1958: 128.
51 Foster 2013: 256.
52 See Padva 2004.
53 Ward 2015.
54 Ward 2015: 28.
55 Halberstam 2011: 88.
56 Merleau-Ponty 2012 (1960).
57 Gail I. Weiss notes that to describe embodiment as intercorporeality is to emphasize that the experience of being embodied is never a private affair, but "is always already mediated by our continual interactions with other human and nonhuman bodies" (Weiss 1999: 5).
58 Fuchs 2017: 9.
59 Foster 2014.
60 King 2014: 199.

4 Odd couples, queer partnerships and gay marriages in pretending-to-be-gay films

There's something intriguingly odd about straight buddies, whether their close friendship is contextualized in a homosocial or, rather, in a mixed gendered environment. Buddies' relationships are typically fueled by unadmitted tension between the protagonists' commitment to prevalent heteronormative imperatives that design a totally platonic, non-sexual connection on one hand, and the unruly, rampageous and free-spirited nature of long-time companions' intimacy on the other hand. Same-sex intimacies between self-identified straight men, with their powerfulness, depth and implications, are changing and developing over time.

Heteronormative frameworks, however, impose strict definitions of what a legitimate, desirable and acceptable straight men's relationship is. Yet intimacies between buddies, with their emergent oppressed *and* erupting passions, are not always easily subdued by the omnipotent, compulsive heterosexuality. This complicacy is at the center of thousands of buddy films in diverse genres, including westerns, military dramas, prison cinemas, TV sitcoms, telenovelas and soap operas, and bromance comedy films. When a mainstream buddy film involves a pretending-to-be-gay scheme, however, the result might be even more complicated, conflicted and dramatically self-contradictory.

The commercially successful Hollywood film *I Now Pronounce You Chuck & Larry*,[1] in particular, centers on two heterosexual men, best friends and co-workers on the New York City firefighter force. Larry Valentine (Kevin James) is a widower whose wife died a little more than a year ago, leaving him with two young children. Chuck Levine (Adam Sandler) is an apparently testosterone-fueled, irresistible heterosexual man with a steady stream of voluptuous dates. Larry is so distraught by the death of his wife that he fails to transfer his survivorship benefits to his children within the required one-year window. A government functionary informs him that the only way he can ensure the healthcare of his children in the event of his death is to remarry.

When Larry sees a newspaper article about New York City's domestic partnership benefits, he realizes another way out of his dilemma. He convinces Chuck to pose as his domestic partner so that he will be able to care for Larry's children in the event of Larry's death. Under pressure from an inspector who suspects a case of fraud, the two Brooklyn men head to Canada for a quick wedding. The two men move in together to Larry's place in order to make their relationship seem more conceivable, and then attempt to make themselves into a stereotypical version of a gay male couple. At the outset, they can only imagine gay men as entirely foreign entities, but as the film progresses, they apparently begin to identify, in a limited and often buffoonish way, with their assumed identities and even pretend to be advocates for gay rights.

At a gay charity costume party, the patrons are confronted by homophobic demonstrators. Chuck punches a bigoted preacher, and the incident is covered by the local news. With their apparent gayness and coupledom, the protagonists are scorned and derogated by their New York City Fire Department (FDNY) counterparts who eventually refuse to work with them and circulate a petition to have Chuck and Larry excluded from the firehouse. Larry discovers it and successfully confronts the crew about embarrassing incidents at the job that he and Chuck helped them overcome. Their only supporter is Fred G. Duncan, a black macho firefighter who comes out to Chuck.

Chuck and their devoted female lawyer Alex McDonough (Jessica Biel) become infatuated but cannot fulfill their love because the lawyer thinks he's gay. Alex becomes Chuck's fag hag. The firemen's pretending-to-be-gay gets complicated when 16 women publicly testify to having sex with Chuck in the recent past, and the couple is called into court to defend their marriage against charges of fraud.

Their fellow firefighters, however, arrive in support. Chuck and Larry, and the other firefighters, are sent to jail, but they are released in a short while, after they agree to provide sexy photos for an AIDS research benefit calendar, and Chuck and Larry are allowed to keep their benefits. Two months later, Duncan and Alex's flamingly gay brother, Kevin, are married in Niagara Falls at the same venue as Chuck and Larry. At the wedding party, Larry overcomes the death of his wife and initially flirts with another woman, while Alex and Chuck dance together and finally kiss passionately.

Notably, *I Now Pronounce You Chuck & Larry* was released in 2007 on the backdrop of final approval of domestic partnership and civil unions and outlawing discrimination on the grounds of sexual orientation in numerous states in America and in Britain. On the opening weekend, the film, which centers on quasi-gay protagonists yet targeted at straight viewers, was distributed to 3,495 screens, and approximately three months after its release, it had grossed almost $120 million.[2]

Interestingly, *I Now Pronounce You Chuck & Larry*'s plotline is highly similar to the story of the Australian film *Strange Bedfellows*[3] about two countrymen who pretend to be gay in order to win tax benefits. The story takes place in the teeny Aussie town of Yackandandah, a place where the movie house still shows classics, and the owner Vince Hopgood (Paul

Hogan) lives in the projection booth. The projectionist has some tax problems, but, lucky for him, the government just passed a new law stating that gay couples are entitled to equal rights tax-wise, and, consequently, he can get five years' worth of rebated deductions if he and his partner file jointly. Vince cunningly convinces his best mate Ralph (Michael Caton), a car mechanic, to go gay with him, at least on paper. Their device is complicated when they are informed that an inspector will be stopping by to investigate the validity of their claim. They quickly learn at the local hairstyling parlor how to look and sound gay, and they hang out at an extremely clichéd gay dance club in Sydney where they meet new friends, mostly bikers in leather and drag queens in glitzy gowns.

Because of a careless mail delivery person, the postmaster sees their application for benefits and tells one person, and soon the whole village knows that Ralph and Vince are a gay couple. When the village's vicious gossipmonger hears about their scheme, and the inspector arrives at the village, Ralph and Vince redecorate Ralph's house in a flamboyant gay style and complete their interview. Then they attend the local Fireman's Ball, in which Ralph performs a big speech scene in which he explains to the locals about the importance of love, which can be read by the other characters as meaning gay love or, rather, a platonic love between old straight buddies. This ambivalence promotes a greater tolerance among the townsfolk. It also eases the inspector's mind and helps Ralph to accept his own daughter Carla's coming-out.

The makers of the American blockbuster *Chuck and Larry* were accused of plagiarism by the producers of *Strange Bedfellows*, which was released three years prior to the Hollywood film. The Australian producers thought that the plot of *Chuck and Larry* was all too familiar. Steven Paul Davies contends that *Chuck and Larry* had the same matey vibe running throughout, "the same rather corny, clichéd comedy and the same warm undercurrent, which crept up on the audience at the end."[4] Jeanette Roan notes that the makers of *Strange Bedfellows* sued Universal Pictures for copyright violation, but withdrew when the Hollywood producers proved that they started processing the script years before it was released and did not plagiarize the Australian production.[5] By the end of 2007, however, *Chuck and Larry* appeared in the Golden Raspberry Awards shortlist, nominated in eight categories including Worst Film and Worst Actor (Adam Sandler).[6]

Teaching faggotry, learning to flame

In *I Now Pronounce You Chuck & Larry* the macho firemen, who pretend to be gay in order to secure the future of Larry's children, feel that they do not know how to pass as gays. They embody a macho culture of New York firemen, which is dramatically contradictory to what they imagine as the perverted flamboyancy of a faggotry culture. When Larry initially offers Chuck to arrange a domestic partnership with him, in order to enable

Chuck to inherit his benefits if he dies and be the one responsible for Eric and Tori, Chuck is reluctant because of the association of gayness and the proposed "domestic partnership." Chuck rebukes Larry "You mean like faggots?!" and the latter is confused: "No... I mean, yeah, but, no, not us, obviously. No, no, not, you know... It's just on paper, really." Chuck is overtly afraid to be perceived as gay. He asks "Paper faggots?!" and Larry replies "Okay, look, the accepted vernacular is 'gay', but, yeah."

Larry finds it difficult to persuade Chuck to accept his offer. He says "Chuck, look at us. We're not gay." Then the latter scorns him "But if we were gay, don't you think I'd be with someone a little hotter-looking than you?" Chuck is clearly insulted and reminds his friend "I'm Mr. February, for God's sake. It would be like the prom king fooling around with a... Tuba player." Larry says "Oh, great, I play tuba." Chuck squirms "Larry, I love you, but I'm not *in love* with you, if that makes any sense."

In this awkward dialogue, these two straight guys suddenly look at each other with gay eyes, judging each other in terms of male beauty. Homophobic Chuck even refers to his modeling for New York firemen's charity calendar that exhibits semi-nude male bodies not only for straight women's pleasure but also to satisfy the eager eyes of many gay men. Although their apparently gay statements should be contextualized as heteronormative jokes uttered by straight men in a comic manner, they do indicate some homo-erotic aspects of Chuck and Larry's homosocial friendship. Likewise, in two incidents in *Strange Bedfellows*, Vince briefly touches Ralph's ass. The numerous homoerotic manifestations and subtleties in these films indicate the intricate, abundant, multidirectional and overflown nature of human sexuality that transcends categorical classifications, social boundaries, ideological restrictions and contested systems of values. In this sense, these films celebrate the choice to be authentic, as much as the choice to pretend *and* the choice to *extend* one's sexuality.

Although these films preserve the protagonists' heterosexuality, they demonstrate a sort of what I initially defined as *extended sexuality*. Although their heterosexuality is not refuted, their (hetero)sexuality gradually comprises a greater vocabulary of erotic feelings, reconsideration of male beauty and the ability to look at themselves, at least momentarily, in a different, queer perspective. These abilities of their extended sexuality, however, do not disrupt their straightness. Although the protagonists remain "paper faggots" who are not *really* gay, *Chuck and Larry* and *Strange Bedfellows* prove that gayness, the cultural expression of homosexuality, is not an *inborn* nature but rather an *acquired* phenomenon with its own knowledge, folklore, heritage and iconography.

In contrast to the prevalent political advocacy of queers who were "born this way," a different, radical perspective suggests that straights and gays were not necessarily born this way but they all *choose* their sexual identification. If the right to be gay is not based on the idea that "this is how we were created, sorry, we don't have any other choice," however, then the advocacy of LGBT rights is based on totally different moral ground: the right to choose, adopt and deploy one's sexual *preference* in the name of sexual democracy, sexual multiculturalism and sexual freedom. According to this existentialist attitude, a person creates her/his own identity, destiny and meaningful life. One's sexuality is not dictated by nature but it is rather a lifetime journey with its own intimate dynamics, experimentations, meditations, twists and dramas, as much as endless confrontation with bigoted regimes that condemns a "sinful choice" or a "pervert lifestyle," a never ending struggle for free speech that embraces and celebrates one's true colors and favorite identification.

Jane Ward, in her advocacy of "sexual fluidity," suggests:

> Sexual fluidity is not a challenge to the fixity of sexual orientation; in many ways, the opposite is true. When we know we are born straight or gay, this knowledge enables us to experiment, to stray, to act out, and to let "shit happen" without fear that we have somehow hidden or misrecognized or damaged our true sexual constitution. More importantly, knowing that our sexual orientation was present at birth allows us to make sense of our discordant behaviors as exceptional, not bound to the same identitarian consequences experienced by true homosexuals (or heterosexuals).[7]

The protagonists' (hetero)sexuality in the discussed films, however, is *not* fluid. Although they are comfortable with their heterosexuality, they make sure that "shit" never "happens"; they never have sex with other men. Their attraction to women *remains* exclusive. Yet their sexuality is slightly extended when they come to terms with the homoerotic subtleties in their mundane heterosexual masculine cultures, and later, when they initially explore gay venues and their varied subcultures.

Chuck and Larry and *Strange Bedfellows* reflect a confused straight world facing the rise of gay marriage and other progressive pro-gay developments, on one hand, and a homophobic backlash of radical conservatives and masculinists, on the other hand. Indeed, as Jeffery Weeks observes, we live in a world of uncertainty, where good guides and firm guarantees by which we can reach any particular destination are in short supply, and where the goals themselves are cloudy and indeterminate.[8] "Nowhere is this uncertainty more acute than in the domain of sexuality," he adds, "which has been the subject in the recent past of apparently endless panics, controversies, anguished moralizing, and the rebirth of the value issue."[9] The erotic, and the relationships which focus on it, in particular, offers a glittering mirror which can reflect back to us the dilemmas of individual choice in an age of uncertainty.[10]

The protagonists in these films highlight their individual choice to secure their heterosexuality and hetero-masculinity while pretending-to-be-gay. Their masquerade, however, is restricted to facets of gayness that do not threaten or undermine their heterosexuality. Unsurprisingly, significant parts of these films highlight the impostors' despisal of faggotry, namely the campy gay subculture that celebrates colorfulness, theatricality, androgyny and subversion of the hegemonic masculinity and its certainties. As members of macho cultures, whether it is a conservative Australian rural community or a tough New York firemen culture, the protagonists detest gay men who supposedly betray "natural" male supremacy and dare to blur gender boundaries. They are explicitly reluctant about effeminacy that they misrecognize, in their straight mind, as deviant, spineless and permeable gay masculinity.

Paradoxically, Chuck and Larry's gateway to the weird world of flamboyant effeminacy is Eric, Larry's own preadolescent son. The kid adores musicals, sassy costumes, cooking brownies and doing the splits, whereas his sporty sister is clearly favored by her dad. Larry finds it difficult to accept his son's campiness and implied homosexuality. He rebukes him "Enough with the splits! Watch baseball!" When Larry complains about his son's transgressive fields of interest, Chuck comforts him in a homophobic tone: "Baton swallowing. I bet he'd be great at that." When Chuck keeps scorning, Larry warns him "I'll stick this pole up your ass, turn you into a lollipop!" and Larry replies: "You talking to me or your son?!" This dialogue demonstrates these men's association of effeminacy with homosexuality. In their eyes, male campiness and permeable male body are the same.

Chuck and Larry presupposes that if Eric is flaming then he might be gay; and if he's gay, he might be joyfully penetrated by a same-sex partner in the future. In particular, homophobic Chuck doesn't miss a single opportunity to emphasize the child's delicacy and stylishness. He mockingly mimics Eric when he says that cockroaches are "ewwy," and he later gives him a straight porn magazine that makes the boy scream and flee the room. Larry is also agonized by his son's effeminacy, but his love for all his children *is* unconditional.

The deceivers' gateway to the gay world in *Strange Bedfellows*, however, is not a family member but a notorious freakish member of their rural community. When Ralph and Larry need "to take a course" in faggotry studies, in order to satisfy the tax department's inspector who suspects their gayness, their only candidate for this job is the local hairdresser Eric (Glynn Nicholas) who is stereotypically portrayed as a swishy flaming guy. The deceivers follow him and find out that he's womanizing the village's wives. They meet him at his local barber shop where he wears a feminine outfit and earrings and speaks in a coyly effeminate voice with expressive gestures. When Eric denies that he's *straight*, though, Vince and Ralph show him photos in which he kisses and hugs his local female lovers. Finally, Eric confesses in a surprisingly masculine tone that he's straight.

In the industrialized western world, in which effeminacy is understood as the opposite of authentic or "real" masculinity, there is gender exclusivity between effeminacy and masculinity. Peter Hennen contends that in such a polarity, a presence of feminine traits automatically implies a deficiency in masculine traits.[11] Eric's character in *Strange Bedfellows*, however, is more complicated. His gay masquerade is connoted with stylish, creative, festive, unique, sensitive and devoted hairstyling. Even if he is not regarded as one of the boys, there aren't any indications that he has ever been despised by the straight townspeople. In this small town, Eric's stereotypic flamboyant effeminacy is synonymous with glamorous professionality and cosmopolitan prestige on one hand, and it serves as a perfect alibi for his sexual liaisons with the local women on the other hand. Hennen notes that although effeminacy is sometimes associated with same-sex interests, it has also been interpreted as the result of a too-ardent interest in the opposite sex.[12] Eric's faggotry, however, is adored by his female clients and forgiven by the local male bigots because his apparent sexual perversion perpetuates his position of the straight majority's servant.

Since Eric is merely a pretender, not really gay, he is never looking for sex with local unmarried and married men. Thus, he never undermines the town's heteronormativity. He is the local clown, in a way, a one-man (freak) show. He is mistakenly perceived by the straight men as an emasculated, androgynous, unsexed and thus unthreatening phenomenon. They never realize that he's an adulterous straight guy who fucks the whole town.[13] Notably, Eric is not perceived as a threat to these men's heterosexuality because his work doesn't involve any physical contact with other *men*; he never touches their hair or any other parts of their bodies. At the same time, they are not worried about his physical contact with their wives' heads and hair (and genitalia) because they do not regard him as a real man, in a heteronormative sense. The epistemological gap between their misbelief and the truth they don't know – Eric's pretended gayness camouflages his (hetero)sexual encounters with his female customers – is at the core of this comedy-of-errors.

In contrast to these local men, however, Vince, Ralph, Eric *and* the viewers of *Chuck and Larry* do know that the hairdresser is a fraud. According to this film's heteronormative politics of perversion, Eric's normalcy (heterosexual desire) is not corrupted by his mundane gay masquerade. His voluptuous hetero-masculine sex life is camouflaged by unruly faggotry, glitzy blouses and expressive mannerisms. His normalcy erects through his frequent sexual encounters with local married women. Eric's gayness is primarily a beneficial commercial device *and* a sexual fraud that masks his promiscuous, unruly heterosexuality. As the town's effeminate homosexual, he acts as a powerful mechanism for policing hegemonic masculinity *and* moralistic agenda.

Vince and Ralph, who are impressed by Eric's ability to sustain a continuous false image of being "the only gay man in town," offer this effeminate womanizer to trade the framing photos for a sort of a gayness course. Interestingly, Eric urges the strange bedfellows, in his special class, to realize that to think gay means to think effeminately. "From now on," he insists in his grotesque class, "it's not 'me' or 'I'. No, no, no. You refer to yourselves as 'she' and 'her', Got it?!" Eric assures Ralph and Vince that it's all a matter of learning some body language and some gestures. He instructs them, "Head up, bum out! Think Marilyn Monroe crossed with a bit of penguin! And left shoulder, right shoulder, left shoulder, right shoulder, left shoulder, pivot!" This caricature encodes the idea that homosexuality is a biological perversion, yet effeminate gayness – the cultural manifestation of homosexuality – should be carefully taught and learned.

According to these logics, authentic masculinity is strictly straight and it implies freedom and control, yet effeminacy is predominantly a ridiculous perversion and theatrical absurdity. In the eyes of *Strange Bedfellows*, effeminacy registers as a form of moral failure. Flaming Eric is prey to his passions, prestige and glam as well as sexual gratification. Richard Dyer regards the effeminate queen as the "in between" in that this was a wretched creature who failed to be one gender or the other. It languished in a "no man's land" in between masculinity and femininity.[14] As Dyer notes, we are familiar with the use of this type of put-down. The form this often takes is the tag that gay men are not "real men," which expresses the assumption that true masculinity is in large measure defined in heterosexual sexuality.[15] Niall Richardson wonders: "If gender is the scaffold for eroticism, but a character fails to perform either one gender or the other, then how can this character fit into any scheme of sexuality at all?"[16] In the uncommon case of *Strange Bedfellows*, however, this pattern is traversed; the effeminate queen is oversexed, rather than unsexed. He is presented as a threat to the straight community, which is unaware of this freak's voracious carnality and his intensive sexual consumption of the local wives.

Eric's inability to control his passion is represented as an effeminate attribute. Paradoxically, his voluptuous appetite for sex with women coincides, according to the heteronormative logic of this film, with his flamboyancy and campiness. In other words, he is not manly enough to look and sound like a proper or real man *and* he is not man enough to control his licentious desire *for women*.[17] Hence, Eric is primarily presented as a joke.

In order to amuse the straight audience, Eric teaches his devoted students, Ralph and Vince, how to walk effeminately, and he demands "to put a bit of swish into it. That's the way. For goodness sake, tummy in! Head up!" In a particularly scornful monologue, he tells them "You boys, you need to immerse yourself in the culture, you need to be where gay rules, where queens abound, where men are men and women are totally superfluous." He motivates them, "You boys need to see what I've seen. You need to walk the walk and dance the dance, hmm? In short, gentlemen, you need to follow the Yellow Brick Road." Ralph, who is not familiar with the iconic status of the film *The Wizard of Oz*[18] and its "Yellow Brick Road" musical number, asks "Yellow? Yellow Brick Road? Where?"

This situation is comic because of Ralph's ignorance in gay culture and its iconography and Eric's impressive proficiency in cultural and historical aspects of gayness, despite his straightness.[19] Eric's reference to *The Wizard of Oz* refers to particularly effeminate gay fandom that adores the glamorous bravado of significantly kitschy, campy and theatrical Hollywood films. Clearly, these *Strange Bedfellows'* learning to be gay predominantly means learning to be ridiculously flaming.

Two Erics, one faggotry

Both Erics are flaming in these films. Despite conspicuous differences between them, in terms of age, assumed sexuality, countercultural identification, social status and degree of theatrical stylishness, these are *two Erics* who demonstrate *one faggotry*. They both emblemize the world of flamboyant effeminacy which is commonly connoted with homosexuality. In these films' straight eyes, they are adored and ridiculed, despised and glamorized, perverted and embraced, at times. They are posited as exclusive ambassadors of a kingdom of eccentricities, peculiarities, idiosyncrasies, festivities and oddities that terrify *and* fascinate the straight majority.

This ambivalence is demonstrated by the gay party sequences in these films. When Chuck and Larry attend a gay venue, dressed as Dracula and Humpty Dumpty, they find themselves in a carnivalesque festivity in which the male patrons are dressed in provocative outfits, freely expressing their sexual appetite and exhibitionistic desires. A semi-naked man in a butterfly outfit jumps in front of them and screams "I'm dirty! Who's dirty? I'm dirty! Who's dirty?" Then he laughs madly and walks away. Larry is shocked: "Oh my god, it's homopalooza!" This cabinet of curiosities is inspected and presented as *terra incognita* and the protagonists (and their straight viewers) negotiate its perversions. When Chuck notices a shaped woman in a golden "bunny" outfit shaking her ass, for example, he approaches her, thinking that this is Alex the lawyer. Chuck, who is dressed as Dracula, covers his mouth with his elbow and shouts in a sinister voice: "I want to suck your blood!" The lady turns to him and he realizes that it's a mustached blond man with a flamboyant wig. The latter is surprised "Suck my what?!… It's cool. You want to suck something." Chuck flees and the bunny man shouts at him "Hey! Don't go, bitch! Don't be a tease! You whore!"

Likewise, the two townspeople in *Strange Bedfellows* go to Sydney and are overwhelmed by men kissing, drag queens and transvestite prostitutes. When Vince and Ralph enter a gay bar, they are shocked by a leather man in faux latex butt cropped pants. Later, Vince buys glitzy colorful tight pants in a gay boutique. When he asks Ralph how he looks, his mate bitterly replies "Like two pound of sausages in a one-pound bag." Ralph himself, however, comes out of a cabin in a leather outfit and the flaming tuxedoed salesman compliments him "Divine!" Ralph refuses to turn around, however, because he's wearing butt cropped pants. When they enter a gay mega-club, they feel like strangers in a den of sins. Vince inspects the partygoers as though he were Alice in Wonderland, hardly believing what he sees.[20]

Clearly, both *Chuck and Larry* and *Strange Bedfellows* tend to present a grotesque, ultra-theatrical, rampageous and sensational version of pretended gayness. The pretenders' grotesque masquerade perpetuates a discriminatory hegemonic hierarchy of masculinities. Their masquerade reconstitutes a dichotomy between dissent and pervert, normative and deviant. Urban gay culture is typically presented in these films as a sort of sinister circus with its own variety of malicious clowns, demonic puppets, corrupt jokers and twisted freaks. Whereas the grotesque and its absurdities, paradoxes and farcicalities are essential to any masquerade, such dark masquerades are cannibalistic in their voracious self-annihilating manner. Their notoriously destructive uncontrollability subverts itself, insatiably consuming its ridiculed objects *and* itself. Such caricatured masquerade promotes bigotry, prejudice and pitiless discriminative propaganda.

The mocking of faggotry in these films acts on *truthiness*. Nicole Smith Dahmen defines truthiness – a term propagated in 2005 by the comedian Stephen Colbert – as the societal acceptance of the appearance of truth as fixed for truth itself.[21] Stephen Colbert proposed the neologism "truthiness"[22] as the quality of stating concepts or facts one wishes or believes to be true, rather than concepts or facts known to be true."[23] Priscilla Marie Meddaugh suggests that the term, used by talk show hosts, news magazines and newspaper columnists, "encapsulates the epistemological uncertainty of modern political knowledge."[24] According to this logic, if thousands of people are already convinced of an essential truth, their combined efforts can discredit almost anything, or anyone.[25]

These films, in their perverting of faggotry, communicate a sexual truthiness which is primarily clichéd. Notably, the use of clichés is a powerfully oppressive mechanism that brutally eliminates complexities, depths, ambivalences, subtleties and uncertainties of the represented phenomena. The faked gayness in *I Now Pronounce You Chuck & Larry* is primarily *clichéd gayness*. The clichéd gayness in this film demonstrates a childishly sensational, superficial and highly superstitious attitude toward subcultural sexual communities. Anton C. Zijderveld stresses that clichés are magically convincing, though, because they produce "a sort of enchantment which needs an emotional participation in the general cadence of the words and the sounds."[26] The pathetically clichéd gayness in *Chuck and Larry* and *Strange Bedfellows* enables the straight majority to become enchanted with its hegemonic masculinities while mocking the gay community. By transforming both gay hedonism *and* gay activism into a series of tacky clichés and visual banalities, these films ridicule both phenomena.

Dropping the soap in a world of disguise and disgust

Many homophobic mainstream films and New Queer Cinema alike deal with common heterocentric connotations of homosexuality and disgust. Whereas bigoted films deploy the politics of disgust in order to misrepresent same-sex attraction as repulsive perversion and condemned inversion, queer melodramas criticize homophobic parents who cruelly bash their children and kick them out of home when they realize that they are "disgusting" young gay men. In both *Chuck and Larry* and *Strange Bedfellows*, the protagonists, in their pretending-to-be-gay, experience various homophobic manifestations of disgust. Their gay disguise makes them vulnerable to bigoted accusations, mundane harassments and daily confrontations with their homosocial environments.

William I. Miller perceives disgust as a moral emotion that – as a generalizing moral sentiment – casts blame on whole styles of behavior and personality.[27] All forms of disgust for Miller relate antithetically to things felt to cause pollution and all produce a common feeling and reaction against those polluting things – senses of disgust, violation and contamination, and the feeling and desire to be rid of the offending sensation.[28] Disgust is cultural yet also visceral. Parts of the body can be very problematic producers of such feelings of disgust, particularly the anus.[29] The male's anus, as a symbol of permeability and emasculation, is at the locus of fear, anxiety and unadmitted desire.

The heteronormative fear that this orifice might stimulate a forbidden male desire for same-sex penetration, is intensified in sites of bodily exposure. The notorious communal showers scene in *Chuck and Larry*, in which the über-masculine firefighters expose themselves, breaks out of narrative via performance and it is presented in slow motion as a comedy action scene.[30] The men's routine is interrupted when semi-naked Chuck and Larry show up after their gay marriage has gone public.

The straight firemen look suspiciously and anxiously at the two men (see Figure 4.1). Tense music plays, providing additional focus and attention. One firefighter drops his soap. His slow-motion concerned reaction distends the anxiety already palpably present. Then another firefighter also does so and the whole "script" of the dangers of dropping the soap in the

Figure 4.1 Larry (Kevin James) and Chuck (Adam Sandler) as potential penetrators in the firemen's communal shower in *I Now Pronounce You Chuck & Larry* (USA 2007) (film still).

shower in a prison drama, as Neil Washbourne points out, is evoked and played out.[31] Conspicuously, the bathing men worry that if they bend over to collect the soap, this will physiologically cause a spread of their buttock's cheeks and a consequent exposure of disgusting *and* enticing anuses. They are primarily afraid that they might be penetrated by their newly uncovered gay peers, Chuck and Larry, who are now regarded by the straight firemen as voyeurs who yearn to penetrate them by their gaze *and* phalluses. Although this scene mocks the straight men's paranoia, it still posits the gays as interrupters and intruders who fuel their peers' (and the straight viewers') worst fears.

The tension at the steaming site is slightly cut, however, by the arrival of Fred Duncan (Ving Rhames), a new, slightly mysterious, reputedly dangerous and potentially violent black firefighter. Fred is a large, broad shouldered and muscular bodybuilder. He nonchalantly picks up one of the dropped bars of soap and washes himself under a centrally positioned shower head. The rest of the firefighters look on in confusion. They do not know how to read his figure and actions. Fred begins slowly to spin under a shower head and starts to sing Chaka Khan's song (now a gay anthem) "I'm every woman" (Chuck and then Larry join in to harmonize). The camera draws back to reveal the words "bad" and "ass" tattooed across the left and right cheeks of his buttocks. I agree with Washbourne that though Fred carries with him unstable and unreadable signifiers ("bad ass"), the heavy muscularity and song he chooses could have been used by the firefighters to construct him as gay or construct him, in a racist discourse, as a tough and dangerous criminal in the prison "script," but at this point they do not do so at all, "perhaps because they are already flooded by their anxious concerns about Chuck and Larry."[32]

Significantly, the firemen find an unadmitted erotic pleasure in showering together, a ritual which is part of their labor *and* leisure. The communal showers are an intriguing sight that enables and demands mutual exposure, yet strictly forbids vulnerability and permeability of the naked male bodies or any manifestations of physical attraction, under any circumstances. Unlike communal shower scenes in prison dramas, however, firemen's communal showers are rarely shown on screen and they are not commonly recognized as sites of sexual assaults and rape. The showering scene in *Chuck and Larry* does not involve any physical violence, though, but it maintains the power relations between hetero- and homosexualities and, particularly, the straight firefighters' anal anxieties.

Fred, who picks up one of the dropped bars of soap, demonstrates impermeable masculinity by his powerful muscular body that connotes black machismo and white men's anxiety about black men's phallic superiority, in particular. Notwithstanding, when Fred (whose gayness is still a secret) dares to bend over to get the soap, he is shot in a way that avoids a spectacle of his spread buttocks and any exposure of his anus. In this way, the power relations between white and black men are not subverted or eroticized.

Another perilous site that involves voluntary mutual exposure of men's genitalia, in this film, is the public toilet. When they attend an LGBT Costume Party for an AIDS charity, they are afraid to use the toilets, where their private parts might be gazed at by the partygoers. Larry, however, has to use the toilets and this is made more difficult for him because he is wearing a giant apple costume which is unwieldy and has back and front flaps for access; the one to the rear of the costume appears easy to access by someone other than Larry himself. This generates panic and feelings of potential humiliation of Larry.[33] The toilets are regarded by *Chuck and Larry* as a disgusting site, not because they are immanently related to urine and excrement and consequent bad smell, but mainly because of their sexual and erotic potential as a cruising site for men who are looking for sex with other men.

While Chuck and Larry never discuss homoerotica, certainly not gay porn, the Australian film *Strange Bedfellows* shows the impostors Vince and Ralph searching the Internet for gay pornography at a local Internet shop. They do so not because they find gay pornography exciting, but because they do not know what gay sex really is. In other words, their interest in gay pornography is not erotic but informative. According to this film's heteronormativity, they do not consider gay porn as a way to free their mind and explore unknown joyful aspects of their sexuality. Rather, they are clearly repulsed by a still image of same-sex anal intercourse (the penetration itself is not shown on screen). When the priest surprises them, Vince doesn't manage to turn off the computer. At the last minute, they unplug the PC and avoid an unpleasant closure of their "gayness" (they do not know that the cleric and all other townspeople already know about their transgression).

Yet the homophobic connotation of homosexuality and disgust is also criticized by *Strange Bedfellows* in a scene in which they prepare themselves for a visit from the inspector who suspects that they are frauds. Vince, who considers himself more open-minded, educated, stylish, verbal and articulate than Ralph the car mechanic, confronts his mate: "I can't believe you! You still find all this disgusting, don't you?!" Ralph denies it but Vince insists: "Yes, you do. After all we've seen, all the people we've met, you still find homosexuality disgusting." Ralph replies that he doesn't find homosexuality disgusting at all and adds: "*I just think it'd be disgusting with you.*" Vince explains to his mate that this is "All the more reason we have *to rehearse.*"

Conspicuously, this dialogue demonstrates and limits these straight protagonists' tolerance. Although they apparently tolerate the gay community, they are disgusted by the idea that their long-time companionship will be "contaminated" by penetrating each other. Their heterosexuality is at the center of their masculinity, normativity *and* friendship, and the possibility that their gay *acting* will be translated into *gay sex* particularly terrifies Ralph, who is clearly repulsed by the very idea of all-male sexual intercourse. The distinction between acting out and gay action is reestablished by Vince's declaration that they need to rehearse their gayness (the cultural manifestation of homosexuality, not homosexual sex) in order to play it better, to pass better as gays. They only wish to improve their deception.

Notably, in both *I Now Pronounce You Chuck & Larry* and *Strange Bedfellows*, one impostor is a macho man who is more anxious about effeminacy, faggotry and, particularly, homosexual desire, whereas his counterpart seems to adjust himself more easily to pretending-to-be-gay. In *Chuck and Larry*, Chuck is the relentless womanizer and homophobe while Larry is slightly more tolerant toward homosexuality. In *Strange Bedfellows*, Ralph is the classic macho, an unsophisticated countryside man who misperceives gayness as a disgusting freak show while Vince is more refined and elegant and tries to be a part of the gay world's aesthetics, and, at times, he seems to enjoy his visit to the Sydney gay club.

The more adjustable deceiver in *Chuck and Larry* is Larry the overweight family man, not the hedonistic muscular bachelor Chuck. In contrast, the physical attributes of the gay-friendlier pretender in *Strange Bedfellows* are quite the opposite. Easy-going Vince is more shaped and fit than the chubby homophobe Ralph (see Figure 4.2). When they visit a Sydney gay venue, a black muscular young man in an open vest tells Ralph, in a coyly effeminate tone, that he and Vince seem like "an odd couple." Ralph instantly replies "Well, we're poofs, aren't we? It doesn't get much odder than that!"

Whereas his new gay friends at the gay club think that he is simply expressing a sense of self-humor, Ralph does despise the "poofs" and the burden of pretending to be one of them. This bigoted man is particularly disgusted *and* frightened when his friend Vince dances together with a group of men in glitzy colorful tight pants and black sleeveless T shirts who perform with a glorious drag queen. Ralph is shocked by Vince's skillful performance and he seemingly suspects, for a brief moment, that his friend has been truly captivated by the flaming freaks and has become one of them. Ralph's angst

Figure 4.2 Ralph (Michael Caton) the "leather man" and Vince Hopgood (Paul Hogan) the "campy man" in *Strange Bedfellows* (Australia 2004) (film still).

reflects the prevalent homophobic fear that homosexuality is contagious and might contaminate and infect even perfectly normal straight guys.

Grotesque masquerade and ludicrous authenticities

The politics of homophobia in the discussed films is intricate, contradictory, multilayered, oscillating between parody and grotesque. For example, Chuck, a day before his official wedding with Larry at Niagara Falls, watches signs of businesses offering wedding services. This bigoted fireman fantasizes homophobic parodies of the signs. When he sees the sign "Wedding Bells," he reads it "Wedding Balls"; he transforms the sign "I Do, I Do" to "I Do, I Do Love Clay Aiken"; he reads the sign "Great Beginnings" as "Great Rear Endings"; and he reads the wedding chapel's sign "Till Death Do Us Part" as "Till Dicks Do Us Part." The same kind of vulgar textuality is exercised in a scene in which Ron the closeted postman tries to seduce Larry. The serviceman assures the pretender

> I make drop-offs... I always deliver... There's no extra postage and it's always first-class... I handle with care... And I'd be happy to come in through the back door... I'm used to holding large packages.

Harpham stresses that the grotesque is a structure of estrangement.[34] Wolfgang Kayser suggests that suddenness and surprise are essential elements in this estrangement; the familiar and commonplace must be suddenly subverted or undermined by the uncanny or alien.[35] Indeed, the textual absurdities in these homophobic scenes exemplify estranging attitude toward gay culture, particularly toward gay sex. Familiar and commonplace signs and idioms are distorted in order to mock same-sex desire and love. Primarily, the "inverted" electric signs and dialogues portray gay men as sexually obsessed and bizarre.

Another grotesque sequence in *I Now Pronounce You Chuck & Larry* is the wedding in Niagara Falls (Canada side) which is primarily played for laughs. It is clearly a fake wedding that is not motivated by the conventionally ascribed rationales of romantic love and long-term commitment between two people but rather the legal, social and economic benefits that come with being married. The Niagara Falls wedding is farcical and grotesque in the extreme. It is presided over by Rob Schneider in an uncredited appearance as an Asian minister in extremely offensive "yellowface" make-up complete with taped-back slanted eyes, large glasses, buck teeth and accented English.[36] Notably, the grotesque depends not only on physical conditions, the deformity of which most people would recognize, according to Harpham, but also on our conventions, our prejudices, our commonplaces, our banalities, our mediocrities.[37]

Notably, the grotesquely racist portrayal of the priest reflects the most prejudiced and banal stigmatization of Asian American people in

Hollywood cinema.[38] The grotesque portrayal of the Asian American clerk demonstrates the absurdity and stupidity of the whole scene that ruthlessly mocks homosexuality, gay marriage and Chuck and Larry's fake gayness. Their witness is a homeless man they found on the street, and at the conclusion of the ceremony, rather than kissing his new husband, Chuck punches him in the face. In a grotesque manner, he explains to the minster that they like to "play rough." The pretenders' kiss is, of course, central to the conventions of the romance, often signaling the confirmation of the couple. This physical gesture of intimacy is what lies beyond Chuck's ability to feign in the name of friendship. No matter though, as Roan contends, this wedding is only a formality intended to allay the suspicions of bureaucrats, and the ceremony leaves no doubt that the entire evening is merely for show.[39] This mockery terminates with the Asian American lady playing the popular Jewish song "Hava Nagila" (meaning in Hebrew: "Let's be happy / Let's be gay / Let's sing cheerfully / Wake up, brothers! / We all must be happy") on the piano. The deceivers dance together in grotesquely mechanic and childish movements, rocking their feet like they were mad. The minister approves that the melody sounds "very Jewish" and the drunken homeless man suddenly joins Chuck and Larry in a traditional East European Kazachok dance until he breaks his leg.

This carnivalesque spectacle turns a gay wedding into a ridiculous circus. Lee Byron Jennings notes that a grotesque object always displays a combination of fearsome and *ludicrous* qualities – "or, to be more precise, it simultaneously arouses reactions of fear and amusement in the observer."[40] The Niagara Falls wedding sequence, in its grotesquely comic integration of stupidities, vanities and conventionalities, aims to disrupt the pretenders' and their straight audience's anxieties.

Harpham suggests that where the norm is truly a norm and not just bait for the grotesque, however, the grotesque might have the effect of raising the specter of insanity or of introducing chaos, even if momentarily, into a world or a work which does not wholly embrace it.[41] In the Niagara Falls wedding sequence, gay marriage, which gradually becomes a norm in significant parts of America, is mockingly represented as a chaotic assemblage of moralities and immoralities, greediness and opportunism, freakery and faggotry.

Flamboyant gayness and grotesque homophobia

Chuck and Larry comprises numerous grotesque perceptions of gayness that reflect some of the most disturbing obsessions and anxieties of the straight world toward sexual minorities. After Chuck punched a homophobic preacher, and his picture was published in New York newspapers, Fitzer the firefighter commander calls the deceivers into his office and rebukes them:

> Gentlemen, I have a very simple philosophy. What you shove up your ass is your own business... Now, it's not my style to get involved in

the personal lives of my firemen. And if sometimes I've given you the impression that I'm your friend, I apologize.

The boss sits down and continues: "However, I seriously doubt that you two are banging each other." He tells Larry that he and his late wife Paula were the most beautiful couple he'd ever laid eyes on. Then he turns to Chuck and denounces this fireman's gayness: "You, if my pencil sharpener had a skirt, I'd have to hide it."

The chief commander clearly doesn't believe they are gays. He complains that "Every flaming fruit bat south of Poughkeepsie wants to come down here to our house and slide up and down our pole!" Then he warns them that if this marriage is something they've cooked up in response to their pension problem,

> you are not taking me down with you! I will report you! You will go to jail where you won't have to pretend to be gay, because your asses will be busier than a test bench in a plunger factory!

The commander blatantly connotes gayness with aberrant sexual practices, particularly anal male permeability.

In the commander's bigoted mind, Chuck is a womanizer and thus it is impossible for him to enjoy anal receptivity. He cannot believe that Chuck's prostate can ever be subjected to anal pleasure. In other words, Fitzer doesn't believe that Chuck would ever wish to be fucked by a man *or* a woman. Men's permeability is associated by this homophobe with homosexuality *and* effeminacy, as he uses the homophobic idiom "flaming fruit bat" and argues that every flaming fruit bat wants "to come down" here to their house and "slide up and down" their pole.[42]

Another grotesquely homophobic scene is Larry's visit to his child's class in which he tells the kids about his work as a fireman, after his partnership with Chuck became public. An African American kid suddenly asks him "I don't like girls, either. Does that mean I'm gay, too?" Larry denies this but then a girl raises a question: "You were married to a woman, right? Does that mean you're half-lesbian?!" And another boy wonders "Do you have two jobs? Because my dad said that you're also a butt pirate." The latter's question reproduces again straight men's obsession with anal intercourse among gay men.

Of course, all these scripted questions are not naïve. These are more than indicators of the children's stupidity or their ignorance of their straight fathers' anal anxieties. Rather, these statements provide the viewers with an opportunity to assert their own worries about the "corruptive" nature of gay lifestyle and politics. Bigots who watch this scene get an opportunity to laugh at homosexuality which is misrepresented here as grotesque perversion that might seriously affect innocent kids' sexual identity and transform them into hopeless perverts.

Another harassment occurs when a policeman identifies Chuck and Larry as "the guys from the newspaper" and tells them about a perpetrator who is lodged in the air duct on a rooftop. The criminal tried to break into an apartment a night before and got stuck. The policeman is thrilled: "You're gonna love this! The guy got stuck upside-down so his ass is still hanging out for you!" In response, Larry says "That's pretty funny. Did your moustache come up with that?!" and the policeman replies "Oh, I'm sorry, I don't speak Gayanese."

Typically, the homophobic mind usually perceives gay men as "bottoms," i.e. penetrated subjectivities who lose their masculine integrity because of their uncontrollable receptive passion, or as "tops," unscrupulous predatory penetrators who do not hesitate to rape helpless anguished men. These doubly grotesque spectacles of masochist and sadist homosexualities show the homophobes' interest in gay sex and the language of deviant desires and abundant pleasures.

Thomas Cramer notes that the grotesque is the feeling of anxiety aroused by means of the comic pushed to an extreme, but conversely, the grotesque is the defeat, by means of the comic, of anxiety in the face of the inexplicable.[43] Hence, the homophobic policeman's fantasy of anal rape integrates horror with delight, deviancy with imaginable joyfulness. He sexualizes potential police brutality and modifies Chuck and Larry's "gay" erections as a means of disciplining and punishing delinquents, petty criminals and burglars. In the homophobic policeman's mind, the deviant's body should be punishingly inserted by deviant law enforcers. He envisions a bacchanalian spectacle of deviancy that embodies a particularly grotesque politics of discipline and punishment.

In elaborating Michel Foucault's *Discipline and Punish*,[44] Kate Gleeson suggests that hegemonic knowledge of the homosexual's body and his desires signified power – the Foucauldian terror of the extensive tentacles of the state that was coming to know, and thereby dictate, the truth of the homosexual.[45] She stresses that modern disciplinary regimes understand the importance of the docile body: "The body that is manipulated, shaped and trained is the body that obeys and responds."[46] Accordingly, the homophobic policeman's fantasy demonstrates the paradoxical disciplining power of Chuck and Larry's undisciplined phalluses in reshaping the burglar's delinquent body as subdued and docile. The pretenders' deviant erections are awkwardly imagined by the policeman as useful tentacles of the state that is coming to know, in a Biblical sense, the delinquent's body and to neutralize his threat to society by enforcing a permeability of his male body.

Dis/played intimacy between real men and their absent gay kiss

The authorities' suspicion that Chuck and Larry are pretenders is at the core of a hearing scene, in which they are unanticipatedly supported by

Fred, the closeted African American fireman, who offers persuasive evidence of the two men's relationship. Fred is coming out in the courtroom and praising Chuck and Larry for inspiring him to seek a male soulmate. What gives the game away, however, is the authorities' invitation to the men to kiss. At first their lawyer objects to the investigator's request because it is a demeaning demand that interrupts their privacy. Gay activists in the courtroom, however, encourage Chuck and Larry "to show how real men kiss." Consequently, the deceivers are left with no choice. As their faces and lips come ever closer together in slow motion, a variety of reactions are shown on screen, from suspense to curiosity to arousal to disgust. Chuck and Larry move toward each other while they are clearly disgusted by the idea of kissing each other.

When they are unwillingly about to make contact, though, their commander calls out "Stop!" and says that he would rather change his grandfather's diapers than see two straight men kiss. Jeanette Roan explains that "in a film that derives much of its humor from the comedy of two straight men trying to play it gay, kissing is the line that they cannot cross."[47]

Typically, in a romantic comedy, there's a "key kiss" near the end of the film that, as Mark Rubinfeld describes it, "signifies an end to resistance, a recognition of romantic love, a declaration of commitment, a portent of permanent union, and a pleasurable closure in the narrative."[48] Roan notes that here, however, the resistance continues. "There is no romantic love, and in case anyone might have begun having doubts, we are reminded in no uncertain terms that Chuck and Larry are friends, not lovers."[49]

Samantha Nogueira Joyce suggests that in-house censorship, ratings, culture and the churches' monopoly of knowledge come together in a powerful and limiting interplay culminating in narrow representational possibilities "and the ultimate absence of the physicality of the long-awaited gay kiss."[50] Notably, if Chuck and Larry were kissing in an unconvincing way, they would be condemned as frauds. And if their theatrical kiss was turning into a passionate, erotic manifestation of their deep feelings toward each other, their gay mask could be synonymous with their true skin and, significantly, this could become a gay film. *Chuck and Larry* deliberately avoids a gay kiss in order not to upset its straight audiences who presumably cannot tolerate sincere, unpretentious love between men.

Straightforwardness for the straight eye

Both *Chuck and Larry* and *Strange Bedfellows* conclude with touching speeches carried out by a deceiver who glorifies the deepness of the relationship between him and the other deceiver. These speeches supposedly convey honesty, directness, transparency and acknowledgment of commitment and intimate desires. But, in fact, these speeches are carefully crafted in a way that primarily appeals to straight audiences who do not wish to watch the protagonists' coming-out.

In *Strange Bedfellows* Vince and Ralph realize that Faith, the village's notorious gossipmonger, already knows about their deception and inspector Russel is about to discover the fraud soon. Additionally, their gay friends from Sydney, the leather bikers and the drag queens, suddenly arrive at the village party. Under these circumstances, the deceivers' confession seems unavoidable.

Vince says:

> Now, I understand there's been a bit of speculation around town about Vince Hopgood and myself. Well, it's nobody's business but ours, what goes on between Vince and I. We've been mates since we were kids. Most of you have known us all your lives. Crikey, we've lived and worked amongst you for years. That's what you should be judging us by, not about what may or may not happen between us in private. Vince has been part of every important event in my life. He was my best man. He was there when my daughter was born… And when my wife, Helen, passed away. He was a tower of strength to me. See, it doesn't matter who you are. If you have one real friend in this life, one person you can truly trust, then you're very lucky indeed. Vince Hopgood has been the best mate a man could have, and, yes, for anyone out there who's interested, I *love* him.[51]

To the sounds of kitschy romantic melody, Vince and Ralph put their arms on each other's shoulders. Ralph declares "I'm not ashamed to admit it." The townspeople, including the flamboyant hairstylist who also pretends to be gay (albeit for different business purposes), are tremendously touched by Ralph's apparently sincere words, looking at him in tearful eyes. The Sydney queers start applauding him and the locals immediately join them to the increasing sounds of sentimental violins. Ralph's straightness is solidified by his whispering, "Did you just grab my ass?!" Vince replies "Yeah, well, I'm only human," and they smile at each other. Notably, Vince's homoerotic gesture is unnoticed by the straight townspeople. Yet Vince's transgressive quick touch doesn't make him gay although it proves that he did come to terms with some hidden aspects of his sexuality *and* his long-term relationship with Ralph.

Ralph's rhetorical maneuvering in this scene, however, is the opposite of sincerity. Ralph deliberately obscures the (heterosexual) nature of his relationship with Vince. He talks about his long-time companionship with him that involves love, yet he never says if it is a platonic or romantic and sexual love relationship. Vince's speech reproduces the notorious claim that "what happens between us is none of your business." In doing so, he redeploys the conservative liberal distinction between the public sphere and "what we do or don't do in our bedroom." In this way, Ralph demonstrates a reactionary standpoint that dramatically contradicts the LGBT activists' argument that the private *is* political. These men's unclear statement is the opposite of coming out. They do not admit to being gay but insist on the right to hide or *not* to admit their (homo)sexuality.

At the same time, in his effort to avoid prosecution, Ralph doesn't admit that he and Vince are impostors who cynically exploited the advanced pro-gay legislation in Australia in order to receive economic benefits from the state. *Strange Bedfellows* praises this speech as a brave and exciting declaration, although it is merely a sophisticatedly deceiving speech that predominantly aims to please the conservative straight audience. This speech is more deceptive, in a way, than their pretending to be gay and, arguably, it is even worse than this film's ridiculing of gay subcultures *and* gay sex.

Unsurprisingly, Ralph's speech satisfies the (straight) establishment which is represented by inspector Russell. The inspector tells them that he's going to be "brutally honest" with them before he admits that he was initially convinced that they were nothing more than "a pair of criminal jokers who deserve the full weight of the law thrown at them." Then he adds that this night he witnessed "something quite special." He praises them for their honesty and a tolerance that, sadly, is very rarely displayed these days. The inspector goes even further to suggest that he doesn't believe he's "likely to encounter a tighter bond or a stronger love between two men for many a day to come." Notwithstanding, Russell urges them to stop the "silly charades" and simply "care for each other." According to his twisted logic, Vince and Ralph's sexual transgression can continue only if their gayness is truly a fraud, not a fact.

In the same spirit, when Chuck and Larry are called before a commission in New York City to testify about their marriage, they speak movingly about the depth of their friendship and affection for each other. Given their recent celebrity status as advocates of gay rights, the city agrees that Larry and Chuck can keep their benefits arrangement if they and their fellow firefighters agree to pose for a benefit calendar for raising money for AIDS research. The closing scene in *I Now Pronounce You Chuck & Larry* moves back to Niagara Falls and the wedding chapel at which Chuck and Larry said their vows. This time, friends, family and co-workers gather to celebrate and make official the gay relationship that has flourished between Alex's voluptuous partygoer brother Kevin (Nick Swardson) and Fred, the newly openly gay firefighter. I agree with Roan that this "real" wedding at the end of the film is mostly an afterthought though, whose primary purpose is to show that after coming out as straight, Chuck *is* now able to openly pursue his sweetheart Alex, who has apparently forgiven him for his deception.[52] Paradoxically, gay marriage is not mocked by this film if and only if it promotes and privileges *straightness*.

Strange Bedfellows and *Chuck and Larry* share the same heteronormative bourgeois ideology that strictly preserves a distinction between private life and public performance. These films are deliberately blurring the homosexual dimension of their protagonists' friendship. Moreover, the glorification of long-term platonic friendships implies that the deceivers' gay masks did not affect their straight skin.

Another ideological similarity between these films is reflected by their attitude toward their gay children. In *Chuck and Larry*, Larry is fully aware, from the very beginning of the film, that his preadolescent effeminate son Eric might be gay. Larry is not at ease with his child's transgressive behavior and language but he respects him, and his love for him is unconditional. Likewise, Ralph in *Strange Bedfellows* accepts and unconditionally loves his coming-out daughter and her female partner. Although pretending to be gay did not make him gayer, and his heterosexual identification is sustained, he does become more tolerant and open-minded when real homosexuality is exposed inside his family. In this manner, the gay mask does have a substantial cognitive influence on its bearer.

Substantially, *Strange Bedfellows* clarifies that two men who enjoy each other in *bed* are *strange*. Likewise, the title *I Now Pronounce You Chuck & Larry* parodies the heteronormative statement "I now pronounce you husband and wife," entailing the idea that pronouncing two men as "husband and husband" is grotesque and absurd. These films primarily demonstrate the straight majority's confusion and anxiety regarding the legalization and official regulations of gay marriages in multicultural Western societies and their implications on traditional moralities and existent homophobic folklores. Arguably, these films uncover the theatricality, excessive festivity and grotesque futility of weddings, marriages and marital performances.

Notes

1 *I Now Pronounce You Chuck & Larry* 2007.
2 *Internet Movie Database.*
3 *Strange Bedfellows* 2004.
4 Davies 2008: 155.
5 Roan 2014: 762 n12.
6 Davies 2008: 155.
7 Ward 2015: 41.
8 Weeks 1995.
9 Weeks 1995: 4.
10 Weeks 1995: 12.
11 Hennen 2008: 35.
12 Hennen 2008: 36.
13 As one of the local bigots puts it, "Eric's the local hairdresser. It'd be a worry if he was the barber." His mate responds, "I'd cut my own hair."
14 Dyer 1993.
15 Dyer 1993.
16 Richardson 2010: 128.
17 Although Eric is regarded by the local straight men as a "soft" man, given to self-indulgence, he is a local businessman (the owner of the local hair salon), an unseparated part of the local capitalist economy, and as homosexual, he apparently never threatens the local (hetero)sexual economy.
18 *The Wizard of Oz* 1939.
19 The 1939 MGM film *The Wizard of Oz* and the fantasy homeland of Oz resonate with many gay men. This film still inspires the names of all manner of gay travel-related companies, such as Rainbow Travel (New York, USA); Friends

of Dorothy Travel (Sydney, Australia); Yellow Brick Road Travel Agency and Toto Tours (Chicago, USA); and Red Shoes Travel (California, USA). Gordon Wiatt and Kevin Markwell note that the use of Wizard of Oz–derived names for these businesses is not just because of the film's cult status among many gay men. This film appeals to many gay men and other oppressed groups who identify with the story of Dorothy, particularly her unhappiness in the family home, her sense of not really belonging, and her desire to go "somewhere over the rainbow" where "the dreams that you dare to dream really do come true" (Wiatt and Markwell 2006: 2).

20 Notably, the gay patrons in this venue belong to numerous gay subcultures, e.g., leather and fetish, bikers, men in uniforms, men in jeans, bodybuilders, tuxedoed men, drag queens and gender-benders. In contrast, real gay parties usually focus on one specific subculture or a theme. *Strange Bedfellows'* (mis) representation of this multiplicity is not really meant to celebrate diversity and sexual pluralisms and contemporary gay communities. Rather, this multiplicity is synonymous with polymorphous perversities celebrated by an intimidating sexual minority.

21 Dahmen 2010.

22 He first used this idiom on the October 17, 2005, segment of "The Word" on Comedy Central's *Colbert Report*.

23 Cited by Munger 2008: 125.

24 Meddaugh 2010: 376.

25 Munger 2008: 126.

26 Zijderveld 1979: 66.

27 Miller 1998: 35.

28 Miller 1998: 100.

29 Miller 1998: 100.

30 Washbourne 2018: 46.

31 Washbourne 2018.

32 Washbourne 2018: 47.

33 Washbourne pointedly emphasizes that Chuck's concern about attending the party leads him to refuse to use the toilets at all, saying that he "peed three times" before he left their house to avoid it (Washbourne 2018: 45–46).

34 Harpham 1976: 462.

35 Kayser notes that "it is our world which ceases to be reliable, and we feel that we would be unable to live in this changed world. The grotesque instills fear of life rather than fear of death" (Kayser 1966: 185).

36 Roan 2014: 757.

37 Harpham 1976: 463.

38 This character clearly echoes the stigmatization of the Asian American neighbor of the white female protagonist in *Breakfast at Tiffany's* (1961). Mr. Yunioshi (Mickey Rooney), the unbearable Japanese neighbor of the lighthearted New York socialite Holly Golightly (Audrey Hepburn). The Asian American neighbor regularly calls Holly and threatens to call the police if the noisy party goes on. Unlike the Niagara Falls priest, Mr. Yunioshi is always furious and hostile, and just like in *Breakfast at Tiffany's*, he wears a disgraceful "yellowface" make-up complete with taped-back slanted eyes, large glasses, buck teeth, and accented English.

39 Roan 2014: 757.

40 Jennings 1963: 10.

41 Harpham 1976: 465.

42 The man in charge refers, of course, to the professional fire pole at the station, but he also alludes to the popular phallic connotations of the pole as a masturbatory device. In this case, however, the commander doesn't regard the pole as

a notorious setting for female exotic dancers who arouse their drooling male clientele by sliding up and down the metal hose. Rather, he uses the pole as a metaphor for the firemen's private erections that might be sexually exploited by eager gay men.

43 Cramer 1966 cited by Steig 1970: 256.
44 Foucault 1979.
45 Gleeson 2007.
46 Gleeson 2007: 337.
47 Roan 2014: 759.
48 Rubinfeld 2001: 6.
49 Roan 2014: 759.
50 Joyce 2013: 60.
51 *Strange Bedfellows* 2014.
52 Roan 2014: 759.

5   Screening compulsory homosexuality

The perilous pleasures of parodying heteronormativity and fantasizing a topsy-turvy martyrdom

Few adolescents worry that they will have to sit down with their parents and confide what they have come to realize about their sexual identity, that is to say "Mom, Dad, I'm straight." Meg I. Striepe and Deborah L. Tolman explain that in our society, heterosexuality is assumed from birth. It is when adolescents show signs of being different than the heterosexual norm that sexual identity becomes a visible aspect of development.[1] Striepe and Tolman note that warning signs of differentness often constitute violations of heterosexual practices, such as not demonstrating signs of being attracted to the opposite sex or, alternately, signs of same-sex attraction, gender-atypical bodily appearance (e.g., body piercings, dress, or comportment), or even speaking in particular ways. "Youth who do not show signs of such violations are simply assumed to be heterosexual unless they state otherwise," they add. In comparison, sexual-minority youth experience a different sexual identity developmental process in which the knowledge that they are different is ever present. "Alone or with the support of others, sexual-minority youth explore and experiment to construct, evaluate, or find their sexual identity."[2]

It is never easy to be part of a minority who has to invent and elaborate its subaltern sexual identity, yearning for a haven island in the middle of a turbulent ocean of daily defamations, harassments, persecutions and violent assaults. Anyone who experiences discrimination and bullying, whether due to race, ethnicity, nationalism or religion, or because of gender assignment or sexuality which is different than the majority group's identification, often fantasizes about a totally different and even a reversed, alternate world where his Otherness is the norm and where those who belong to the hegemony, in the real world, suddenly find themselves in a position of a subaltern group that cannot oppress and humiliate different ethnicities and sexualities. Minority members who pretend to be socially, politically and ethically powerful and influential do not necessarily immerse themselves in ridiculous delusions.

At the heart of the ambition to change the world and to promote an egalitarian agenda are revolutionary imagination and fantasy that creatively produce an inspiring and motivating utopia. The carnival, in particular, provides an opportunity to experiment in a topsy-turvy world that cele-brates transformations, masquerades, festive performances and transgres-sive identifications that vibrantly mock the conventional and familiar power relations, hierarchies and dichotomies. The carnival enables minorities and unprivileged groups, in particular, to fulfill their forbidden desires, undis-ciplined fantasies, unruly role-playing and deceptive mannerisms without judgmental bigotry and terrorizing methods of discipline and punishment and corrective technologies.

The complexity of the carnival and its multiple, diverse and often con-tradicted potentialities – oscillating between triumphant revolution, reac-tionary tendencies and ruthless nihilism – is at the heart of the Alternate Gay World Cinema. This group of independent American films made in the 2000s and 2010s features an imaginative world in which gay is the norm and straight is deviated, a world in which merciless homonormativity replaces the oppressive heteronormativity and in which straight "breeders" are the new "faggots."

Voracious carnivals and cannibalistic masquerades

Mikhail Bakhtin connotes the carnival with the intensely indulgent, explo-sively playful and deeply communal experience that involves turning of the world upside down. He perceives the carnivalesque as a highly interactive performative mode based upon ritual spectacles, comic verbal compositions and various billingsgate such as curses and oaths.[3] The carnival offers a "second world" that is neither "finished nor polished" to stand in opposi-tion to the official, the ecclesiastical, the political and the serious.[4] This is a world marked by "loudness," defined by a "sensuous character and [...] strong element of play," and "organized on the basis of laughter."[5] The carnivalesque is a shared public experience that involves all present as par-ticipants rather than separating performers from audiences and makes it dif-ficult "to trace any clear dividing line between symbol and reality."[6] Hence, carnival laughter is festive, universal in scope and ambivalent, "a deliberate and abundant confusion of the social order."[7]

Notwithstanding, carnivals are not always revolutionary and emanci-patory. Their unruliness is often, if not always, limited, formulated, con-fined and scripted according to omnipotent essentialist social structures. Carnivalesque practices regularly discipline humor, criticism and revolution-ary anarchism. Embodied forms of carnival often serve as subtle but power-ful rhetorical maneuvers that invite subaltern cultures to tame themselves through the pleasures of momentary liberation and alternate oppositeness. Following Bakhtin, Stephen Gencarella Olbrys criticizes the colonization of the festive world by the systems world that leaves us today in a very tenu-ous circumstance, "bound by an impoverished laughter that merely encour-ages satirists to place themselves above the objects they mock rather than share in a comedy of errors."[8] Carnivalesque scripts are often not written to embrace a liberating grotesque criticism but rather to tame it, to transform it and to discipline its potential for transgression under a familiar hierarchical ordering of bodies. In this respect, carnivals often ambiguate the tensions between the carnivalesque and the hegemonic, even as the official script moves to fortify and emphasize the joys of an inverted world that is supposedly uninhibited, uncensored and undisciplined.

An exuberantly corpulent, irreverent, vulgar, obscene, excessive, low-brow, sensational and revolutionary carnival, however, can dramatically become a self-institutionalized oppressive regime that uses notorious disciplinary procedures to brutally control and surveil subaltern communities and countercultures. M. Lane Bruner insists that in carnivals, hegemonic social roles were reversed and usual restrictions on public behavior were officially relaxed, ultimately to *reinforce* "normal" public order.[9] Hence, carnivalesque masks merely signify a momentary breaking away from ordinary time and entrance into fictive or sacred time via anonymity and the loss of normal roles. Role reversals – or the turning of the world upside down – signify a divine instance of group fusion as people enter liminal spaces where normally highly disciplined social roles are only temporarily exchanged or discarded.[10]

The carnival is an arena of experienced freedom, improvisation, humor and parody that deviates the traditional sexual order. Hence, in queer eyes, the carnival provides a dialogical, multi-vocal and polyphonic framework that subverts discriminative sexual standpoints. In particular, the carnival vividly produces an alternate, inverted topsy-turvy world (*Le monde à l'envers*) that celebrates an excessive, theatrical and grotesque world that challenges the heteronormative agenda and promotes an open, exuberant and passionate negotiation of sexual values, conventions, rules and conducts.

In terms of the sexual world, however, the carnival framework with its misconducted lustfulness and transgressive debauchery provides a precarious means of critical reexamination of sexual scripts and sexual hegemonies. The carnival, as a liminal space, is the locus of popular, if symbolic, resistance. Yet the carnival's symbolic usurpation of power is also reactionary as it is acceptable just in order to be contained and to firmly restore the current social order when the unruly festivity is over.[11]

Carnivalesque masquerade, with its multiple ideological aspects, is at the core of screening queer fantasies and anxieties about a world pretending to be gay, in particular. The Alternate Gay World Cinema, fantasizing a world in which gays are the sexual majority and straights are a persecuted minority, comprises films about carnivalesque sexual disguise, the ethics of sexual revolutions and uncompromising sexual radicalism.

Tyrrell Shaffner's *Different*[12] is a short film that initiated this carnivalesque cinema. It focuses on Justin (Ben Hogestyn), a closeted straight student at Liberty High School who lives in an all-gay world. Bobby (Kay Stratton), the muscular captain of the football team, asks him to go on a date to the homecoming dance. Justin, however, is attracted to Joanne (Emily Brook Hands), a female student. Justin finds it difficult to come to terms with his transgressive sexuality and to fulfill his love and desire for his sweetheart. The protagonist finally gives up and arrives at the Prom with Bobby. He is courted by another female student, however, but he does not dare to follow his attraction to her. Justin eventually dances reluctantly with arrogant Bobby.

Marc Moody's *Almost Normal*[13] centers on Brad Jenkins (J. Andrew Keitch), a 40-year-old academic approaching a mid-life crisis and tired of being different because he is gay. Clearly, he is still uncomfortable in his own skin. After an argument with his mother, he furiously leaves his home, claiming that he is going somewhere where he is more normal. Surrealistically, a sudden car accident forces him back to his youth and into a fantastic world in which gay is "normal" and straight is discriminated against and persecuted. Brad has to decide whether to stay in the past and be "normal" or to try and return to his previous life. Roland Davis (Tim Hammer), a local blond athlete who disregarded him before, now dates him. However, he now grows attracted to a woman, his schoolmate Julie Erwin (Joan Lauckner), who, in real life, is his adorable sister-in-law and cynical fag hag. The minoritized straight couple struggles to fulfill its forbidden love in an intolerant homonormative world. They experience daily hardship, including physical brutality, as they come to terms with their (almost) normalcy. They eventually come out and celebrate their transgressive straightness at the high school's Blue Jean Ball. Brad, however, returns to his life as a gay professor and rejoins Roland, who turns out to be the gay father of one of Brad's devoted students.

Tom Gustafson's *Were the World Mine*[14] is a musical gay adaptation of Shakespeare's play *A Midsummer Night's Dream*[15] that focuses on Timothy (Tanner Cohen), an anguished gay student at an all-boys private school outside of Chicago. As Timothy and the other schoolmates from the school football team are in their graduating year at prep school, they are all obliged to take part in the springtime play as chosen by the colorful and eccentric English and Drama teacher Ms. Tebbit (Wendy Robie). Considering the Elizabethan acting customs of the time, Ms. Tebbit decides to put on an adaptation of Shakespeare's *A Midsummer Night's Dream* where some of the boys are cast in female roles. Providing some classic context to the rampageous homophobic athletes, Ms. Tebbit requires the young actors to flirt and romantically involve themselves with each other.

After Timothy auditions and secures the role of Puck, Oberon's honest but naughty faerie servant, Timothy learns the secret recipe of the love potion within the pages of his play's script. Pulling together all of the ingredients, Timothy creates the famed love-in-idleness flower, a purple pansy, and he vividly turns student and adult alike into lust-thirsty lovers. In particular, he puts the spell on his beloved Jonathon (Nathanial David Becker), a previously straight athlete, who miraculously responds to infatuated Timothy.

While many of the townspeople became gay, the local straight majority challenges this utopia and demands to reestablish and reinforce heteronormativity. After Timothy brings the situation back to normal, however, he fears that Jonathan's love for him will vanish together with this handsome boy's gayness.

Kim Rocco Shields' awarded short film *Love Is All You Need?*[16] has garnered 45 million YouTube views.[17] It articulates the hardship of Ashley (Lexi DiBenedetto), a preadolescent girl who is coming to terms with her heterosexuality in an alternative gay world where straight people are rejected and condemned as deviants. Ashley is severely bashed by straightphobic students after they discover her infatuation with a boy of her age. Ashley is denounced by a school teacher who claims that her (hetero)sexuality is just a phase and blames her for the brutality against her. Her lesbian parents also do not support her, and her biological mother, in particular, considers her daughter as a pervert. Consequently, Ashley cuts her veins and it is doubtful whether her mothers manage to rescue her or not.

Love Is All You Need?[18] is an extended version of Shields' 2012 short film by this name. The main plot is transformed from middle school to a university in which Jude Klein (Briana Eviga), a female quarterback, is infatuated with the handsome journalist Ryan Morris (Tyler Blackburn). The picture-perfect celebrated quarterback is outed for being a heterosexual or a "breeder." In the alternate gay world, Jude and Rian's transgressive sexuality is overtly and publicly loathed, persecuted and bashed. The long version of *Love Is All You Need?* also comprises a subplot that resembles the central story in the shorter version of this film, concentrating on Emily Curtis (Kyla Kenedy), a high school student who is romantically and sexually interested in Ian Santilli (Jacob Rodier). When Ian's sister Paula (Ava Allan) discovers his forbidden love for a woman, she and her friends bash Emily who allegedly seduced Ian to act against nature and to practice a despicably shameful and obscene (hetero)sexual perversion.

In the topsy-turvy worlds of the short and long versions of *Love Is All You Need?*, however, the church is presented as a bigoted institution that discriminates and deceits against sexual minorities. The prevalent "heterophobia" in this cinematic fantasy is conducted by a prejudiced society that also persecutes an overweight student because of his size, and it maltreats an idealistic teacher who dares to promote sexual tolerance. Following these occurrences, the townspeople are gradually coming to terms with the tragic consequences of their community's narrow-mindedness and they realize the moral cost of fanatic attitudes.

These films negotiate sexual bigotry and prevalent heterocentric fanaticism by allegorical inversion of the power relations between the straight majority and the gay and lesbian minorities. Yet turning the current sexual oppression on its head does not necessarily signify an unruly queer deconstruction of the borderline between hetero- and homosexuality, nor it liquidizes the distinction between privileged hegemonic masculinities and subaltern masculinities and its consequent distinctions between sissies and machos, abusers and victims, bullies and martyrs, normalcies and perversities. I will show that positioning gays and lesbians at the top of the (alternate) world does not necessarily challenge the ubiquitous hierarchy of male physique, particularly at the crucial stage of male adolescence. This chapter criticizes the screening of an alternate gay world which is based on a fantasized "compulsory homosexuality." It examines the perilous pleasures of parodying heteronormativity and reevaluates the spectacles of topsy-turvy martyrdom in these films which are based on dichotomized sexual regime, stereotyped sexualities and hierarchized masculinities, femininities and effeminacies.

Realistic gay bashing and surrealistic salvations

The short film *Different* and the short and long versions of *Love Is All You Need?* take place, from their very beginning, in an alternate gay world which is dominated by same-sex attraction and which brutally discriminates against the straight minority. In contrast, the films *Almost Normal* and *Were the World Mine* alternately present two realms. They dramatically move between the mundanely oppressive heteronormative world and the imagined world that pretends to be gay, a fantasy that oscillates between egalitarian utopia and destructive dystopia. Thus, *Almost Normal* and *Were the World Mine* present their protagonists' angst in the real world that motivates them to fantasize a gay haven. In other words, these films not just settle on allegorical educative fantasy but also present the daily hardship experienced by gay adolescents and adults in reality.

At the beginning of *Almost Normal*, Brad the frustrated mid-life gay professor looks at semi-naked muscular men playing basketball. He looks eagerly at their sweaty perfect physique. Then he stares passionately, and pathetically, at one of the basketball players, a particularly handsome semi-naked blond guy. The guy nonchalantly lifts his arms and crosses his fingers behind his neck, revealing his shaved armpits. When Brad keeps looking at him desperately like a hush puppy, the athlete blows a kiss in the air, mocking Brad's same-sex desire. Blowing a kiss in the air signals the blond guy's dissatisfaction with Brad's erotic interest in him. In a homophobic culture, this facial expression also dares Brad not to objectify another guy. This apparently gay gesture ridicules the possibility that the young sportsman will ever be involved in sexual contact with another man or, rather, it rejects the possibility that this young muscular guy, even if he *is* gay, would ever be attracted to Brad, who is much older and less attractive than him. Whether the blond guy's refusal is heteronormative, homophobic, ageist or both, Brad's face expresses disappointment after he was rejected and humiliated.

Later, Brad visits his parents and realizes that his mother would always treat him as the family's black sheep as she blatantly favors his deceased brother over him. Brad aims to leave the house. His mother asks him, where he is going, and he angrily replies "Some place where I'm not so God damn different!" This phrase anticipates his wild driving, the car accident and his resultant coma in which he fantasizes an alternate gay world. The homophobia he experiences catalyzes his envisioning of a utopian realm in which being *gay* primarily means being normal.[19] In contrast, the protagonist's homosexuality in *Were the World Mine* is never changed or subverted. It is disrespected in the real heteronormative world whereas it is greatly appreciated in his fantastic alternate gay world. Contrary to the dramatic inversion of Brad's sexual identification, Timothy remains gay in both realistic and surrealistic domains. Unlike Brad, the eternal protagonist who is alienated by both the real world, where he is gay who is mocked by the heteronormative dominance, and the world of fantasy in which he is straight who struggles with brutal gay authoritarianism, Timothy's gay fantasy is his haven. In the real world, he is routinely abused in gym class, in particular, where he is scorned and bullied by his homophobic classmates.[20]

Timothy's peers interpret the fact that he dislikes sports and see his artistic sensitivity as signs of effeminacy *and* gayness and, consequently, they attack him physically and verbally. Just before Timothy is slammed by a heavy red ball that his classmates brutally throw at him, for example, the ball freezes in the air and the screen turns white. Then Timothy heads toward the door of the hall, and hallucinates that these boys, wearing sexy red vests, begin to dance, caressing red balls with glittering points. In his utopian fantasy, the boys dance with the balls in a classic Busby Berkeley style, honoring Timothy, who walks between the rows, awed and respected by his peers. In this way, the violent gay bashing is metamorphosed into a utopian vision of highly sensual all-male interaction. Their aggressive sport training is turned into a graceful, homoerotic dance. In this musical fantasy, the boys, who were previously wearing cherry dark red T-shirts, are now wearing sexy tight undershirts by the same color with white splashes, exposing their muscular shoulders and sparsely haired boyish armpits.

This dreamlike spectacle ends abruptly, however, when Timothy's sordid dystopian routine reemerges. He returns to the devastative reality when the ball hits his face. His classmates and their coach look at him with a smirk and leave him alone with his pain. In the social Darwinism in Timothy's gym class, this marginalized boy finds himself at the bottom of the hierarchy of masculinities. As a result, he is the scapegoat of the male adolescents and their angsts, tensions, sex drives and (un)concealed desires.

The homophobes' interest in all-male sex, masqueraded as a spectacle of mockery, however, is initially embodied by the coach's sexual referral to Timothy's "fancy feet." Then one of the boys in the sports hall scorns the protagonist "Timothy needs a ball!" and another boy giggles: "He needs my balls!" Timothy sneers "You wish." Homophobia, as such, is more than the irrational fear of gay men, more than the fear that straights might be perceived as gay men. The semi-naked boys' referrals to Timothy's testicles in the locker room – a site of communal exposure of pubescent male bodies and their anxieties – perilously and excitingly blur the boundaries between mockery and faggotry, ridicule and passion, bullying and forbidden desires, alienation and authentic desires. The homophobes' erotic interest in Timothy's body anticipates the abusers' (homo)sexual conversion in an alternate gay world fantasy.

Whereas *Almost Normal* distinctly separates between the protagonist's real world and his salvation fantasy, *Were the World Mine* inquires the intricacies of the interrelationship between reality and imagination, authenticity and masquerade, realism and surrealism. The high school student's sordid reality is interwoven with redemptive daydreams and inspiring illusions which are both escapist and empowering. The ability to dream about a gay world, full of beauty and magic, proves to the protagonist that his soul is free, despite the brutalities that he experiences at school. Yet the surrealistic scenes of fantasy do not underestimate the sordid reality that many gay boys face every day. The homoerotic fantasies provide Timothy with a sense of power and control of his hostile environment and they vividly, at least momentarily, free his spirit (see Figure 5.1). *Were the World Mine* demonstrates the ability of surrealism to impact on reality, to transcend it *sur* ("above") reality, and to change it dramatically.

The cinematic fantasy about an alternate gay world in these films is characterized by interwoven realisms and surrealisms. The very idea of turning the power relations between hetero- and homosexualities on its head is an alluringly illusionary, surrealistic enterprise that derives its power from its improbability in the real world. At the same time, the topsy-turvy world, in which the hegemony is gay and its scapegoats are straights, is portrayed in a rather realistic way that sincerely reflects the mundane anxieties and everyday horrors of coming of age while struggling for popularity among the adolescent peers and fulfilling youth desires under constant social pressure. The boys attempt to prove both their "proper" masculinity and their sexual normalcy.[21] Notably, they sustain their hetero-masculinity in deviating and humiliating Timothy, the sexual Other.

Figure 5.1 Timothy (Tanner Cohen) embraces his fantasy about a gay world in *Were the World Mine* (USA 2008) (film still).

Pretending-to-be-gay as perilous parody

These fantasized gay worlds are primarily parodies. Linda Hutcheon stresses that parody involves "repetition with *critical difference*."[22] Chuck Kleinhans insists that parodies are not necessarily regressive or progressive.[23] Parody can be considered regressive if its only aspiration is aesthetic or if its primary goal is to entertain the audience by a spectacularly paradoxical topsy-turvy world that yields an irreverently clownish comedy-of-errors.

Parody can be political, however, if it presupposes that people can change things around them. As we can see in Brad's attempt to confront and reshape his sordid gay youth by imagining an alternate gay world, and by Timothy's coloring the seedy world pink, parody becomes deep and cutting against the past, against the status quo, against what holds people back. Kleinhans maintains that such parody is fused with anger in art and political expression. He contends that parody begins to function in art to indicate richness, diversity, possibility and hope for the future "precisely because it seems a whole culture can be transformed. Parody sets up the opportunity to make new connections."[24]

Notably, these films are parodying heteronormativity by spectacular visualization of a fantastic homonormative world. Elizabeth Atkinson and Renée DePalma note that imagining the homonormative means imagining a norm that may never actually exist in the official structure of broader society, but can exist in brief carnivalistic bursts as a sort of momentary reversal of conventions. "As peasants performed rituals where they were momentarily reinscribed as kings in societies that would eventually begin to level the power differential between the two," they explain, "reinscribing homosexual identities in (seriously) playful imaginaries may open possibilities for weakening the power of the heteronormative."[25] Lisa Duggan, however, depicts the features of what she calls "the new homonormativity" as a politics that does not contest dominant heteronormative assumptions and institutions, but upholds and sustains them, "while promising the possibility of a demobilized gay culture anchored in domesticity and consumption."[26]

The parodic alternate gay worlds on screen dissolve the illusion of justice for all, sexual multiculturalism, open-mindedness and an exuberant carnivalesque celebration of multiple desires. In fact, these films often equalize gayness and totalitarianism by presenting the straights as victims of a heartless gay hegemony. Although this strategy is meant to disrupt any compulsory sexuality whatsoever, it can be easily embraced by homophobes who routinely claim that gays take over the world. In this respect, the discussed films apparently visualize the homophobe's greatest fear that the gay community attempts to deviate children, adolescents and adults alike while disrupting natural instincts. While such paranoia can be easily challenged by a closer look at these movies that actually reject any totalitarian sexual regime, however, the main problem with these films is their limited scope on hetero- and homosexualities and their interrelations.

Steven Seidman agrees that normative heterosexuality creates a structural order of gender binarism, heterosexual-homosexual division, male dominance and heterosexual privilege.[27] This sexual-gender hierarchical order is embedded in Western psyches, classification schemes, social organizations and public rituals. "Under these conditions," he approves, "heterosexuality becomes compulsory."[28] Indeed, individuals do not choose to organize their lives around heterosexuality. Instead, heterosexuality is imposed as a condition of social existence. The state, laws, social institutions, culture and informal social regulations enforce heterosexuality and gender difference as compulsory.[29] Under social conditions of compulsory heterosexuality, homosexuality becomes a distinct and oppressed social identity in a dynamic of sexual difference and hierarchy, not just of power.

Seidman insists that compulsory heterosexuality produces not the homosexual, however, but differences, conflicts and hierarchies among homosexualities at the level of identity, culture and politics.[30] He supports pluralization of sexual lifestyles and identifications and recognition of multiple heterosexualities and homosexualities which are not dichotomized or confined by traditional gender roles and stereotypic connotations of machismo, butchness, effeminacy, sissyness, normativity, deviancy, etc. Seidman emphasizes that it is not just homosexuality that is disrespected under conditions of compulsory heterosexuality; so, too, are heterosexual practices that deviate from models of what is considered normal heterosexuality, e.g., the sex worker, the libertine or the pornographer.

Seidman prefers sexual politics that exceed the politics of gender preference and sparking, for example, conflicts over the purpose of sexuality (procreation, love, pleasure, expressive values), over norms of intimate behavior and arrangements (marriage, cohabitation, monogamy), over gender norms of sexuality, over norms regulating sex and the private-public sphere and so on. "These conflicts have their own distinct patterns of division and hierarchy," he explicates, "as well as their own strategies of regulation and resistance."[31] Seidman does not suggest the abandonment of the notion of compulsory heterosexuality, though, which remains "indispensable for understanding the structural sources of sex and gender difference and hierarchy."[32] However, he contends that this concept should be used in a more reflexive way that is attentive not only to what it makes possible but also to what it obscures.

The discussed Alternate Gay World films, with their spectacles of carnivalesque compulsory homosexuality, are politically committed to confronting homophobia. Yet they present a rather limited scale of homosexualities and heterosexualities. In other words, almost all the gays in these films are presented as fanatics who cannot tolerate sexual otherness while virtually all straight guys are victimized as destitute martyrs who are regularly tortured by the tremendously bigoted gay majority. In these cinematic topsy-turvy worlds, none of the adolescents is self-identified as flexible heterosexual, bi-curious homosexual, bisexual, pansexual, omnisexual or any other sexuality that transgresses the rigid monosexual framework of homo- and heterosexualities. Furthermore, all the straight guys are portrayed in these films as sad young men (or a sad young girl, in the short and long versions of *Love Is All You Need?*) who are typically less masculine, muscular and popular than their straight peers.[33]

In these pretending-to-be-gay worlds *heterosexuality* poses a challenge to conventional masculinities. Being victimized reinvokes shame that is rooted in failure or unwillingness to uphold homonormative masculine norms. For the closeted straight men in these grotesque realms, victimization has connotations of nonmasculinity that makes a scapegoat an unwanted position, yet that status must be demanded to stimulate the viewers' sympathy. The outcasts yearn for a tolerant world where they can find a supportive community and a sense of belongingness, "suturing into the story" through which their identities arise. Such belonging is, partly, in the imaginary (as well as the symbolic) and is therefore, "always, partly constructed in fantasy, or at least within a fantasmatic field."[34]

Straights don't cry and heterosexualities are never queer?

The gay world is fantasized on screen as an extremely dichotomized and polarized world with a distinct homosexual majority and heterosexual minority which are never interwoven. The borderlines between the two camps are never blurred, diffused, hybridized or crossed over; straights never fall in love with same-sex friends and gays are never attracted to the opposite sex or both sexes; if a *gay* male adolescent is infatuated with a girl, it is because he is not gay at all but a closeted *straight*. Conspicuously, there are no "queer masculinities" in these films that perpetuate dichotomous straight and gay masculinities.

Robert Heasley defines "queer masculinity" as "ways of being masculine outside hetero-normative constructions of masculinity that disrupt, or have the potential to disrupt, traditional images of the hegemonic heterosexual masculine."[35] Under these circumstances, the hegemonic masculine guy is presumed to be straight and holds stereotypically masculine beliefs, attitudes and values unless and until they present themselves as other. The straight "Others" are males who are perceived to be queer or actively disrupt both heteronormativity and hegemonic masculinity. Thus, straight males-with-queerness may be identified as deviant or pathologized for being gender inappropriate or sexually confused. Those who are openly queer straight males are often stigmatized or seen as a curiosity. Consequently, "they find themselves positioned along with gay males in a world that is 'other' and thus vulnerable to homophobic oppression."[36]

In *Different* and *Almost Normal*, though, the hegemonic masculinity is gay but it is presented as oppressively hegemonic, powerful, undefeated and arrogant masculinity. In contrast, the closeted straights in the alternate worlds are sissified and victimized. No single hegemonic "homo-masculine"

guy shows tenderness, vulnerability, sensitivity or empathy toward the tormented straight scapegoats. In this respect, no "hetero-masculine" gay guy
in these films is ever "queering" his heterosexuality.

Consequently, most of these films produce one-dimensional characters
who are either devils or saints. Even in the short version of *Love Is All
You Need?* the closeted straight boy Ian betrays Ashley and blames her for
harassing him. He is portrayed as an opportunist boy who prefers to masquerade his sexual otherness and his love for Ashley in order to appease the
(homo)sexual majority and survive the hostile school environment and his
bigoted family. All the other "real" straight guys, from the female leader
of the abusers to Ian's bully brother, are tremendously evil. None of them
shows kindness or solidarity with the victims of the hegemonic sexual group.
Consequently, Ashley, Brad and Justin feel devastated, isolated, abandoned
and doomed. They do not find any allies among their peers who uniformly
and collectively persecute them.

On one hand, the schematic portrayal of the gay majority as oppressors
and the straight minority as glorious martyrs emphasizes the absurdity and
cruelty of sexual bigotry. On the other hand, such simplistic articulation of
"the good guys" and "the bad guys" fails to recognize the intricacies, complexes, complicities and subtleties of the interrelations between straights
and gays, as much as diverse heterosexualities and homosexualities, and
the multiplicity of attitudes toward sex roles, masculinities, effeminacy,
machismo, sexual otherness and transgressive desires.

Delusive happiness and new martyrdom in a perfect gay world

At first, the gay worlds in *Almost Normal* and *Were the World Mine* pretend
to be fantastically emancipatory and fabulously open-minded. For example,
Brad, whose fantasy sends him back to his adolescence, fantasizes that he's
a gay teen whose parents – two fathers and two mothers – play scrabble
together and are amused by the emergent word "straight" (in his real life,
his parents mocked the word "gay"). Brad's utopian world is aestheticized
by warm, lively, bright colors. This is a lively imagery that comprises green
trees, smooth light-skinned youthful physique, a metallic red-brown car,
flamboyant, colorful and flowery outfits and extravagant hairstyles.

In this fantasy, beautiful blond cheerleaders in theatrical yellow and
blue skirts and tight blouses are not afraid to hold hands in the middle of
the schoolyard, and two handsome boys in T-shirts and jeans passionately
kiss. It is a bright, sunny world, in which shirtless muscular workers loudly
complement Brad's sexy body. In such a perfect world, same-sex attraction
is most desired and these youths' pubescence is predominantly queer (see
Figure 5.2).

In *Were the World Mine*, agonized Timothy is saved by the theatre.
He plays Puck, the trickster fairy in Shakespeare's *Midsummer Night's
Dream*, who is the beloved servant of Oberon, the Fairy King. Inspired by

Figure 5.2 Brad Jenkins (J. Andrew Keitch) is hugged by his semi-naked boyfriend Roland Davis (Tim Hammer) at their homonormative school in *Almost Normal* (USA 1999) (film still).

Shakespeare's plotline, Timothy successfully recreates the love concoction used in the play. While reviewing his lines, he discovers the recipe for creating the flower love-in-idleness. When he sprays his schoolmates with his pansy flower's love elixir, in the middle of their rehearsal of *A Summer Night's Dream*, the boys on stage start acting queer. These youths, who initially regarded *Midsummer Night's Dream* as "Shakes-queer craps," start caressing and kissing each other passionately.

When the tough coach steps into the gym hall, he first roars "Gentlemen!," but then he informs the newly queer students in a coyly effeminate voice with theatrical gestures: "This afternoon, we'll focus on ballet and coordination." He claps his hands when the boys dance around him in theatrical gracious movement. The trainer explicates: "Essential skills to hone for football won!" In this way, *Were the World Mine* connotes homosexuality with highbrow culture, sublime beauty, artistic refinement, transcendent delicacy and youthful enthusiasm. The boys, who previously bullied Timothy, are now dancing, kissing and making love to each other everywhere.

Then Timothy bewitches his loveable football player Jonathon (Nathanial David Becker), who is cast as Lysander in the play, and Jonathon immediately falls in love with him. When the boys kiss, Timothy says "I don't want to go back to real life." Jonathon replies that this *is* real. "Yah," Timothy whispers, "but this is so far from the way I woke up this morning." *Were the World Mine* portrays the emergent gay world in Timothy's boys' school as a haven of blissful freedom. Since all the students and teachers become gay, no one in school is persecuted for his straightness.

Yet not everybody in town is happy with this spatially restricted change. For instance, Jonathon, who is now in love with Timothy, dumps his girlfriend and ruthlessly offends her: "Don't mock my love! Who would not change a raven for a dove?! Fly away!" The girl's agony is ridiculed just like the misery of Frankie, Timothy's fag hag, after the latter mistakenly sprayed the gay love potion at her boyfriend Max's eyes, in this comedy-of-errors, thus causing him to be infatuated with him. The abandoned girlfriends are furious. Jonathon's ex-girlfriend even starts beating him up until Timothy, with his love concoction, turns her into a lesbian.

Infatuated Max pushes Frankie to the ground, telling her that he doesn't love her anymore. Afterward, he is severely beaten by Jonathon during their fight over Timothy's heart. Problematically, *Were the World Mine* conveys the message that all revolutionary progress is accompanied by painful yet unavoidable personal tragedies, broken marriages, devastated partners and deserted love ones. The passionate gay upheaval entails an unprecedented yet unavoidable oppression of the straights. In other words, when you chop wood and carve out a brave new gay world, straight chips fly.

However, a tragic, heartbreaking and totally unamusing portrayal of oppressed straights in a gay world is manifested by the short film *Different*. At the beginning of this film, a female pastor preaches passionately at a church: "Men and women are not meant to be together in sexual relations." In this homonormative world, Justin is notified by his friend that Bobby, the captain of the football team, would like to take him to the school prom, but he's not enthusiastic about this offer. Bobby, who's arrogantly unwilling to accept "no" as an answer, violently pushes Justin into the empty classroom during a break and threatens him: "So, what's up? I heard you don't have a date and you won't be coming. Are you waiting for someone special?!... Are you playing hard to get?!" In this alternate gay world, the high school's beauty is replaced by a handsome, delicate closeted straight adolescent in order to parody the heteronormative chauvinism and its worshipping of Alpha-male captains.

In *Almost Normal* the new gay world's intolerance toward non-gays is embodied by a violent encounter between Brad, his platonic friend Bill (Kehry Anson Lane) and the straight student Dwayne Twillis (Jowl Egger), a martyred blue-eyed boy with angelic face in a bright yellow polo shirt and curly brown hair. Bill yells at the straight boy "Fuck you, breeder! Fucking hole puncher!" He explains to Brad why he hates the straight guy so much: "You know. He's a breeder! A straight! *He likes girls so much he even acts like one.* God, it makes me sick!" In this interesting inversion of the common gay bashing script, the straight boy is mocked for his straightness, a marginalized and despised phenomenon in the fantasized gay world. Moreover, the common hegemonic connotation of *heterosexuality* and proper masculinity is changed into an association of *homosexuality* and proper masculinity. Whereas gays are often criticized by straights for not being manly enough because of their "effeminate" attraction to other men, the straight boy is abused, here, because of his assumed "effeminate" similarity to his feminine subjects of desire. Paradoxically, the straight boy's masculinity is questioned, in this gay fantasy, because of his transgressive interest in the *opposite sex* like he was girly as the girls he likes.

Although Brad is more masculine, muscular and popular than Dwayne, he is also scorned as a "breeder" when his peers find out about his forbidden love for Julie (in the real world, she is Brad's beloved sister-in-law). Julie tells Brad "I feel like a freak!" and accuses him of confusing her. She shouts at him "Leave me alone! Haven't you done enough?!" Brad is devastated because of his own sexual confusion and his sweetheart's angst. In a satiric reversal of conventional coming-out scenes in the 1990s New Queer Cinema, Brad is sanctioned by his lesbian mother, who finds it difficult to accept her son's *heterosexuality*. He tells her that his lover's name is Julie and the parent gazes at him: "That's disgusting! How can you say that?! How can you even think that?!"

In this emotional crisis, Brad yells at his mother "There's nothing for me to be ashamed of!" but his parent insists: "It's wrong! Tell that to the neighbors. Tell that to your father." Brad, however, confronts his bigoted lesbian mother: "Oh, yah. The guy you have had to have sex with to have me." His mother explains that "It's not the same. It's love, but not like that. I could have never been with someone of the opposite sex in that way!" Brad replies: "Good for you, but I can." Then his mother determines that "It's a sin" and the agonized son frowns at her: "Then I'd go to hell. And guess? You don't!"

As this melodramatic confrontation continues, his mother slowly sits down on the couch, turning her back to him. Brad reaches out his hand to comfort her. The anguished parent takes a deep breath and sobs. Brad tries to ease her mind: "Mom, I'm alone. I got stacked with that life I didn't want." Sentimental music is playing while Brad repeats every possible coming-out scenes' cliché: "I don't know if that's the life that I chose or it chose me." His mother wonders, like young Eric's mother (played by Stephanie McVay) in *Edge of Seventeen*:[37] "You're just eighteen, you're so young. What are you talking about?!" Brad gazes at his parent, who doesn't know that this is *not* her original son but an alternate straight version of him. Brad tells his mother: "I'm back, mom. I've come back, trying to make things right."

In a sense, this statement reflects his situation as a man from another era who unwillingly found himself re-experiencing his boyhood. His "coming back" can also be interpreted, however, as a yearning to live his authentic, unconcealed sexuality, and his consequent refusal to pretend to be what he is not. Brad's mother gently puts her hands on his face. "If God would want men and women to be together," She bursts into tears and leaves the room, completing her sentence off-screen: "He would have made women like football!" This dialog reflects an intricate epistemological framework in which Brad is perceived by the viewers as a gay person who pretends to be straight who pretends to be gay who confesses about his straightness. This amalgamation of pretenses and insincerities reveals hidden authenticities and inescapable truths alike.

The spectacle of emotional crisis is typical of the genre of melodrama, which is often articulated as an attempt to intensify the viewer's emotions through excessive reproduction of structural and stylized conventions and to generate unjustifiably tragic feelings by one-dimensional characters that experience personal, social and family difficulties on their way to romantic unification.[38] Although melodramas are criticized for their lack of authenticity and for their theatrical, exaggerated and even fabricated visualization of interpersonal conflicts and crisis, it is important to note that authenticity is also formulated and stylized. It is never natural or transparent but instead is designated according to cultural codes of presentation and representation.[39]

Further, the suffering protagonist in mainstream melodramas is the agonized straight woman whereas in queer adolescent melodramas it is the closeted gay or lesbian pubescent; and in the allegorical Alternate Gay World films it is the closeted straight adolescent or young adult. Melodramas usually concentrate on the point of view of the victim, and sometimes even manage to present all the characters convincingly as victims.[40]

The young protagonist in the coming-out scenes in these films, in particular, feels devastated, desperate and isolated. He feels that any attempt to refute his sexuality is an attempt to refute his whole personality and subjectivity at the critical stage of his coming of age. Significantly, these films' melodramatic and enthusiastic campaign for coming out during one's teen years in the New Queer Cinema does not confront sufficiently the difficulties of coming-out, treating coming-out as healing, therapeutic, or at least better than not coming-out, and thus romanticizing an extremely dichotomized choice. In this sense, the message of the alternate gay world melodramas appears to be that sexual minorities' coming-out is essential and purifying, no matter what the price of this martyrdom might be.

Unmasking the particularities and subtleties of queer martyrdom

In *Almost Normal* Brad is a closeted straight guy who faces unbearable hostility both at home and at school, where he is heavily mocked because of his transgressive straightness. His hardship resembles the suffering of gay protagonists in queer adolescent melodramas who cannot escape their mundane torment.

When adolescent Brad dances with Julie, in the final part of the film, he is confronted by a bigoted black teacher who scolds them:

> We can't keep your kind out but I can certainly keep you from doing something as disgusting as what you're doing! What you are doing is vulgar! And if you think that we'll sit around and be enforced to see such a disgusting spectacle then you just think again!

In response, Brad intends to leave the ball but Julie refuses to give up. When the orchestra plays again, Roland asks a black female student to dance with him, and a goodhearted teacher offers a female colleague to join him. About a dozen opposite-sex couples join Brad and Julie.

As Brad and Julie leave the hall, however, Billy bashes Brad and calls him "a freak." Brad is bleeding. Roland confronts Billy: "You'll never hurt him again!" The basher responds "I'm going to fucking kill you!" but Brad rebukes the attacker "Billy, shut up! Nobody listens to you!" The students gather around them and Brad confesses in an overdramatized Frank Capra style: "I'm straight. I like women. There's nothing you can say or do that is ever gonna change that. There's nothing I would do to ever change that."

Then Brad tells Julie, "I wanted you as a friend and got you as a girl-friend." Then he applies to Roland: "I wanted you as a boyfriend, then got you as a friend." Like the speech of the sensitive gay student Steven in the gay youth melodrama *Get Real* (UK 1998), in which the boy publicly and emotionally uncovers his (homo)sexuality at his graduation ceremony, Brad's speech in *Almost Normal* replaces shame with pride. It reflects his coming to terms and self-acceptance of his subaltern sexuality. This edu-cative coming-out moment is both parodic and magnificent, particularly because it is performed in an allegorical gay film by a straight martyr who challenges the homosexual majority's righteous and heartless collectivism.

In the short version of *Love Is All You Need?* the tormented straight pro-tagonist Ashley recalls how she played with her friends in "Daddy and Daddy and Mommy and Mommy." Ashley dares to suggest that she and one of the boys would be "Mommy and Daddy." In response, her female friend says "it's really disgusting" and suspects that Ashley is "some kind of breeder." The protagonist confesses that after this incident, she tried very hard "to be normal." Her friends kept taunting her, however, particularly after they saw her flirting with a boy named Ian, "Ashley likes boys! Ashley likes boys!" In a bigoted world that despises straight people, it is no wonder that her biologi-cal mother instructs her to change her walk to school so that she wouldn't be exposed to the deviant lifestyle of a notorious heterosexual couple. Her mother explains: "It just makes me sick thinking about that. So revolting." Then Ashley notices that the garage door of the notorious straight couple was sprayed with graffiti "God Hates Hetero!" The straights in her small town powerfully presented as martyrs are unjustly sanctioned and persecuted.

In the same spirit, the long version of *Love Is All You Need?* (aka *Love Is Love?*) portrays the hardship of Jude Klein (Briana Evigan), a closeted straight captain of a women's football team whose partner is the ambitious blond politician Emily Curtis (Kyla Kenedy) (see Figure 5.3).

Jude gradually comes to terms with her (hetero)sexual attraction to Ryan Morris (Tyler Blackburn) however, a handsome pledge student. They all live in a topsy-turvy Christian college that sanctifies same-sex family val-ues, sanctions homosexuality and glorifies heterophobia. In such a hostile, bigoted campus culture, the local Hetero Alliance student organization is despised and mocked by most of the students and faculty, and Jude and Ryan's forbidden love and rendezvous are melodramatically accompanied by the voice of a female priest who preaches to her congregation "They teach our innocent children that they can love whomever they want to love,

Figure 5.3 Jude Klein (Briana Evigan) kisses her girlfriend Emily Curtis (Kyla Kenedy) in the long version of *Love Is All You Need?* (USA 2016) (film still).

even someone of the opposite sex!" She warns her churchgoers: "Our god that tells us, 'thou shalt not kill', is the same god that says, 'mankind shall not lie with womankind'."

This hate speech also accompanies scenes of innocent love between a pre-adolescent boy and a girl. After the girl Emily agrees to play Juliet in a "subversive" straight version of Shakespeare's *Romeo and Julio*[41] "invented" by their liberal male teacher, Emily is humiliated by her peers who dare her to kiss her beloved Romeo, surrounding and pushing her off while shouting: "Ro! Ro! Ro! Ro!" Later, Emily's female classmate holds her hair and drowns her face in a toilet while another girl rips Emily's notebooks apart.

In another bashing scene, Ryan's fraternity bullies a black overweight "pledge," comparing him to a pig. Ryan, who leaves the abusive fraternity, tries to convince the other victim to join him but the latter tearfully refuses, too scared to be lonely and isolated. The bullying in this film is also directed at Jude, who is in love with Ryan. When she breaks up with Kelly Williams (Emily Osment), the latter publicly shames her by spreading dozens of posters across the campus featuring a photo of Jude and Ryan kissing entitled "Slut!" and "Jude Kissin' a Hetero!"

A dramatic tune accompanies shots of Jude's alienated friends who demonstratively ignore her. Later, the martyrdom of Emily, who is chased and beaten by her classmates who shout "Smear the queer" is alternated with shots of Jude going on a field with her teammates toward an important football match. At the end of these alternated sequences, Jude is sprawled on the lawn after her teammates, along with members of their rival team, have attacked her wildly, and Emily is sprawled on the floor, shocked and crying, after the brutal bashing she went through. Jude is rushed to hospital by an ambulance and Ryan is kidnapped and tortured by bullies from his former fraternity who record their deeds on a smartphone.

Dominic Janes, in his book *Visions of Queer Martyrdom: From John Henry Newman to Derek Jarman*,[42] suggests that martyrdom is a social formation and requires the witness not just of the martyr but of others who will

attest to one. Notably, queer martyrdom is established as outside normative social roles of gender and sexuality. It combines Christian witness with
aspects of gender and sexual transgression, enabling men to live powerful
queer lives that also give them a route to salvation. Janes notes that if this
cultural formation as a whole has not provided a direct path toward gay
liberation it can, nevertheless, still be hailed as an example of the idea that
"if at first you don't succeed, failure may be your style."[43] Janes explains:
"Queer tears defied heteronormative expectations of manhood in the nineteenth century and continue to do so today."[44]

Robert Mills contends that bodily torment, in particular, is the means by
which martyrs negotiate their transition from positions of male-controlled
wealth and power to a state of de-phallicized humility and fleshliness.
Male martyrs express their rejection of the phallus through "a lengthy
process of social and economic abnegation, demonstrative exhibition-
ism – and even potentially 'feminizing' torment – that leads to their final,
castrating death."[45] The screening of queer martyrdom in Alternate Gay
World films, however, does not necessarily follow this pattern. In *Almost
Normal* the gay protagonist, whose nightmarish fantasy posits him as a
closeted and persecuted straight youth, is seemingly reborn as a confident
gay adult who even reunites with the guy he was secretly infatuated with
in his high school days.

Likewise, *Were the World Mine* glorifies the protagonist's victorious fulfillment of his love for another boy who miraculously continues to be infatuated with the protagonist even after the magic has expired and the world is
heteronormative again. In *Different*, however, the closeted guy *is* symbolically
de-phallicized when he's humiliatingly forced to date the gay football captain
instead of following his true sexual desire. And in the short version of *Love
Is All You Need?* the protagonist is a girl, not a boy; thus she cannot become
de-phallicized. Notwithstanding, she involuntarily goes through a lengthy
process of social abnegation and demonstrative tormenting that apparently
leads to her final self-annihilation that terminates her unbearable otherness.

When Ashley hesitantly holds hands with a boy of her age, the scene is
accompanied by a voice-over of a female pastor who preaches to her congregation (in the same spirit of the preaching clergywoman in *Different*):

> The Holiness reminds us, and I quote, "It is a sin, for a man, to lust after
> a woman. It is an abomination for a woman to lie with a man outside
> of the breeding season. Any such person harboring lust for the opposite
> sex will burn in Hell!" Let us pray.

Ashley and Ian are caught by their peers. Ian claims that she forced herself
upon him. Ashley's classmates, incited by the religious sexual bigotry, try to
drown her head in the toilet. A teacher who suddenly enters the restroom
stops this action. Instead of punishing the abusers, however, he blames the
victim. The bearded educator rebukes the abused girl:

You know, Ashley, this school has zero tolerance for this kind of behavior. Imagine your mother seeing you holding hands with a man in public! I should really call both of your parents but I'll let this be punishment enough.

Ashley says "Thank you Sir" and the teacher gently encourages her: "This is just a phase that you're going through. You'll grow out of it." Ashley replies "Yes, sir" and the teacher shakes his head and leaves.

Compassionate, sentimental music accompanies this difficult incident when the educator turns around and whispers "You know, Ashley, maybe if you got yourself a girlfriend, this teasing would stop. Now finish cleaning up and go back to class!" Ashley comments, in a voice-over, that she really had hoped that this was just a phase as Mr. Thompson had said. But then she remembered how strong it felt and what that kissing had done to her. Ashley walks the edge of a swimming pool, considering whether to drown herself to end her suffering when the voice-over continues: "And I knew that it wasn't a phase." At the end of this potentially suicidal scene, Ashley looks at her reflection in the deep water and she adds in a voice-over "And I hated myself for it."

In this scene, Ashley explicitly portrays herself as a queer martyr, a state that she applies to create a sense of exalted drama around the sufferings and privations of transgressive sexuality. Queer martyrdom is employed in her personal script of the creation of the deviated self. Ashley's misery proves that queer martyrdom is by no means the sole province of men. It applies to certain aspects of lesbianism (allegorized here as female straightness in a gay world).[46] Further, Ashley's reflection corresponds to a martyrdom iconography that embodies a masochistic structure of suspense – it is, above all, an art of stillness and deferral, representing actions about to be fulfilled as much as things already carried out.[47]

Yet the short version of *Love Is All You Need?*'s aestheticization of pain is definitely *not* in the service of pleasure. Ashley, a closeted straight girl who lives in a compulsory gay world, is doomed to be a martyr. She's certainly not a masochist who expects pain as the condition that will finally ensure (both physically and morally) the advent of pleasure.[48] As Mills points out, images of martyrdom, male and female, although on the surface they might suggest sadism, habitually align the viewer with the victim-as-hero.[49] The viewers' gratification that derives from watching gay martyrs suffer, however, is concomitantly sadistic and masochistic and involves fantasies of mutilation, agony and corporeal abjection.

Hopelessly devoted "heteros" and their gay tormentors

All the discussed films dramatize a crisis in the romantic relationship of the closeted straight boys and girls caused by his or her hostile environment. In the short version of *Love Is All You Need?* for example, Ian breaks up with Ashley after his older brother found out about this forbidden love. The brother threatened to tell their parents who might kill Ian if they found out. Ashley says that they won't do it because they love him but Ian replies "You don't know my dads. My aunt Sara came out and the entire family scared her off. We're not even allowed to say her name. My papas are full of hate, bigots, and they're sure that those are gonna be burnt in hell."

Ashley asks Ian if she can kiss him just for the last time. The boy hesitates and Ashley urges him "Please, I don't know if I ever get to kiss a boy again [sic]." They tenderly kiss but Ashley's female classmates surprise them: "Got you!" The boy shakes Ashley off, shouting "What are you doing?! Get away from me" and telling the girls: "I don't know why she keeps touching me like this. I was just trying to be nice to her. I hate you, Ashley Curtis! STAY AWAY FROM ME! [sic]" One of the girls rebukes him: "That's the problem. You can't be nice to heteros [sic]" and the girls chase Ashley. In dramatizing this traumatic experience, the chase is filmed in slow motion from the perspective of the helpless victim who tries to escape her peers. Ian does not go with the other boys who join the girls who chase Ashley, but he does not try to defend her.

The persecuted girl finally arrives at the gym hall. Her classmates and some older students surround her. Ian's brother says "So this is the little queer who dared to touch my brother's hand." Ashley confronts him: "He wanted me to." Ian's older brother insists: "No, he didn't. You forced him." One of the girls adds: "We saw them kissing just now" and the other girls confirm it. Ian's brother scolds her "You freakin' breeder!" and orders his friends: "Grab her!" A black male student holds Ashley tight when Ian's brother punches her face and the leader of the abusive girls scorns her "You queer!" and kicks Ashley, who is lying on the floor. Then the children shout "Smear the queer! Smear the queer!" and kick her while the female leader of the abusers tells Ashley in a sinister tone: "Do us all a favor and kill yourself!"

In both the short and long versions of *Love Is All You Need?*, Ashley returns home bruised and bleeding while the word "HETERO" is written in black marker on her forehead like a mark of Cain. Ashley sobs and her biological mother scorns her: "Well, you did it to yourself, didn't you?!" The other mother whispers "That's enough!" but the furious biological mother orders her daughter: "March upstairs and have yourself cleaned up!" When the girl goes upstairs, the mother shouts that Ashley is gonna start karate lessons.

Ashley cries in her bed when she hears her mothers quarrel about their daughter's deviancy. Suddenly, hooligans go by their house, shouting "Fucking breeder, we're watching you!" when Ashley receives dreadful text messages: "Ashley Curtis is a breeder! Gross!!," "Dirty queer!" and "Why don't you just kill yourself, faggot?!" Ashley locks herself in the bathroom and fills the bath with water.

In the long version of this film, the girl watches the online broadcast of the atrocious bullying of Ryan by the fraternity's bullies (the title of this broadcast is "Fraternity hazing of hetero student"). The bullies tie Ryan to the carousel where he and Jude used to meet secretly and beat him up over and over again. The victim's face and body are bleeding but the main abuser, incited by the horrendously "straightphobic" Reverend to commit this heinous offense, doesn't leave the crime scene before he cites the Bible with tears, caressing Bryan's forehead: "The seventh angel poured out his vial into the air. And there came a great voice out of the kingdom of heaven, from the throne, saying, 'it is done!'."[50] Ryan whispers "please help me." The torturer ignores Ryan's cry for help, turns to his people and shouts: "WE ARE DOING GOD'S WORK!!" and hits the boy again.

Devastated by this bashing and the horrifying online broadcast of Ryan's lynch, the devastated straight girl commits suicide. In both versions of *Love Is All You Need?* the shots of the girl's bruised face with the mark "HETERO" alternate with the accumulating water in the bath and flash-backs in which her classmates urge her to kill herself. In the short version of *Love Is All You Need?* Ashley wonders in her voice-over: "Why is everyone hating me?" She wonders whether to take pills from the medicine cabinet to end her life. Then Ashley bursts into tears and cleans her forehead of the mark "HETERO." In both versions, the girl then cuts her veins with a piece of broken glass. Her blood drips into the reddening water. Her suicide is accompanied by celestial music, a soundtrack that wittily ironizes the righteous church and its horrifying Christian fanaticism. The sentimental music is intensified while her mothers break into the bathroom. Her legs are shown in the red water when she is removed from the bath. It is unclear whether the women managed to save her life or not.

However, this scene embraces the transcendence of the flesh and its assumption into heaven. Pain, never experienced as delight by this martyred girl, is a symbol of her ultimate queer triumph over the body that is regularly tormented by Ashley's gay peers. In a way, she's divine. The short version of *Love Is All You Need?* terminates with a stirring subtitle: "All the events that took place in this film are true stories from victims of bullying." A second subtitle clarifies:

> This film is dedicated to any child who has ever felt such darkness due to other's hatred and misunderstanding. Always know that love is meant to be within and you should never feel wrong or alone by being who you are… Unique.

This queer martyr, in her imitation of Christ, is ultimately saying, *Take me back into your heart.*[51]

In the long version of *Love Is All You Need?*, however, the straight girl is saved. She shows up with her mothers at Ryan's funeral. The film continues with a coming-out speech from Jude, the straight football captain, in which she tearfully confesses that she truly believes that once in your life a person meets someone who just changes her or his whole world. Her words are interspersed with flashbacks of her and Ryan's romance. "I thank god for showing me how to love someone, for giving me Ryan," she says. "Give me my Romeo, and when he shall die, take him and cut him out into little stars, and he will make the face of heaven so fine. Because the only thing that lasts forever is love." When the mourners leave, Emily sits near Jude. She looks at the "straightphobic" demonstrators who hold signs "God Hates Fags" to justify the bashing of Ryan. Then she asks the captain: "Why do people hate us so much?" Jude replies: "I guess they don't understand love like ours. Maybe they never will." Emily wonders "Isn't our love the same as theirs?" Jude says that it is, and the girl comments: "Maybe someone should teach them that."

Motivated by the girl's wish, Jude visits the inciting Reverend in jail. The captain recalls her devastating visits to the confession cell at the Reverend's church. Jude tries to educate the Reverend: "First book of Peter, verse four, line eight. 'Above all, love each other deeply, because love covers over a multitude of sins'. I think that covers my sin. How about yours?!" In the next scene, Jude sits on the carousel where she and Ryan used to meet secretly and where Ryan was tortured to death for his sexual otherness. She listens to one of his recorded message that now, under the tragic circumstances, gains a new, transcendental and spiritual meaning: "Hey, you, I just wanted to let you know that I was safe, and from where I am right now, I have an amazing view of you in all of your glory. I love you. See you soon." Magnificently, Ryan appears behind Jude for a brief moment and disappears. Jude bursts into tears and listens again to his message and smiles.

The film credits sequence, in the long version of *Love Is All You Need?*, is accompanied by newspaper clippings of reports about the horrendous homophobic murder of Matthew Shepard, and reports about suicides among LGBT youth, as well as reports about homophobic demonstrations of fanatic, bigoted Christians and Jews. In this way, the film readdresses its criticisms at the real world, which is notoriously and murderously homophobic, not straightphobic. The unmasked, painfully factual credits sequence is accompanied by the song "You Paint Me Black" in which Danielle Parente promises that you can paint her black and call her your shadow or you can paint her white and call her a song. "I've got nothing to give, nothing to borrow," she explains in her angelic voice, "but in the light you can watch me bloom."[52]

Significantly, Ashley's tragic death, in the short version of *Love Is All You Need?*, and Ryan's tragic death, in the long version of *Love Is All You Need*, are yearnings for unconditional love that transcends a brutally enforced sexual conformity. Ashley's bleeding body, rising from the red water, is a sublime and visceral spectacle at the same time. Although the alternate gay world she lives in is a theatrical and often grotesque mirror image of the heteronormative world, Ashley's death is not theatrical but realistic. Her victimhood is not a stage she goes through on the way to becoming a survivor; her victimhood is fatal and deterministic.

In contrast to Brad in *Almost Normal*, however, the young men who exercise agency in "fighting back," that is, resisting further queerocentric victimization, recovering and celebrating their (hetero)sexual authenticity, Ashley is sieged by a totalitarian sexual regime whose agencies are invincible. The tragic ending of the short version of *Love Is All You Need?*, though, uncovers the atrocious aspects of masquerade and the alluring spectacle of alternate victimhood.

The guilty pleasures of screening dichotomized alternate gay worlds

In an interview published in the early 1980s, Jacques Derrida dreams about a world in which there might be further alternatives which would lie "beyond the binary difference that governs the decorum of all codes, beyond the opposition feminine/masculine, beyond bisexuality as well, beyond homosexuality and heterosexuality, which come to the same thing."[53] Derrida stresses that it is not impossible that desire for a sexuality without number can still protect us, like a dream, from an implacable destiny which immures everything for life in the number 2. Notwithstanding, he wonders: "Does the dream itself not prove that what is dreamt of must be there in order for it to provide the dream?"[54]

The cinematic depictions of alternate gay worlds, however, problematize sexual oppression, on one hand, and do not deconstruct the essentialist sexual binary, on the other hand. In these films, alternating the sexual power relations means only an inversion of the powerfulness of heterosexuality and the subaltern position of homosexuality – the gays become oppressors and the straights become victims. The two sexualities, however, remain distinct, oppositional and contradicted to each other.

Although the protagonists' transgressive sexuality manifests a somewhat Butlerian standpoint that "disturbs a certain conventional idea of gender in which there is believed to be coherence and continuity among sex, gender, sexual practice and desire,"[55] the borderlines between heterosexuality and same-sex desire are never blurred or overruled. In other words, these films are about a world pretending to be gay, not about a world which is sexually undefined, polymorphic, exuberant, multidirectional and, arguably, truly emancipated.

These films are far from an emancipatory *queer* utopia that yearns for a world without frontiers which is free of deceptive bigotry and constraining libidinal conventionalities. Indeed, as José Ésteban Muñoz suggests, queerness is not yet here. Queerness is an ideality. Put another way, "we are not yet queer. We may never touch queerness, but we can feel it as the warm illumination of a horizon imbued with potentiality."[56] I agree with Muñoz that we must dream and enact new and better pleasures, other ways of being in the world, and ultimately new worlds. Indeed, "Queerness is a longing that propels us onward, beyond romances of the negative and toiling in the present. Queerness is that thing that lets us feel that this world is not enough, that indeed something is missing."[57]

Nevertheless, this something which is missing in the Alternate Gay World films – a cinematic representation of a broader scale of sexual and gender identifications – is also conspicuously powerful. Two decades ago, Rob Cover problematized the ideological tendency in the New Queer Cinema to promote a rigid dichotomy between heterosexuality and homosexuality that is contrasted with any notion of *real* or *latent* bisexuality or, alternatively, of a *sexual fluidity* or a sexuality that might be understood along lines *other* than gender-object-choice.[58] The overemphasized differentiation between hetero- and homosexualities in the Alternate Gay World films reflects a premise that there *is* a distinction, perhaps even an essentialist dichotomy, between straight and gay sexualities and one should realize what one is and live one's true erotic identity properly. Although this notion may sound too essentialist, too rigid and narrow, and too solid, it still has its benefits. These films emphasize that the problem is not sexual otherness but sexual bigotry; homosexuality is not the problem but the prevalent homophobia (allegorically disguised in these films as "straightphobia").

Moreover, Butler notes that identifications are never fully and finally made; they are incessantly reconstituted, and, as such, are subject to the volatile logic of iterability. They are that which is constantly marshalled, consolidated, retrenched, contested and, on occasion, compelled to give way.[59] Confused queer adolescents and young adults who suffer from the forced socialization demanded by their family, school and community desperately need a stable identity, however, that can locate them in a certain position in regard to themselves, their families, friends and institutions. Their formation of a distinguished gay or lesbian identity will enable them to enjoy their desires, loves and devotions.

The radical notion of sexual fluidity and misidentification with any particular sexual identity is not always liberating. It can sometimes aggravate a youth's agony in her or his search for self and social definition – knowing who she or he is, what she or he wants, and what kind of sexual, social and cultural lifestyle to choose or to aspire to.

These films apparently reproduce a reactionary plotline that centers on the brutal death of the gay or lesbian protagonist.

According to these movies, being a young gay or lesbian often means being tortured to death by prejudiced, cannibalistic predators (Ryan's ending in the long version of *All You Need Is Love*); or being miraculously saved from a suicide attempt caused by horrific hardships (Emily's survival in the long version of *All You Need Is Love?*); or failing to be miraculously saved from a suicide attempt that stems from endless suffering (Ashley's implied death in the short version of *All You Need Is Love?*); or living a sordid, unlivable life while alienating one's authentic passions and unfulfilling one's true love (the tormented student Dwayne in *Almost Normal*); or paying a heavy price, in terms of professional careers, for ideological solidarity and support of a persecuted minority (the forced resignation of the male teacher in the long version of *All You Need Is Love?* after he dared to write an alternate, straight version of Shakespeare's *Romeo and Juliet* in a hostile homonormative world).

Notwithstanding, some of these films glorify the coming-out of abused and tortured protagonists, who publicly come to terms with their authentic sexuality. Like a wounded, bleeding phoenix who is reborn out of fire and ashes, spreading its wounded wings, scoring the darkness and heading toward the rainbow, some protagonists prove a sexual renewal and heroic emancipation: Brad, who confronts his attackers at the end of *Almost Normal* and demands to live freely and openly with his sweetheart Julie, as well as Brad's reunion in the "real" life with Roland that he secretly desired during his sordid high school days; Timothy, who fulfilled his love for Jonathon in *Were the World Mine*, both in the alternate, fantastic gay world *and* in the "real" world; and Jude, who comes out following her appointment as football captain and after the murder of her boyfriend Ryan, and her confrontation with the murderous female Reverend, in the long version of *Love Is All You Need?*.

These screenings of compulsory homosexuality are compelling and heavily melodramatic. Of course, they do not intend to strengthen homophobic fears of a gay takeover of the world. Rather, they powerfully mirror the atrocious consequences of bigotry, prejudice, Christian fanaticism and its congregations' mob mentality directed by ruthless hate speech. Yet the pleasure of parodying heteronormativity *is* perilous because it often employs clichés, stereotypes, frameworks and conventionalities that produce a one-dimensional, schematic portrayal of the tremendously complicated, multilayered interrelations between sexual majorities and minorities. In fantasizing a topsy-turvy martyrdom, these films create powerful spectacles of brutality and painfulness, oblivion and salvation, loss and resurrection. These cinematic worlds, masked as gay, extravagantly and melodramatically unmask awful truths about America's poisoned apple pie.

Notes

1 Striepe and Tolman 2003.
2 Striepe and Tolman 2003: 523.
3 Olbrys 2006: 242.
4 Bakhtin 1984: 6.
5 Bakhtin 1984: 7–8.
6 Olbrys 2006: 245.
7 Olbrys 2006: 242.
8 Olbrys 2006: 243.
9 Bruner 2005: 138, emphasis added.
10 Bruner notes that closing formalities (e.g., orderly processions, ritual reinstatement of officials) occur at the end of the carnival period *to signify a return to the normal world of humorless repression* (Bruner 2005: 139–140, emphasis added).
11 Davis 1965.

12 *Different* 2004.
13 *Almost Normal* 2005.
14 *Were the World Mine* 2008.
15 Shakespeare 2014 (originally published in 1595–1596).
16 *Love Is All You Need?* 2012.
17 Anders 2014.
18 *Love Is All You Need?* (aka *Love Is Love?*) 2016.
19 In a way, *Almost Normal* is a modern version of Jonathan Swift's *Gulliver's Travels* in which he is alternately magnified and miniatured, depending on the nature of his surrounding environment, whether it is Lilliput, the land of dwarves, or Brobdingnag, the land of giants. In each case, however, the traveler feels like an outcast freak and is being sensationalized, perverted and persecuted by the intolerant locals who mistreat him like he was an exhibit in their cabinet of curiosities.
20 Padva 2014.
21 See Kimmel 2001.
22 Hutcheon 1095: 7, emphasis added.
23 Kleinhans 1994.
24 Kleinhans 1994: 198–199.
25 Atkinson and DePalma 2008: 31.
26 Duggan 2002: 179.
27 Seidman 2009.
28 Seidman 2009: 19.
29 Shelley 1992 (1972); Wittman 1992 (1972); Young 1992 (1972).
30 Seidman 2009: 23, emphasis added.
31 Seidman 2009: 24.
32 Seidman 2009: 27.
33 An exceptional case is young Brad in *Almost Normal* whose physique *is* muscular and he is popular and loveable among his peers until he comes out as straight.
34 Hall 1996: 4.
35 Heasley 2005: 310.
36 Heasley 2005: 311.
37 *Edge of Seventeen* 1998.
38 Alderice 1965; Feuer 1984.
39 Padva 2004.
40 Vicinus 1981.
41 Based on Shakespeare's classic play *Romeo and Juliet* (see Shakespeare 2000; originally published in 1591–1595).
42 Janes 2015.
43 Quentin Crisp cited by Halberstam 2011: p. 96.
44 Janes 2015: 9.
45 Mills 2001: 9.
46 She is designed as a sexual scapegoat, in the spirit of Radclyffe Hall's *The Well of Loneliness* (1928) in which Stephen Gordon, the invert heroine of the novel, is told that "you were made for a martyr" (Hall 1928: 443).
47 Mills 2001: 71.
48 Deleuze 1989 (1967): 71.
49 Mills 2001: 35.
50 *Revelations*, chapter 17, verse 16.
51 Jane 2015: 167.
52 "You Paint Me Black" 2015.
53 Derrida 1982: 108.
54 Derrida 1982: 108.

55 Butler 1990: 17.
56 Muñoz 2009: 1.
57 Muñoz 2009: 1.
58 Cover 2000: 77.
59 Butler 1993: 105.

Afterword

When gay masks gaze at the deceiver's straight skin: the grotesque screening of deceptive horrors and delights

Unmasking the abundance, ferocity, theatricality and unanticipated pleasures of pretending to be gay on screen is a journey to sexual conventionalities and potentialities. Yet a critical examination of cinematic representations of sexual deception not only subverts heteronormativity and its formulation of gayness, it also questions the reality itself in which the straight majority eagerly frames, deviates, visualizes, parodies, eroticizes and playfully theatricalizes homosexuality. The powerful gay–straight binary is a cage for members of sexual majorities and minorities and the mask, i.e. the deceivers' pretending to be gay, enables them to fly. The gay masquerade provides a precious opportunity for sexual introspection and experimentation beyond the prevalent straight and narrow bigotries. Despite the emancipatory potentiality of pretending to be gay, however, the discussed films conspicuously limit the countercultural vocabulary that the deceivers are allowed to adjust.

Typically, the cinematic fraudsters are only interested in the visual attributes of gayness, or faggotry, which is its radically effeminate and flamboyant manifestation. They never wish to have sex with a person of their own gender, and they often regard gay sex as disgusting. The interrelations between disguise and disgust are extensively analyzed in this book as a mechanism that signifies the limits of (false) identification. Notwithstanding, pretending to be gay is a powerful, vibrant experience for the deceivers, even if they were homophobic before they started to pretend to be gays.

Through their gay mask, they not only gaze at subcultural otherness; their mask also gazes at their own (hetero)sexual identification and reconsiders their relationship with sexual minorities. The mask is a highly two-way process in which the masquerade also penetrates the impersonator's mind and generates an intimate process of self-examination of one's basic assumptions, lifestyle, primordial premises, and desires and traditional sexual axioms. In this manner, the gay mask is an invaluable means of counter-discourse that readdresses its wearer's sexual accountability and his over-idealized heterosexual recognition.

Sexual pretending is revealed as both intimidating and an empowering experience for the deceiver who initially negotiates disruptive bodies and an unknown, countercultural sexual capital. The gay mask secures the pretenders' difference yet fortifies the artificiality and arbitrariness of an apparently dichotomous sexual regime and its discursive strategies. Although straight men pretending to be gay usually re-inscribe gender norms, they dramatically demonstrate the cost of the social pressure of hetero-masculinity. Their masquerade *is* a distorted and distorting image. Although it is often meant to caricaturize gayness, it grotesquely uncovers sexual uncertainties and reveals the discursive production of male sexiness and masculine authenticity.

Murray Healey notes that the very overcompensatory nature of hyper-masculinity, the very effort to authenticate manliness, threatens to expose rather than allay that anxiety. "Masculinity, as a conscious act or a pose before the camera," he notes, "is then revealed to be inauthentic. Real men are not supposed to admit it, but masculinity is always problematic; even at an experiential level, there is an unavoidable contradiction in *trying* to be a real man."[1] When protagonists like Lance and Ralph in *Strange Bedfellows*,[2] Shushan in *Kicking Out Shoshana*[3] and Steve in *Cruising*[4] pretend to be gay, they concomitantly masquerade *and* flaunt their hetero-masculinity. Their desperate endeavors to secure their authentic straight masculinity, however, denaturalize their hetero-masculine authenticity. These straight guys' epistemology of the closet deconstructs itself when it recurrently exposes the performativity and theatricality of hegemonic masculinity. Although their masquerade is primarily meant to mock gay masculinity's apparent effeminate perversity, their pretending exposes the deceptive, inauthentic aspect of all masculinities.

Ernst H. Gombrich, in his analysis of the power of masks in indigenous people's lives, suggests that as hunters, they know the true shape of the eagle's beak, or the beaver's ears, much better than any of us. "But they regard one such feature as quite sufficient," he explains, "a mask with an eagle's beak is an eagle."[5] Likewise, the pretenders in the discussed films play the gay identity with only a few characteristics of gayness. In their heteronormative eyes, a limp-wristed gesture, a swishy walk, an effeminate coy voice, a glitzy androgynous outfit, a leather accoutrement or wearing heavy make-up is sufficient for playing it gay. Such oversimplified articulation of a subcultural phenomenon, however, demonstrates the artificiality of the hegemonic masculinity as well. The mask both falsifies itself *and* distorts its wearer's naturalness. In its carnivalesque passion, the deceiver's mask serves as a totemic, distinctive mark of the hegemonic group *and* its unruly outlaws. The mask itself is liminal, separating and reattaching the two identities.

Deforming mirrors and sincere anxieties

The gay mask, in particular, is essentially merged with its wearer's straight skin, in diverse degrees, and generates an abundant, exuberant "thirdspace" in which traditional straight and gay authenticities are subversively put on an act. In *Strange Bedfellows*,[6] for example, Lance and Ralph's masquerade

changes their perspective on their long-term companionship, heteronormativity, homosexuality (including Ralph's coming to terms with his daughter's lesbian identity) *and* the somewhat homoerotic potentiality of their
friendship (manifested by Lance touching Ralph's behind after the latter's
confessional speech). In the same spirit, the undercover policeman Steve's
heterosexual identification is affected and remodified by his dramatic experiences in subcultural gay leather venues *and* his consequent joyful sexual
encounters with other men.

Hence, these deceivers' gay mask is a *pars pro toto* of the transformation
of their apparently straight body into the gay image.[7] The mask is a face,
human aspect, representation; but it is something material, rigid, unalter-
able, as if it's dead.[8] The stability and instability conveyed by the mask
affect these cinematic protagonists' lives. They feel both trapped and eman-
cipated by wearing it. Their straightness and its borderlines and limitations
are reformulated and redesigned by their masquerade.

In contrast to Pizzorno's association of mask and death, however, their
gay masks do not show proximity to death but are rather a vivid, dynamic,
energetic and exciting adventure and exploration for them. In *Kicking Out
Shoshana*,[9] for instance, Shushan the soccer player is initially devastated
by his enforced gay camouflage that explicitly contradicts his traditional
background and his love and devotion to his sweetheart. Yet his fabricated
gayness, to his surprise, turns out to be an effective means of having sex
with two attractive women who desire him precisely because of his non-
heterosexual pretense.

Although gayness is extremely different than the deceiver's previous daily
routine, this pretender finds himself playing a role model and a source of
inspiration for a closeted gay fan. Notably, although the title of this book
relates to *Gay Masks* (a plurality of masquerades) and *Straight Skin* (a singular sort of straight "authenticity"), I now realize that these movies also
pluralize "straight skins." They diversify straightness, showing multiple
hegemonic and non-hegemonic straight masculinities. In this respect, these
mostly heteronormative films' representation of hetero-masculinities oscil-
late between brutality and sensitivity, fascism and humanism, and discriminatory and egalitarian attitudes toward other men and women.

These screens are deforming mirrors that grotesquely misrepresent the
intricacy and multidimensionality of gayness. Yet they accurately portray
contemporary incongruities, inconsistencies and anxieties of the straight
majority. These films' ambivalent attitude toward straight–gay relationship
reflects the heteronormative society's coming to terms with the greater social
acceptance of LGBT people, progressive pro-gay legislation and recognition
of the right for same-sex marriage, the realization of the financial power of
the gay community and the emergent sexual multiculturalism that unapolo-
getically challenges traditional family values and sex roles, machismo and
homophobia. Hence, in these films we are indeed faced with grotesque
masks, yet, as Youssef Ishaghpour contends, the meaning of grotesque needs

to be understood in a modern sense, because of this inextricable mingling between the comic and the horrific[10] within which the (mis)representation of the gay body and soul appears substantially.

Impenetrable and inhuman through their masks, yet cinematic deceivers like Steve in *Cruising*[11] and the sassy fashion designer Evaristo in *Macho*[12] show their fragility at the moment of physical contact with a same-sex partner, a contact that, in their eyes, is always traumatic and aims at penetrating and cutting the body,[13] or rather at its destruction. And, as Jelena Reinhardt suggests, the fear of being touched is the greatest fear of humankind. Especially frightening is the idea of being touched by somebody or something unknown. Thus, man always tends to avoid physical contact with anything strange.[14]

The terrorizing mask and its new erotic pleasures

Strangeness, in regard to sexualities, is subversively redirected by the Alternate Gay World films that feature a dystopian fantasy about a world pretending to be gay. The "gay world" films critically allegorize the prevalent homophobia in America by representing it as "straightphobia." The atrocious mundane persecutions experienced by millions of adolescents and young adults, because of their homosexuality, are dislocated to topsy-turvy worlds in which gay men and lesbians control the world and straights are defamed as "breeders!" Didactically, *Almost Normal*,[15] the short and long versions of *Love Is All You Need?*[16] and the short film *Different* show the straight viewers the injustice and cruelty of sexual intolerance, and how they would feel if they were the victims rather than the victimizers.

Although the gay world films represent inverted power relations, they replicate the familiar identification patterns and the disparity between hegemonic and marginalized sexualities. The politics of gay masks and straight skins is more complicated in these films, however, because they necessitate and revalidate an extremely dichotomous sexual world in which every person is straight *or* gay, every boy is admirably muscular or, shamefully, a sissy.

Notably, the straight mask, imposed on the protagonist's gay skin, is perceived by these screens as a burden that they must get rid of. According to the ideological imperative of this cinema, members of a subaltern sexual minority must come out to their family, friends, co-workers and classmates, no matter what the price of this act might be. According to the logics of the Alternate Gay World films, the mask is not transitional, not a precious opportunity for a journey of self-discovery, but a constant obstacle in the young protagonists' lives. These "breeders'" straight mask is a disruptive business that does not allow them to move from a precarious stance to a new position of power. Their (hetero)sexuality is deformed and ruptured by the mask that they are forced to wear.

Indeed, in many cases, the mask *is* an unbearable construction that terrorizes both its wearer and the people who look at it. Charles Dickens wonders:

When did that dreadful Mask first look at me? Who put it on, and why was I so frightened that the sight of it is an era in my life? It is not a hideous visage in itself; it is even meant to be droll; why then were its stolid features so intolerable? [...] Was it the immovability of the Mask? [...] Perhaps that fixed and set change coming over a real face, infused into my quickened heart some remote suggestion and dread of the universal change that is to come on every face, and make it still? [...] The mere recollection of that fixed face, the mere knowledge of its existence anywhere, was sufficient to awaken me in the night all perspiration and horror, with, "O! I know it's coming! O! The Mask!"[17]

Masks are remarkably powerful, effective, influential and frequently revealed as means of survival and intimidation, entertaining escapism and devastating confrontation with familiar and estranged environments, enemies, persecutors and abusers of all kinds. The sexual masks involved in pretending to be gay, in particular, are forcefully worn and removed, invented and manipulated by members of the powerful straight majority. These masks mediate their wearers' fears *and* curiosity toward gay subcultures and lifestyles *and* gay sexual practices that the protagonists in most of the discussed films never dare to experience. Their gay masks are frontlines and borderlines, facade and new faces, rescuing and risking their wearers.

The pretending-to-be-gay cinema mostly reproduces an essentialist perception of a dichotomous sexual world, in which people are either straight or gay, men or women, persecutors or persecuted, abusers or martyrs. This cinema often misrecognizes a wider spectrum of sexual, erotic, romantic, social and cultural shades, innuendos, subtleties and intricacies. Yet its protagonists, oscillating between the tropes, embody the irrefutable inconsistencies and unpredictability of human sexualities that can never be totally and completely surveilled and dominated by social, cultural, political and economic forces and their gazing cameras. The uncategorized, voluptuous, unruly and emancipating power of our sexualities erupts on the discussed screens in precious, inescapable moments that undermine their own ideological premises and moralistic fixations.

Consider the moments in which Steve in *Cruising*,[18] for example, cannot police his attraction to the gay leather scene any longer, Avaristo's straight campiness in *Macho*[19] questions its own straightness, and Brad finds out in *Almost Normal*[20] that his gayness camouflages romantic feelings for a woman. In these valuable cinematic moments, the multiple straight skins and their numerous gay masks are blurred, intermingled and immersed into each other. This is an amazing grace erected by forbidden loves, uncontrollable desires, undefeated erections, insatiable anuses, invincible vaginas, carnivalesque honesties and visceral masquerades. This is a quest of new frontiers and their perilous screens of pleasures.

Notes

1 Healey 1994: 88.
2 *Strange Bedfellows* 2004.
3 *Kicking Out Shoshana* 2014.
4 *Cruising* 1980.
5 Gombrich 1950, cited in Reinhardt 2016: 1.
6 *Strange Bedfellows* 2004.
7 See Belting 2002.
8 Pizzorno 2008: 27.
9 *Kicking Out Shoshana* 2014.
10 Ishaghpour 1990: 54.
11 *Cruising* 1980.
12 *Macho* 2016.
13 See Reinhardt 2012: 357–366.
14 Reinhardt 2016: 9-10.
15 *Almost Normal* 2005.
16 *Love Is All You Need?* 2012; *Love Is All You Need?* (aka *Love Is Love?*) 2016.
17 Dickens 1850, cited in Wilson 1970: 9–10.
18 *Cruising* 1980.
19 *Macho* 2016.
20 *Almost Normal* 2005.

References

Alderice, Nicole. 1965. *The Theatre and the Dramatic Theory*. London, UK: Harrap.

Alderson, David. 2016. *Sex, Needs and Queer Culture: From Liberation to the Postgay*. London, UK: Zed Books.

Altman, Dennis. 1982. *The Homosexualization of America: The Americanization of the Homosexual*. New York, NY: St. Martin's Press.

Altman, Dennis. 1993 (1971). *Homosexual Oppression and Liberation*. New York, NY: New York University Press.

Anders, Charlie Jane. October 15, 2014. "In this Film's Topsy-Turvy World, The Gay Majority Persecutes Straights." Retrieved October 10, 2019 (https://io9. gizmodo.com/this-is-silly-first-you-post-something-that-i-respond-1647257260).

Appiah, Kwame Anthony. 1992. *My Father's House*. New York, NY/Oxford, UK: Oxford University Press.

Arendt, Hannah. 1958. *The Human Condition*. Chicago, IL: University of Chicago Press.

Arendt, Hannah. 1961. "What Is Freedom?" Pp. 143–171 in *Between Past and Future: Eight Exercises in Political Thought*, edited by Hannah Arendt. New York, NY: Viking.

Atkinson, Elizabeth and Renée DePalma. 2008. "Imagining the Homonormative: Performative Subversion in Education for Social Justice." *British Journal of Sociology of Education* 29(1): 25–35.

Babuscio, Jack. 1978. "The Cinema of Camp (*Aka* Camp and the Gay Sensibility)." *Gay Sunshine Journal* 35; reprinted in pp. 117–136 in *Camp: Queer Aesthetics and the Performing Subject*, 1999, edited by Fabio Cleto. Edinburgh, UK: Edinburgh University Press.

Baila, Morgan. August 13, 2018. "Movies that Make Us Want to Go Back to College." Retrieved July 28, 2019 (https://www.refinery29.com/en-us/2016/0 7/116748/best-college-movies).

Bakhtin, Mikhail. 1968 (1965). "Carnival"; reprinted in pp. 216–221 in *Performance Analysis: An Introductory Coursebook*, edited by Colin Counsell and Laurie Wolf. London, UK/New York, NY: Routledge.

Bakhtin, Mikhail. 1984. *Rabelais and His World*. Bloomington, IN: Indiana University Press.

Barnard, Ian. 2018. "Queer: Good Gay, Bad Gay, Black Gay, White Gay?" *QED: A Journal in GLBTQ Worldmaking* 5(2): 105–111.

Bartle, Chris. 2015. "Gay/Queer Dynamics and the Question of Sexual History and Identity." *Journal of Homoseuality* 62(4): 531–569.

Baudrillard, Jean. 2010. *Carnival and Cannibal, or the Play of Global Antagonism.* Translated by Chris Turner. London, UK: Seagull Books.

Beckson, Karl (Ed.). 1970. *Oscar Wilde: The Critical Heritage.* London, UK: Routledge.

Bell, Deborah. 2015. "Introduction." Pp. 1–17 in *Masquerade: Essays on Tradition and Innovation Worldwide*, edited by Deborah Bell. Jefferson, NC: McFarland & Company.

Belting, Hans. 2002. *Bild-Anthropologie: Entwürfe für eine Bildwissenschaft.* Padeborn, Germany: Wilhelm Fink Verlag.

Berlant, Lauren and Michael Warner. 1998. "Sex in Public." *Critical Inquiry* 24(2): 547–566.

Boone, Brian. September 4, 2018. "The 25 Best College Comedies of All Time." Retrieved July 28, 2019 (https://www.vulture.com/article/25-best-college-comedies-ever.html).

Braddy, Jon and Billy Huff. 2016. "Queerness Underground: The Abject, the Normal, and Pleasure in *Cruising* and *Interior. Leather Bar.*" Pp. 101–120 in *Exploring Erotic Encounters: The Inescapable Entanglement of Tradition, Transcendence and Transgression*, edited by John T. Gider and Dionne van Reenen. Oxford, UK: Inter-Disciplinary Press.

Breward, Christopher. 2011. "Aestheticism in the Marketplace: Fashion, Lifestyle and Popular Taste." Pp. 194–205 in *The Cult of Beauty: The Aesthetic Movement 1860–1900*, edited by Stephen Calloway and Lynn Federle Orr. London, UK: V&A Publishing.

Brickell, Chris. 2006. "Sexology, the Homo/Hetero Binary, and the Complexities of Male Sexual History." *Sexualities* 9(4): 423–447.

Bristow, Joseph. 1997. *Sexuality: The New Critical Idiom.* New York, NY: Routledge.

Bruner, M. Lane. 2005. "Carnivalesque Protest and the Humorless State." *Text and Performance Quarterly* 25(2): 136–155.

Burston, Paul. November 1998. "So Good It Hurts." *Sight and Sound* 8(11): 24.

Butler, Judith. 1990. *Gender Trouble: Feminism and the Subversion of Identity.* London, UK: Routledge.

Butler, Judith. 1993. *Bodies that Matter: On the Discursive Limits of 'Sex'.* New York, NY/London, UK: Routledge.

Button, Simon. July 2000. "Best Friends." *Attitude* 75: 46–48.

Campbell, Alyson and Stephen Farrier. 2015. "Queer Practice as Research: A Fabulously Messy Business." *Theatre Research International* 40(1): 83–87.

Carver, Terrell. 2009. "Sex, Gender and Heteronormativity: Seeing *Some Like It Hot* as a Heterosexual Dystopia." *Contemporary Political Theory* 8(2): 125–151.

Cascais, Antonio Fernando and Joao Ferrera. 2014. *Queer Film and Culture.* Lisbon, Portugal: International Queer Film Festival.

Champagne, John. 2000. "Pornography." Pp. 701–703 in *Gay Histories and Cultures: An Encyclopedia*, edited by George E. Haggerty. New York, NY: Garland Publishing.

Clagett, Thomas. 2003. *William Friedkin: Films of Aberration, Obsession and Reality.* Los Angeles, CA: Silman-James Press.

Clum, John A. 1992. *Acting Gay.* New York, NY: Columbia University Press.

Clum, John M. 2000. *Still Acting Gay*. New York, NY: St. Martin's Griffin.

Coates, Jennifer. 1993. *Women, Men and Language*. London, UK: Longman.

Connell, R. W. 2005. *Masculinities*. Berkeley, CA: University of California Press.

Core, Phillip. 1984. *Camp: The Lie that Tells the Truth*. New York, NY: Delilah Books.

Cover, Rob. 2000. "First Contact: Queer Theory, Sexual Identity, and 'Mainstream' Film." *International Journal of Sexuality and Gender Studies* 5(1): 71–89.

Crain, Caleb. 1994. "Lovers of Human Flesh: Homosexuality and Cannibalism in Melville's Novels." *American Literature* 66(1): 25–53.

Cramer, Thomas. 1966. *Das Groteske bei E. T. A. Hoffmann*. Munich, Germany: Wilhelm Fink.

Crisp, Quentin. 1968. *The Naked Civil Servant*. London, UK: Cape.

Cross, R., A. Errigo, Robyn Karney, Joel W. Finler, D. Oppedisano, Ronald Bergan and C. Hirschhorn (Eds.). 2004. *Cinema Year by Year 1984–2002*. London, UK: Dorling Kindersley.

Curtis, Val, Robert Aunger and Tamer Rabie. 2004. "Evidence that Disgust Evolved to Protect from Risk of Disease." *Proceedings of the Royal Society: Biology Letters* 271 Supplement 4: S131–S133.

Dahmen, Nicole Smith. 2010. "Construction of the Truth and Deconstruction of 'A Million Little Pieces'." *Journalism Studies* 11(1): 115–130.

Dargis, Manhola. March 4, 2014. "A Heavy Bass Beat, a Wreath of Smoke, an Aura of Sweat." Retrieved July 7, 2019 (https://www.nytimes.com/2014/03/05/movies/interior-leather-bar-spun-from-recreated-lost-footage.html).

Davidson, Guy. 2005. "Contagious Relations: Simulation, Paranoia, and the Postmodern Condition in William Friedkin's *Cruising* and Felice Picano's *The Lure*." *GLQ* 11(1): 23–64.

Davies, Steven Paul. 2008. *Out at the Movies: A History of Gay Cinema*. Harpenden, UK: Kamera Books.

Davis, Natalie Zemon. 1965. "Strikes and Salvation at Lyons." *Archiv für Reformationsgeschichte* IVI: 48–64.

Deleuze, Gilles. 1989 (1967). *Présentation de Sacher Masoch*. Translated by Jean McNeil. New York, NY: Zone Books.

Derrida, Jacques. 1995 (1982). *Points: Interviews 1974–1994*. Redwood City, CA: Stanford University Press.

Diawara, Manthia. 1996. "The Absent One: The Avant-Garde and the Black Imaginary in *Looking for Langston*." Pp. 205–224 in *Representing Black Men*, edited by Marcellus Blount and George P. Cunningham. New York, NY/London, UK: Routledge.

Dilley, Patrick. 1999. "Queer Theory: Under Construction." *International Journal of Qualitative Studies in Education* 12(5): 457–472.

Duggan, Lisa. 2002. "The New Homonormativity: The Sexual Politics of Neoliberalism." Pp. 175–194 in *Materializing Democracy: Toward a Revitalized Cultural Politics*, edited by Russ Castronovo and Dana Nelson. Durham, NC: Duke University Press.

Dyer, Richard. 1977. "Stereotyping." Pp. 27–39 in *Gays and Film*, edited by Richard Dyer. New York, NY: Zoetrope; reprinted in pp. 297–301 in *The Columbia Reader on Lesbian & Gay Men in Media, Society, & Politics* (1999), edited by Larry Gross and James D. Woods. New York, NY: Columbia University Press.

Dyer, Richard. 1993. *The Matter of Images: Essays on Representations*. London, UK: Routledge.

Edwards, Lisa and Carwyn Jones. 2009. "Postmodernism, Queer Theory and Moral Judgement in Sport: Some Critical Reflections." *International Review for the Sociology of Sport* 44(4): 331–344.

Ellis, Havelock. 1938. "Sadism and Masochism." Pp. 30–32 in *Basic Writings of Sigmund Freud*, edited by A. A. Brill. New York, NY: Modern Library.

Evans, Nicola. 1999. "A Becoming Amplitude: Fag Hags and Gay Men in Fiction and in Theory." *Discourse* 21(2): 21–46.

Fahraeus, Anna. 2014. "Proustian Desire and the Queering of Masculinity in Gay Cinematic Romance." *Masculinities: A Journal of Identity and Culture* 1(1): 28–59.

Fanon, Frantz. 1988 (1952). *Black Skin, White Masks*. London, UK: Pluto Press.

Feldman, Adam. February 28, 2014. "James Franco, Voyeur." Retrieved July 7, 2019 (https://www.out.com/movies/2014/2/28/james-francos-hardcore-interior-leather-bar-hits-cinemas).

Feuer, Jane. 1984. "Melodrama, Serial Form and Television." *Screen* 25(1): 4–16.

Fiske, John. 1986. Television: Polysemy and Popularity. *Critical Studies in Mass Communication* 3(4): 391–408.

Fortier, Mark. 2002. *Theory/theatre: An Introduction*. London, UK/New York, NY: Routledge.

Foster, David William. 2013. "*Plan B* (film review)." *Chasqui* 42(1): 255–256.

Foster, David W. 2014. "Marco Berger: Filmar las masculinidades queer en la Argentina." Retrieved July 20, 2014 (http://www.asaeca.org/imagofagia/index.php/imagofagia/article/view/513).

Foucault, Michel. 1979. *Discipline and Punish: The Birth of the Prison*. Translated by Alan Sheridan. Harmondsworth, UK: Penguin.

Freud, Sigmund. 1905. "Three Essays on the Theory of Sexuality." Pp. 135–243 in *The Standard Edition of the Complete Psychological Works of Sigmund Fred* (1953–1974), vol. 7. Translated by James Strachey *et al*. London, UK: The Hogarth Press and the Institute of Psycho-analysis.

Fuchs, Thomas. 2017. "Intercorporeality and Interaffectivity." Pp. 3–23 in *Intercorporeality: Emerging Socialities in Interaction*, edited by Christian Meyer, Jürgen Streeck and J. Scott Jordan. New York, NY: Oxford University Press.

Gamman, Lorraine and Merja Makinen. 1994. *Female Fetishism: A New Look*. London, UK: Lawrence & Wishart.

Gates, Henry Louis Jr. 2002. "Foreword." Pp. xi–xii in *Gay Rebel of the Harlem Renaissance: Selections from the Work of Richard Bruce Nugent*, edited by Thomas H. Wirth. Durham, NC/London, UK: Duke University Press.

Genet, Jean. 1990 (originally published in 1943). *Our Lady of the Flowers*. Translated by Bernard Frechtman. London, UK: Faber and Faber.

Girard, René. 1976. *Deceit, Desire and the Novel: Self and Other in Literary Structure*. Translated by Yvonne Freccero. Baltimore, MD: Johns Hopkins Press.

Gleeson, Kate. 2007. "Discipline, Punishment and the Homosexual in Law." *Liverpool Law Review* 28: 327–247.

"Go West" (pop song). 1979. Lyrics and music: Jacque Morali, Henri Belolo, and Victor Willis. Performance: The Village People. Casablanca Records. 4:10 min.

Goffman, Erving. 1986 (1963). *Stigma: Notes on the Management of Spoiled Identity*. New York, NY: Touchstone.

"Gonna Make You Sweat (Everybody Dance Now)" (pop song). 1990. Lyrics and music: Robert Clivillés and Fredrick B. Williams. Performers: C+C Music Factory featuring Freedom Williams and Martha Wash. Columbia Records. 4:06 min.

Graham, Paula. 1995. "Girl's Camp? The Politics of Parody." Pp. 163–181 in *Immortal, Invisible: Lesbians and the Moving Image*, edited by Tamsin Wilson. London, UK/New York, NY: Routledge.

"The Great Pretender" (pop song). 1955. Lyrics and music: Buck Ram; performed by Tony Williams and The Pretenders, Mercury Records, 2:36 min.; covered by Freddie Mercury (1987); Polyphone Records, 3:25 min.

Gross, Larry. 1988. "The Ethics of Misrepresentation." Pp. 188–202 in *Image Ethics*, edited by Larry Gross, John Katz and Jay Ruby. New York, NY: Oxford University Press.

Gross, Larry. 1989. "Out of the Mainstream: Sexual Minorities and the Mass Media." Pp. 130–149 in *Remote Control: Television, Audiences and Cultural Power*, edited by Ellen Seiter, Hans Borchers, Gabriele Kreutzner, and Eva-Maria Warth. London, UK: Routledge.

Gross, Larry. July 1994. "You're the First Person I've Ever Told I'm Gay: Letters to a Fictional Gay Teen." *Paper presented at the International Communication Association Annual Conference.* Sydney, Australia.

Gross, Larry. 1998. "Minorities, Majorities and the Media." Pp. 87–102 in *Media, Ritual and Identity*, edited by Tamar Liebes and James Curran. London, UK/New York, NY: Routledge.

Guignon, Charles. 2013. "In Search of Authenticity: A Heideggerian Quest." *The Humanistic Psychologist* 41: 204–208.

Guzmán, Isabel Molina and Angharad N. Valdivia. 2004. "Brain, Brow, and Booty: Latina Iconicity in U.S. Popular Culture." *The Communication Review* 7: 205–221.

Hadleigh, Boze. 2001 (1993). *The Lavender Screen: The Gay and Lesbian Films.* New York, NY: Citadel Press.

Halberstam, Jack. 2011. *The Queer Art of Failure.* Durham, NC/London, UK: Duke University Press.

Hamdan, Sameer. 2011. "Identifying the Linguistic Genderlects of the Style of Writing of Arab Male and Female Novelists." *Journal of Education Culture and Society* 2: 55–62.

Hall, Radclyffe. 1982 (originally published in 1928). *The Well of Loneliness.* London, UK: Virago.

Hall, Stuart. 1996. "Introduction: Who Needs 'Identity'?" Pp. 1–17 in *Questions of Cultural Identity*, edited by Stuart Hall and Paul Gay. London, UK: Sage.

Harpham, Geoffrey. 1976. "The Grotesque: First Principles." *Journal of Aesthetics and Art Criticism* 34(4): 461–468.

Harris, Daniel. 1997. *The Rise and Fall of Gay Culture.* New York, NY: Ballantine.

Hart, Kylo-Patrick R. 2013. *Queer Males in Contemporary Cinema: Becoming Visible.* Lanham, MD, Toronto, Canada, and Plymouth, UK: The Scarecrow Press.

"Hava Nagila" (traditional Hebrew song). Lyrics, music and original performer: Unknown.

Hayes, Hutton. August 28, 2003. "Prison Camp." Retrieved January 1, 2004 (http://www.advocate.com/html/stories/897/897_hayes.asp).

Healey, Murray. 1994. "The Mark of a Man: Masculine Identities and the Art of Macho Drag." *Critical Quarterly* 36(1): 86–93.

Heasley, Robert. 2005. "Queer Masculinities of Straight Men." *Men and Masculinities* 7(3): 310–320.

Hennen, Peter. 2008. *Faeries, Bears and Leathermen: Men in Community Queering the Masculine*. Chicago, IL/London, UK: The Chicago University Press.

Hennessy, Rosemary. 1993. "Queer Theory: A Review of the 'Differences', Special Issue and Wittig's 'The Straight Mind'." *Signs: Journal of Women in Culture and Society* 18(4): 964–973.

Hines, Claire. 2009. "Armed and Fabulous: Miss Congeniality's Queer Rom-Com." Pp. 117–131 in *Falling In Love Again: Romantic Comedy in Contemporary Cinema*, edited by Stacey Abbott and Deborah Jermyn. London, UK: I.B. Tauris.

Hutcheon, Linda. 1985. *A Theory of Parody: The Touching of Twentieth-Century Art Form*. New York, NY: Methuen.

"I Will Survive" (pop song). 1978. Lyrics and music: Freddie Perren and Dino Fekaris. Performer: Gloria Gaynor. Polydor. 4:56 min.

Icard, Larry. 1986. "Black Gay Men and Conflicting Social Identities: Sexual Orientation Versus Racial Identity." *Journal of Social Work and Human Sexuality* 4: 83–93.

"I'm Comin' Out" (pop song). 1980. Lyrics and music: Nile Rodgers and Bernard Edwards. Performer: Diana Ross. Motown. 5:27 min.

"I'm Every Woman" (pop song). 1978. Lyrics and music: Nickolas Ashford and Valerie Simpson. Performer: Chaka Khan. Warner Bros. 4:07 min.

Ingraham, Chrys. 2005. "Introduction: Thinking Straight." Pp. 1–11 in *Thinking Straight: The Power, the Promise, and the Paradox of Heterosexuality*, edited by Chrys Ingraham. New York, NY/London, UK: Routledge.

Internet Movie Database. December 2, 2008. "Box Office/Business for *I Now Pronounce You Chuck & Larry*." Retrieved January 10, 2009 (http://www.imdb.com/title/tt0762107/business).

Ishaghpour, Yussef. 1990. *Elias Canetti. Métamorphose et identité*. Paris, France: La Différence.

Jackson, Earl Jr. 1995. *Strategies of Deviance: Studies in Gay Male Representation*. Bloomington and Indianapolis, IN: Indiana University Press.

James, Henry. 2010 (originally published in 1903). "The Beast in the Jungle" (1st ed.). Martin Secker edition by David Price. Retrieved July 15, 2019 (http://www.gutenberg.org/files/1093/1093-h/1093-h.htm).

Janes, Dominic. 2015. *Visions of Queer Martyrdom: From John Henry Newman to Derek Jarman*. Chicago, IL/London, UK: University of Chicago Press.

Jennings, Lee Byron. 1963. *The Ludicrous Demon: Aspects of the Grotesque in Post-Romantic German Prose*. Berkeley and Los Angeles, CA: University of California Press.

Joyce, Samantha Nogueira. 2013. "A Kiss Is (Not) Just a Kiss: Heterodeterminism, Homosexuality, and TV Globo Telenovelas." *International Journal of Communication* 7: 48–66.

Kayser, Wolfgang. 1966. *The Grotesque in Art and Literature*. New York, NY: McGraw-Hill.

Kellerman, Robert. 2004. "Village People." Pp. 266 in *The Queer Encyclopedia of Music, Dance & Musical Theatre*, edited by Claude J. Summers. San Francisco, CA: Cleis Press.

Kermode, Mark. November 1998. "Cruising Control." *Sight and Sound* 8(11): 22–24.

Kimmel, Michael. 2001. "Masculinity as Homophobia: Fear, Shame, and Silence in the Construction of Gender Identity." Pp. 266–287 in *The Masculinities Reader*, edited by Stephen M. Whitehead and Frank J. Barnett. Oxford, UK/Malden, MA: Polity.

King, Claire Sisco. 2014. "*A Single Man* and a Tragic Woman." *Feminist Media Studies* 14(2): 190–205.

Kleinhans, Chuck. 1994. "Taking Out the Trash: Camp and the Politics of Parody." Pp. 182–201 in *The Politics and Poetics of Camp*, edited by Moe Meyer. London, UK and New York, NY: Routledge.

Klinger, Barbara. 1984. "'Cinema/Ideology/Criticism' Revisited: The Progressive Text." *Screen* 25(1): 30–40.

Korn, Andrew. 2016. "Male Intimacy in Marco Berger's *Plan B* and *Hawaii*." *Queer Studies in Media and Media Popular Culture* 2(3): 323–337.

Lee, Nathan. March–April 2014. "Review: *Interior. Leather Bar*." Retrieved July 7, 2019 (https://www.filmcomment.com/article/review-interior-leather-bar-james -franco-travis-mathews/).

Lemish, Dafna. 2004. "'My Kind of Campfire': The Eurovision Song Contest and Israeli Homosexuals." *Popular Communication* 2(1): 41–63.

"Macho Man" (pop song). 1978. Lyrics and music: Jacque Morali, Henri Belolo, Victor Willis, and Peter Whitehead. Performer: The Village People. Casablanca Records. 3:30 min.

Mackay, Daniel. 2001. *The Fantasy Role-Playing Game*. Jefferson, NC/London, UK: McFarland.

Maddison, Stephen. 2000. *Fags, Hags and Queer Sisters; Gender Dissent and Heteroseocial Bonds in Gay Culture*. Basingstoke, UK: Palgrave Macmillan.

Martin, Alfred L. Jr. 2014. Scripting Black Gayness: Television Authorship in Black-Cast Sitcoms. *Television & New Media* 16(7): 648–663.

Martinez, Katherine. 2018. "BDSM Role Fluidity: A Mixed-Methods Approach to Investigating Switches Within Dominant/Submissive Binaries." *Journal of Homosexuality* 65(10): 1299–1324.

Mathers, Lain A. B., J. E. Sumerau and Ryan T. Cragun. 2018. "The Limits of Homonormativity: Constructions of Bisexual and Transgender People in the Post-gay Era." *Sociological Perspectives* 61(6): 1–19.

McCluskey, Martha T. 2009. "How Queer Theory Makes Neoliberalism Sexy." Pp. 115–134 in *Feminist and Queer Legal Theory: Intimate Encounters, Uncomfortable Conversations*, edited by Martha Fineman, Jack E. Albertson and Adam P. Romero. Farnham, UK: Ashgate.

McPhail, Beverly A. 2004. "Questioning Gender and Sexuality Binaries." *Journal of Gay & Lesbian Social Services* 17(1): 3–21.

Meddaugh, Priscilla Marie. 2010. "Bakhtin, Colbert, and the Center of Discourse: Is There No 'Truthiness' in Humor?" *Critical Studies in Media Communication* 27(4): 376–390.

Mercer, Kobena. 1991. "Skin Head Thing: Racial Difference and the Homoerotic Imaginary." Pp. 169–210 in *How Do I Look? Queer Film and Video*, edited by Bad Object Choice. Seattle, WA: Bay Press.

Merleau-Ponty, Maurice. 2012 (1960). *Phenomenology of Perception*. New York, NY: Routledge.

Miller, D. A. 2007. "Cruising." *Film Quarterly* 61(2): 70–73.

Miller, Michael S. 2008. "Activism in the Harlem Renaissance." *The Gay & Lesbian Review* 15(1): 30–33.

Miller, William I. 1998. *The Anatomy of Disgust*. Cambridge, MA: Harvard University Press.

Mills, Claudia. 1999. "'Passing': The Ethics of Pretending to Be What You Are Not." *Social Theory and Practice* 25(1): 29–51.

Mills, Robert. 2001. "'Whatever You Do Is a Delight to Me!': Masculinity, Masochism, and Queer Play in Representations of Male Martyrdom." *Exemplaria* 13(1): 1–37.

Moon, Dawne. 1995. "Insult and Inclusion: The Term Fag Hag and Gay Male 'Community'." *Social Forces* 74(2): 487–510.

Moradi, Bonnie, Marcie C. Wiseman, Cirleen Deblaere, Melinda B. Goodman, Anthony Sarkees, Melanie E. Brewster, and Yu-Ping Huang. 2010. "Stigma, Internalized Homophobia, and Outness: Comparisons of LGB of Color and White Individuals' Perceptions of Heterosexist Anti-White Racism Among Blacks." *The Counseling Psychologist* 38(3): 397–424.

Morris, Charles E. and John M. Sloop. 2006. "'What Lips These Lips Have Kissed!' Reconfiguring the Politics of Queer Public Kissing." *Communication and Critical Cultural Studies* 3(1): 1–26.

Munger, Michael C. 2008. "Blogging and Political Information: Truth or Truthiness?" *Public Choice* 134(1/2): 125–138.

Muñoz, José E. 2009. *Cruising Utopia: The Then and There of Queer Futurity*. New York, NY: New York University Press.

Murray, Heather. 2015. "The Pathos of the Closet and the Generations: Gay Professors and Their Students During and Post Gay Liberation in the United States." *Journal of Homosexuality* 62(5): 644–663.

Murray, Raymond. 1996. *Images in the Dark: An Encyclopedia of Gay and Lesbian Film and Video*. Philadelphia, PA: TLA Publications.

Needham, Gary. 2014. "Bringing Out the Gimp: Fashioning the SM Imaginary." *Fashion Theory* 18(2): 149–168.

Nolletti, Arthur. 1982. "Gay Trappings and Straight Truths: A Study of Blake Edward's *Victor/Victoria*." *Film Criticism* 6(3): 41–52.

Nunley, John W., Cara McCarty, John Emigh, and Lesley Ferris. 1999. *Masks: Faces of Culture*. New York, NY: Harty N. Abrams, Inc. Publishers.

Olbrys, Stephen Gencarella. 2006. "Disciplining the Carnivalesque: Chris Farley's Exotic Dance." *Communication and Critical/Cultural Studies* 3(3): 240–259.

Ormond, Leonee. 2011. "'Punch' and Satire." Pp. 212–215 in *The Cult of Beauty: The Aesthetic Movement 1860–1900*, edited by Stephen Calloway and Lynn Orr Federle. London, UK: V&A Publishing.

The Oxford Dictionary & English Usage Guide. 1996. Oxford, UK/New York, NY: Oxford University Press.

Padva, Gilad. 2000. "*Priscilla* Fights Back: The Politicization of Camp Subculture." *Journal of Communication Inquiry* 24(2): 216–243.

Padva, Gilad. 2004. "Edge of Seventeen: Melodramatic Coming-Out in New Queer Adolescence Films." *Communication and Critical/Cultural Studies* 1(4): 355–372.

Padva, Gilad. 2008. "Educating *The Simpsons*: Teaching Queer Representations in Contemporary Visual Media." *Journal of LGBT Youth* 5(3): 57–73.

Padva, Gilad. 2014. *Queer Nostalgia in Cinema and Pop Culture*. Basingstoke, UK: Palgrave Macmillan.

Padva, Gilad and Miri Talmon. May 24–28, 2001. "When *Hairstylist* Meets a Criminal: Screening Oriental Masculinities in Israeli 'Bourekas' Films." A paper presented at *Communication Research Matter: The 51st Annual Conference of the International Communication Association (ICA)*. Washington, DC.

Pizzorno, Alessandro. 2008. *Sulla Maschera*. Bologna, Italy: Il Mulino.

Plummer, David. 2007. "Homophobia and Heterosexism." Pp. 310–314 in *Routledge International Encyclopedia of Men and Masculinities*, edited by Michael Flood, Judith Kegan, Bob Pease and Keith Pringle. London, UK/New York, NY: Routledge.

Plummer, Ken. 2003. "Queers, Bodies and Postmodern Sexualities: A Note on Revisiting the 'Sexual' in Symbolic Interactionism." *Qualitative Sociology* 26(4): 515–530.

Poole, Ralph J. 2018. "'Rise Like Two Angels in the Light': Sexualized Violence Against Queers in American Film." *European Journal of American Studies* 13(4): 1–22.

Proust, Marcel. 1996 (originally published in 1921–1922). *In Search of Lost Time*, vol. 4: *Sodom and Gomorrah*. New York, NY: Vintage Classics.

Queen, Carol. 1997. "Beyond the Valley of the Fag Hags." Pp. 76–84 in *PomoSEXUALS: Challenging Assumptions About Gender and Sexuality*, edited by Carol Queen and Lawrence Schimel. San Francisco, CA: Cleis Press.

Queen, Carol and Lawrence Schimel (Eds.). 1997. *PomoSEXUALS: Challenging Assumptions About Gender and Sexuality*. San Francisco, CA: Cleis Press.

Raymond, Diane. 2003. "Popular Culture and Queer Representation: A Critical Perspective." Pp. 98–110 in *Gender, Race, and Class in Media*, edited by Gail Dines and Jean Humez McMahon. Thousand Oaks, CA: Sage.

Reinhardt, Jelena. 2012. "Segni sul corpo. Canetti e la scure dell'armeno." Pp. 357–366 in *Pensando tra gli oggetti. Dai Greci ai giorni nostril*, edited by Giovanni Falaschi. Perugia, Italy: Morlacchi.

Reinhardt, Jelena. 2016. "The Grotesque Masks of Elias Canetti: Monads with no Doors or Windows." *Between* 6(12): 1–14.

Rich, Adrienne. 1980. "Compulsory Heterosexuality and Lesbian Existence." *Signs* 5(4): 636–660.

Richardson, Niall. 2010. *Transgressive Bodies: Representations in Film and Popular Culture*. Farnham, UK/Burlington, VT: Ashgate.

Riviere, Joan. 1929. "Womanliness as Masquerade." *International Journal of Psychoanalysis* 10: 303–313.

Roan, Jeanette. 2014. "Fake Weddings and the Critique of Marriage: *The Wedding Banquet* (1993), *I Now Pronounce You Chuck and Larry* (2007), and the Marriage Equality Debate." *Quarterly Review of Film and Video* 31(8): 746–763.

Robertson, Pamela. 1996. *Guilty Pleasures: Feminist Camp from Mae West to Madonna*. Durham, NC: Duke University Press.

Rodger, Gillian. 2004. "Drag, Camp and Gender Subversion in the Music and Videos of Annie Lennox." *Popular Music* 23(1): 17–29.

Ross, Andrew. 1988. "Uses of Camp." *Yale Journal of Criticism* 2(1); reprinted in pp. 308–329 in *Camp: Queer Aesthetics and the Performing Subject: A Reader*, edited by Fabio Cleto. Edinburgh, UK: Edinburgh University Press.

Rubidge, Sarah. 1996. "Does Authenticity Matter? The Case for and Against Authenticity in the Performing Arts." Pp. 219–233 in *Analysing Performance:*

A Critical Reader, edited by Patrick Campbell. Manchester, UK/New York, NY: Manchester University Press.

Rubinfeld, Mark D. 2001. *Bound to Bond: Gender, Genre, and the Hollywood Romantic Comedy*. Westport, CT/London, UK: Praeger.

Rumens, Nick. 2016. "Sexualities and Accounting: A Queer Theory Perspective." *Critical Perspectives on Accounting* 35: 111–120.

Russell, Eric M., Danielle J. DelPriore, Max E. Butterfield and Sarah E. Hill. 2013. "Friends with Benefits, but Without the Sex: Straight Women and Gay Men Exchange Trustworthy Mating Advice." *Evolutionary Psychology* 11(1): 132–147.

Russo, Vito. 1987 (1981). *The Celluloid Closet: Homosexuality in the Movies*. New York, NY: Harper & Row.

Sedgwick, Eve Kosofsky. 1985. *Between Men: English Literature and Male Homo-Social Desire*. New York, NY: Columbia University Press.

Sedgwick, Eve Kosofsky. 1986. "The Beast in the Closet: James and the Writing of Homosexual Panic." Pp. 148–186 in *Sex, Politics, and Science in the Nineteenth-Century Novel*, edited by Ruth Bernard Yeazell. Baltimore, MD: Johns Hopkins University Press; reprinted in pp. 182–212 in *Epistemology of the Closet*, edited by Eve Kosofsky Sedgwick (1990). Berkeley, CA/Los Angeles, CA: University of California Press.

Sedgwick, Eve Kosofsky. 1989. "Tide and Trust." *Critical Inquiry* 15(4): 745–757.

Sedgwick, Eve Kosofsky. 1990. *Epistemology of the Closet*. Berkeley and Los Angeles, CA: University of California Press.

Sedgwick, Eve Kosofsky. 1990. "Introduction: Axiomatic." Pp. 1–63 in *Epistemology of the Closet*, edited by Eve Kosofsky Sedgwick. Berkeley, CA/Los Angeles, CA: University of California Press; reprinted in pp. 243–268 in *Cultural Studies Reader* (1993), edited by Simon During. London, UK/New York, NY: Routledge.

Sedgwick, Eve Kosofsky. 1994. *Tendencies*. London, UK: Routledge.

Sedgwick, Eve Kosofsky. 1998. "A Dialogue on Love." *Critical Inquiry* 24(2): 611–631.

Seidman, Steven. 2009. "Critique of Compulsory Heterosexuality." *Sexuality Research & Social Policy Journal* 6(1): 18–28.

Severiche, Guillermo Abel. 2019. "From the Face to the Crotch: Intersubjectivity, Affective Schemas and the Politics of the Close-Up in *Los Labios/The Lips* (Fund and Loza, 2010) and *Plan B* (Berger, 2009)." *Studies in Spanish & Latin American Cinemas* 16(2): 271–288.

Shakespeare, William. 2000 (originally published in 1591–1595). *Romeo and Juliet*, edited by Jill L. Levenson. Oxford, UK: Oxford University Press.

Shakespeare, William. 2014 (originally published in 1595–1596). *Midsummer's Night Dream*. Scotts Valley, CA: CreateSpace Independent Publishing Platform.

Shelley, Martha. 1992 (1972). "Gay Is Good." Pp. 31–33 in *Out of the Closets: Voices of Gay Liberation*, edited by Karla Jay and Allen Young. New York, NY: New York University Press.

Simpson, Mark. 2001. "Foreword." Pp. ix–xii in *Sissyphobia: Gay Men and Effeminate Behavior*, edited by Tim Bergling. New York, NY: Harrington Park Press.

Sinfield, Alan. 1994. *The Wilde Century: Effeminacy, Oscar Wilde and the Queer Moment*. New York, NY: Columbia University Press.

Somerville, Siobhan. 2000. *Queering the Color Line: Race and the Invention of Homosexuality in America*. Durham, NC/London, UK: Duke University Press.

Sontag, Susan. 1964. "Notes on Camp." *Partisan Review* 31(4): 515–530; reprinted in pp. 53–65 in Camp: Queer Aesthetics and the Performing Subject, 1999, edited by Fabio Cleto. Edinburgh, UK: Edinburgh University Press.

Stebbins, Robert A. 1982. "Serious Leisure: A Conceptual Statement." *The Pacific Sociological Review* 25: 251–272.

Steig, Michael. 1970. "Defining the Grotesque: An Attempt at Synthesis." *Journal of Aesthetics and Art Criticism* 29(2): 253–260.

Stein, Arlene and Ken Plummer. 1994. "'I Can't Even Think Straight': 'Queer' Theory and the Missing Sexual Revolution in Sociology." *Sociological Theory* 12(2): 178–187.

Stephens, Elizabeth. 1999. "Masculinity as Masquerade: 'Gay' Macho in the Novels of Jean Genet." *Journal of Interdisciplinary Gender Studies* 4(2): 52–63.

Striepe, Meg I. and Deborah L. Tolman. 2003. "'Mom, Dad, I'm Straight': The Coming Out of Gender Ideologies in Adolescent Sexual-Identity Development." *Journal of Clinical Child and Adolescent Psychology* 32(4): 523–530.

Stryker, Susan. 2008. "Transgender History, Homonormativity and Disciplinarity." *Radical History Review* 100: 145–157.

Sullivan, Nikki. 2003. *A Critical Introduction to Queer Theory*. Edinburgh, UK: Edinburgh University Press.

Swift, Jonathan. 2003 (originally published in 1726). *Gulliver's Travels*, edited by Robert J. DeMaria. London, UK: Penguin.

Tannen, Deborah. 1990. *You Just Don't Understand: Women and Men in Conversation*. New York, NY: Morrow.

Tannen, Deborah. 1993. *Gender and Conversational Interaction*. New York, NY: Oxford University Press.

Taylor, Charles. 1989. *Sources of the Self*. Cambridge, MA: Harvard University Press.

Taylor, Charles. 1991. *The Ethics of Authenticity*. Cambridge, MA: Harvard University Press.

Taywaditep, Kittiwut Jod. 2002. "Marginalization Among the Marginalized." *Journal of Homosexuality* 42(1): 1–28.

Thompson, Deborah. 2004. "Calling All Fag Hags: From Identity Politics to Identification Politics." *Social Semiotics* 14(1): 37–48.

Tinkcom, Matthew. 2001. *Working Like a Homosexual: Camp, Capital, Cinema*. Durham, NC/London, UK: Duke University Press.

Tucciarone, Krista M. 2007. "Cinematic College: National Lampoon's Animal House Teaches Theories of Student Development." *College Student Journal* 41(4). Retrieved July 28, 2019 (https://eds-b-ebscohost-com.ezproxy.haif a.ac.il/eds/detail/detail?vid=0&sid=d4b4f6fa-46ba-45bd-ac2e-ee63c0296c3e %40sessionmgr103&bdata=JnNpdGU9ZWRzLWxpdmUmc2NvcGU9c2l0ZQ %3d%3d#AN=28351180&db=a9h).

Van Leer, David. 1989. "The Beast of the Closet: Homosociality and the Pathology of Manhood." *Critical Inquiry* 15(3): 587–605.

Vicinus, Martha. 1981. "Helpless and Unfriended: Nineteenth Century Domestic Melodrama." *New Literary History* 13(1): 127–143.

Villarejo, Amy. 2014. *Ethereal Queer: Television, Historicity, Desire*. Durham, NC/London, UK: Duke University Press.

Waitt, Gordon and Markwell, Kevin. 2006. *Gay Tourism Culture and Context*. London, UK/New York, NY: Routledge.

Wallace, Robert. 1994. "Towards a Poetics of Gay Male Theatre." *Essays on Canadian Writing* 54: 212–236.

Ward, Jane. 2015. *Not Gay: Sex Between Straight White Men*. New York, NY/ London, UK: New York University Press.

Warner, Michael. 1991. "Introduction: Fear of a Queer Planet." *Social Text* 29: 3–17.

Warner, Michael. 1993. *Fear of a Queer Planet: Queer Politics and Social Theory*. Minneapolis, MN: University of Minnesota Press.

Warner, Michael. 1999. *The Trouble with Normal: Sex, Politics, and the Ethics of Queer Life*. New York, NY: Free Press.

Washbourne, Neil. 2018. "Adam Sandler as (Questionable) Masculine 'Role Model': Towards an Analysis of Disgust and Violence in Adam Sandler's Comedian Comedy." *Comedy Studies* 9(1): 36–49.

Watney, Simon. 1982. "Hollywood's Homosexual World." *Screen* 23(3–4): 107–121.

Weeks, Jeffrey. 1995. *Invented Moralities: Sexual Values in an Age of Uncertainty*. New York, NY: Columbia University Press.

Weiss, Gail I. 1999. *Body Images: Embodiment as Intercorporeality*. New York, NY: Routledge.

Wilson, Alexander. 1981. "Friedkin's *Cruising*, Ghetto Politics, and Gay Sexuality." *Social Text* 4: 98–109.

Wilson, Angus. 1970. *The World of Charles Dickens*. London, UK: Viking Press.

Wittman, Carl. 1992 (1972). "A Gay Manifesto." Pp. 330–341 in *Out of the Closets: Voices of Gay Liberation*, edited by Karla Jay and Allen Young. New York, NY: New York University Press.

Yaya, Isabel. 2008. "Wonders of America: The Curiosity Cabinet as a Site of Representation and Knowledge." *Journal of the History of Collections* 20(2): 173–188.

"You Paint Me Black" (pop song). 2015. Lyrics, music and performer: Danielle Parente. Gravelpit Music/Danielle Parente Music. 4:10 min.

Young, Allen. 1992 (1972). "Out of the Closets, Into the Streets." Pp. 6–30 in *Out of the Closets: Voices of Gay Liberation*, edited by Karla Jay and Allen Young. New York, NY: New York University Press.

Young, Ian. 1995. *The Stonewall Experiment: A Gay Psychohistory*. London, UK/ New York, NY: Cassell.

Zeichner, Amos and Reidy, Dennis E. 2009. "Are Homophobic Men Attracted to or Repulsed by Homosexual Men? Effects of Gay Male Erotica on Anger, Fear, Happiness, and Disgust." *Psychology of Men & Masculinity* 10(3): 231–236.

Zijderveld, Anton C. 1979. *On Clichés: The Supersedure of Meaning by Function in Modernity*. London, UK: Routledge and Keegan Paul.

Filmography

3rd Rock from the Sun (TV series). Creators: Bonnie Turner and Terry Turner. NBC. 1996–2001.

4th Man Out. Director: Andrew Nackman. Performers; Parker Young, Evan Todd, and Chord Overstreet. Tait Productions / Moving Pictures / Moving Pictures Artists. 2015.

Almost Normal. Director: Marc Moody. Performers: J. Andrew Keitch, Joan Lauckner, and Tim Hammer. Tenure Track Productions. 2005.

Aquarius (TV series). Creator: John McNamara. Performers: David Duchovny, Grey Damon, and Gethin Anthony. NBC. 2015–2016.

Beach Rats. Director: Eliza Hittman. Performers: Harris Dickinson, Madeline Weinstein, and Kate Hodge. Cinereach / Animal Kingdom / Secret Engine. 2017.

Beautiful Thing. Director: Hettie Macdonald. Performers: Glen Berry, Linda Henry, and Meera Sylal. Channel Four Films / World Productions. 1996.

The Beauty and the Beast. Directors: Jean Cocteau and René Clément. Performers: Jean Marais, Josette Day, and Mila Parély. DisCina / Les Films André Paulvé. 1946.

Beginners. Director: Mike Mills. Performers: Ewan McGregor, Christopher Plummer, and Mélanie Laurent. Plympus Pictures / Parts and Labor / Northwood Productions. 2010.

Bend It Like Beckham. Director: Gurinder Chadha; Performers: Parminder Nagra, Keira Knightley, and Jonathan Rhys Meyers. Kintop Pictures / Film Council / Filförderung Hamburg / British Sky Broadcasting (BSkyB) / British Screen Productions / Helkon Media / The Works / Scion Films / Bent It Films / Roc Media / Road Movies Filmproduktion / Future Films / Redbus Pictures. 2002.

Big Wednesday. Director: John Milius. Performers: Jan-Michael Vincent, William Katt, and Gary Busey. A-Team. 1978.

Billy Elliot. Director: Stephen Daldry. Performers: Jamie Bell, Julie Walters, and Jean Heywood. StudioCanal / Working Title Films / BBC Films / Arts Council of England / Tiger Aspect Productions / WT2 Productions. 2000.

Boat Trip. Director: Mort Nathan. Performers: Cuba Gooding Jr., Horatio Sanchez, and Roselyn Sanchez. Motion Picture Corporation of America / International West Pictures (IWP) / ApolloMedia / Boat Trip LLC / Erste Productions KG / Gemini Film. 2002.

Boy Meets Boy (TV series). Creators: Douglas Ross, Dean Minerd, and Tom Campbell. Bravo. 2003.

Boys. Director: Mischa Kamp. Performers: Gijs Blom, Ko Zandvliet, and Jonas Smulders. Pupkin Films / NTR. 2014.

Breakfast in Tiffany's. Director: Blake Edwards. Performers: Audrey Hepburn, George Peppard, and Patricia Neale. Jurow-Shepherd. 1961.

Bromance: My Brother's Romance. Director: Wenn V. Deramas. Performers: Sanjoe Marudo, Cristine Reyes, and Arlene Muhlach. ABS-CBN Film Productions / Skylight Films. 2013.

Call Me By Your Name. Director: Luca Guadagnino. Performers: Armie Hammer, Timothée Chalamet, and Michael Suhlbarg. Frenesy Fim Company / La Cinéfacture / RT Features / Water's End Productions / M.Y.R.A. Entertainment / Ministero per I Beni e le Attività Culturali (MiBAC) / Lombardia Film Commission. 2017.

Close Encounters of the Third Kind. Director: Steven Spielberg. Performers: Richard Dreyfuss, François Truffaut, and Teri Garr. Julia Phillips and Micahel Phillips Productions / EMI Films. 1977.

The Closet (aka *Le Placard*). Director: Francis Veber. Performers: Daniel Auteuil, Gérard Depardieu, and Thierry Lhermitte. Gaumont / EFVE / TF1 Films Production / Canal+. 2001.

Colbert Report (TV show). Created by Stephen Colbert, Ben Karlin, and Jon Stewart. Director: Jim Hoskinson. Performer: Stephen Colbert. Comedy Central. 2005–2014.

Connie and Carla. Director: Michael Lembeck. Performers: Nia Vardalos, Toni Collette, and David Duchovny. Universal Pictures / Spyglass Entertainment / CCLA Productions / Epsilon Motion Pictures. 2004.

Cruising. Director: William Friedkin. Performers: Al Pacino, Paul Sorvino, and Karen Allen. CiP Europaische Treuhand AG / Lorimar Film Entertainment. 1980.

Days of Our Lives (TV series). Creators: Ted Corday and Betty Corday. Performers: Lucas Adams, Kristian Alfonso, and Lemon Archey. NBC. 1965–present.

Death in Buenos Aires. Director: Natalia Meta. Performers: Mónica Antonópulos, Hugo Arana, and Fabián Arenillas. Utopica Group. 2014.

Different. Director: Tyrrell Shaffner. Performers; Ben Hogestyn, Emily Brooke Hands, and Kay Stratton. USC School of Cinema and Television. 2004.

Dog Gone Love. Director: Rob Lundsgaard. Performers: Alexander Chaplin, Jordan Ladd, and Tom McGowan. Lucky Dog Film Group. 2004.

Dostana. Director: Tarun Mansukhani. Performers: Abhishek Bachchan, John Abraham, and Priyanka Chopra. Black Dog Jib Productions / Dharma Productions. 2008.

Edge of Seventeen. Director: David Moreton. Performers: Chris Stafford, Tina Holmes, Andersen Gabrych, and Stephanie McVay. Luna Pictures / Blue Streak Films. 1998.

The Exorcist. Director: William Friedkin. Performers: Ellen Burstyn, Max von Sydow, and Linda Blair. Warner Bros. / Hoya Productions. 1973.

Fag Hags: Women Who Love Gay Men (documentary film). Director: Justine Pimlott. Writer: Maya Gallus. Performer: Carole Pope. Red Queen Productions. 2005.

The Falls. Director: Jon Garcia. Performers: Nick Ferrucci, Benjamin Farmer, and Brian J. Saville Allard. Radical Media / Absolute Entertainment. 2012.

For a Lost Soldier. Director: Roeland Kerbosch. Performers: Andrew Kelley, Jeroen Krabbé and Maarten Smit. Sigma Film Productions. 1992.

Frantz Fanon: Une Vie, Un Combat, Une Oeuvre (documentary film). Director: Cheikh Djemaï. RFO / La Lanterne. 2001.

Frasier (TV series). Creators: David Angell, Peter Casey, and David Lee. Performers: Kelsey Grammer, Jane Leeves, and David Hyde Pierce. NBC. 1993–2004.

The French Connection. Director: William Friedkin. Performers: Gene Hackman, Roy Scheider, and Fernando Rey. Philip D'Antoni Productions / Schine-Moore Productions. 1971.

Freshman Orientation. Director: Ryan Shiraki. Performers: Sam Huntington, Marla Sokoloff, and Mike Erwin. Element Films / L.I.F.T. Production / Persistent Entertainment. 2004.

Friends (TV series). Creators: David Crane and Martha Kauffman. Performers: Jennifer Aniston, Courtney Cox, and Lisa Kudrow. NBC. 1994–2004.

G.B.F. Director: Darren Stein. Performers; Michael J. Willett, Paul Iacono, and Sasha Pieterse. School Pictures / Parting Shots Media / Logolite Entertainment / ShadowCatcher Entertainment / Steakhaus Productions. 2013.

The Gay Deceivers. Director: Bruce Kessler. Performers: Kevin Coughlin, Brooke Bundy, and Lawrence P. Casey. Fanfare Films. 1969.

Get Real. Director: Simon Shore. Performers: Ben Silverstone, Brad Gorton, and Charlotte Brittain. Arts Council of England / British Screen Productions / Distant Horizon / Graphite Film Productions. 1998.

Hairspray. Director: John Waters. Performers: Divine (Harris Glenn Milstead), Sonny Bono, and Ruth Brown. New Line Cinema / Stanley F. Buchtal / Robert Shaye Production. 1988.

Halloween. Director: John Carpenter. Performers: Donald Pleasence, Jamie Lee Curtis, and Tony Moran. Compass International Pictures / Falcon International Productions. 1978.

Handsome Devil. Director: John Butler. Performers; Fionn O'Shea, Ardal O'Hanlon, and Amy Huberman. Treasure Entertainment / Windmill Lane Pictures. 2016.

Happy, Texas. Director: Mark Illsley. Performers: Jeremy Northam, Steve Zahn, and William H. Macy. Marked Entertainment / Miramax. 1999.

Heads or Tails. Director: Claude Fournier. Performers; Roy Dupuis, Patrick Guard, and Charlotte Laurier. Malofilm Productions / Rose Films / Réseaux Premier Choix / Société de Développement des Entreprises Culturelles (SODEC) / Téléfilm Canada. 1997.

A Home at the End of the World. Director: Michael Mayer. Performers: Colin Farrell, Dallas Roberts, and Robin Wright. Hart Sharp Entertainment / John Wells Productions / Killer Films / Plymouth Projects / True Film Fund / Window Pane Pictures. 2004.

How to Seduce a Woman. Director: Charles Martin. Performers: Angus Duncan, Angel Tompkins, and Heidi Brühl. Forward. 1974.

"I Love the Nightlife." Lyrics and music: Alicia Bridges and Susan Hutcheson. Performer: Alicia Bridges. Polydor. 1978.

I Love You Phillip Morris. Directors: Glenn Ficarra and John Requa. Performers: Jim Carrey, Ewan McGregor, and Leslie Mann. EuropaCorp / Mad Chance / Consolidated Pictures Group. 2009.

I Now Pronounce You Chuck & Larry. Director: Dennis Dugan. Performers: Adam Sandler, Kevin James, and Jessica Biel. Universal Pictures / Relativity Media / Happy Madison Productions / Shady Acres Entertainment. 2007.

If You Only Knew. Director: David Snedeker. Performers: Johnathon Schaech, Alison Eastwood, and James Le Gros. Cinerenta Medienbeteiligungs KG / Two Sticks Productions. 2000.

Interior. Leather Bar. Directors: James Franco and Travis Mathews. Performers: Val Lauren, Christian Patrick, and James Franco. RabbitBandini Productions. 2013.

Jonathan. Director: Piotr J. Lewandowski. Performers: Jannies Wiewöhner, André Hennicke, and Julia Koschpitz. Kordes & Kordes Film GmbH / Südwestrundfunk (SWR) / Westdeutscher Rundfunk (WDR) / Hessischer Rundfunk (HT) / Arte / CinePostproduction / FunDeMental Studios / CS Filmproduktion. 2016.

Kenny vs. Spenny (TV series). Creators and performers: Kenny Hotz and Spencer Rice. Showcase. 2005–2010.

Kicking Out Shoshana (aka *Shoshana Halutz Merkazi*). Director: Shay Kanot. Performers: Oshri Cohen, Gal Gadot, and Eli Finish. Artza Productions / United King Films. 2014.

The Ladies' Hairdresser. Director: Ze'ev Revach. Performers: Ze'ev Ravah, Tikva Aziz, and Alik Arma. April Films / Shapira Films. 1984.

Latter Days. Director: C. Jay Cox. Performers: Wes Ramsey, Steve Sandvoss, and Mary Kay Place. Funny Boy Films / Davis Entertainment Filmworks. 2003.

The Life and Loves of Oscar Wilde (documentary film; *Reputations* series). Producer: Annie Paul. BBC. 1995.

Little Britain (TV series). Creators: David Williams and Matt Lucas. Performers: Matt Lucas, David Walliams, and Tom Baker. British Broadcasting Corporation (BBC) / Little Britain Productions. 2003–2006.

Locked Up (aka *Gefangen*). Director: Jörg Andreas. Performers: Marcel Schlutt, Mike Sale, and ralph Steel. Cazzo Film Berlin. 2004.

The Lost Language of Cranes. Director: Nigel Finch. Performers: Brian Cox, Eileen Atkins, and Angus Macfadyen. British Broadcasting Corporation (BBC). 1991.

Love and Death on Long Island. Director: Richard Kwietniowski. Performers: John Hurt, Jason Priestley, and Fiona Loewi. Arts Council of England / British Broadcasting Corporation (BBC) / British Screen Productions / Mikado Film / Nova Scotia Film Development Corporation / Skyline Films / The Sales Company / Téléfilm Canada / imX Communications. 1997.

Love Boat (TV series). Creator: Wilford Lloyd Baumes. Performers: Gavin MacLeod, Bernie Kopell, and Ted Lange. Aaron Spelling Productions / Douglas S. Cramer Company / The Love Boat Company. 1977–1986, 1990.

Love Is All You Need? (short version). Director: Kim Rocco Shields. Performers: Lexi DiBenedetto, Carrie Lazar, and Sheri Levy. Genius Pictures / Wingspan Pictures. 19 min. 2012.

Love Is All You Need? (aka *Love Is Love?*) (long version). Director: Kim Rocco Shields. Performers: Briana Evigan, Tyler Blackburn, and Kyla Kenedy. Genius Pictures / Love Is All You Need Productions. 121 min. 2016.

Love, Simon. Director: Greg Berlanti. Performers: Nick Robinson, Jennifer Garner, and Josh Duhamel. Fox 2000 Pictures / New Leaf Literary & Media / Temple Hill Entertainment / Twisted Media. 2018.

M.A.S.H. (TV series). Developer: Larry Gelbart. Performers: Alan Alda, Wayne Rogers, and McLean Stevenson. CBS. 1972–1983.

Macho. Director: Antonio Serrano. Performers: Cantante, Mario Iván Martínez, and Sophia Gómez. Astillero Films / Labodigital / Rodarte Entertainment. 2016.

Manhattan. Director: Woody Allen. Performers: Woody Allen, Diane Keaton, and Mariel Hemingway. Jack Rollins & Charles H. Joffe Productions. 1979.

The Matthew Shepard Story. Director: Roger Spottiswoode. Performers: Stockard Channing, Shane Meier, and Wendy Crewson. Alliance Atlantis Communications / Canadian Film or Video Production / Canadian Television (CTV) / Cosmic Entertainment. 2002.

Mondo Trasho. Director: John Waters. Performers: Mary Vivian Pears, Divine (Harris Glenn Milstead), and David Lochary. Dreamland. 1969.

My Best Friend's Wedding. Director: P.J. Hogan. Performers: Julia Roberts, Dermot Mulroney, and Cameron Diaz. TriStar Pictures / Zucker Brothers Productions / Predawn Productions. 1997.

My Friend Rachid. Director: Philippe Barassat. Performers: Nordine Mezaache, Jonathan Reyes, and Mathieu Demy. La Vie Est Belle Films Accociés / Les Productions de l'Amour Fou. 1998.

National Lampoon's Animal House. Director: John Landis. Performers: John Belushi, Karen Allen, and Tom Hulce. Universal Pictures / Oregon Film Factory / Stage III Productions. 1978.

The Nation's Situation (aka *Matzav Ha'Umah*) (TV satire show). Creators: Avi Cohen and Lior Schleien. Performers: Guri Alfi, Orna Banai, and Einav Galilee. Channel 2 / Reshet. 2010–2015.

Next Best Thing. Director: John Schlesinger. Performers: Madonna, Rupert Everett, and Benjamin Bratt. Lakeshore Entertainment / Paramount Pictures. 2000.

The Object of My Affection. Director: Nicholas Hytner. Performers: Jennifer Aniston, Paul Rudd, and Kali Rocha. Twentieth Century Fox. 1998.

Partners. Director: James Burrows. Performers: Ryan O'Neal, John Hurt, and Kenneth McMillan. Paramount Pictures / Aaron Russo Productions. 1982.

Pink Flamingos. Director: John Waters. Performers: Divine (Harris Glenn Milstead), Mary Vivian Pears, and David Lochary. Dreamland. 1972.

Plan B. Director: Marco Berger. Performers: Manuel Vignau, Lucas Ferraro, and Mercedes Quinteros. Rendez-vous Pictures / Oh My Gomez! Films / Brainjaus Producciones / Universidad del Cine. 2009.

Polyester. Director: John Waters. Performers: Divine (Harris Glenn Milstead), Tab Hunter, and Edith Massey. New Line Cinema. 1981.

Pride. Director: Matthew Warchus. Performers: Bill Nighy, Imelda Staunton, and Dominic West. Pathé / BBC Films / Proud Films / British Film Institute (BFI) / Canal+ / Ciné+ / Calamity Films. 2014.

Queer as Folk (TV series). Created by Russell T. Davies; Developed by Ron Cowen and Daniel Lipman. Performers: Gale Harold, Randy Harrison, and Scott Lowell. Showtime / Showcase. 2000–2005.

Queer Eye for the Straight Guy (TV series). Creator: David Collins. Performers: Carson Kressley, Ted Allen, Thom Filicia, Kyan Douglas, and Jai Rodriguez. Bravo. 2003–2007.

The Raging Bull. Director: Martin Scorsese. Performers: Robert De Niro, Cathy Moriarty, and Joe Pesci. Chartoff-Winkler Productions. 1980.

The Ritz. Director: Richard Lester. Performers: Jack Weston, Rita Moreno, and Jerry Stiller. Courtyard Films / Warner Bros. 1976.

Saturday Night Live (TV program). Creator: Lorne Michaels. Developer: Dick Ebersol. NBC. 1975–1980; 1985–present.

Shelter. Director: Jonah Markowitz. Performers: Trevor Wright, Brad Rowe, and Tina Holmes. GP Pictures / here! Films. 2007.

"Shoop Shoop Song (It's In His Kiss)" (music video). Lyrics and music: Rudy Clark. Director: Marty Callner. Performer: Cher. Geffen Records. 1990.

The Simpsons (animated TV series). "Homer's Phobia" (15th season, 8th episode). Creator: Matt Groening. Director: Mike B. Anderson. Scriptwriter: Ron Hauge. Fox. 1997.

Some Like It Hot. Director: Billy Wilder. Performers: Jack Lemon, Tony Curtis, and Marilyn Monroe. Ashton Productions / The Mirisch Corporation. 1959.

South Park (TV animation series). Creators: Trey Parker and Matt Stone. Comedy Central. 1997–present.

South Park (animated TV series). "South Park Is Gay!" (7th Season, 8th episode). Creators: Trey Parker and Matt Stone. Scriptwriter: Trey Parker. Comedy Central. 2003.

Strange Bedfellows. Director: Dean Murphy. Performers: Michael Caton, Alan Cassell, and Andy Pappas. Instinct Entertainment. 2004.

Three Sisters (TV series). Creators: Eileen Heisler and DeAnn Heline. Performers; Katherine LaNasa, David Alan Basche, and Vicki Lewis. NBC. 2001–2002.

Three's Company (TV series). Creators: Don Nicholl, Michael Ross, and Bernard West. Performers: John Ritter, Joyce DeWitt, and Suzanne Somers. ABC. 1976–1984.

Titanic. Director: James Cameron. Performers: Leonardo DiCaprio, Kate Winslet, and Billy Zaner. Twentieth Century Fox / Paramount Pictures / Lightstorm Entertainment. 1997.

Victor Victoria. Director: Blake Edwards. Performers: Julie Andrews, James Garner, and Robert Preston. Metro-Goldwyn-Mayer / Buckhantz-NMC Company / Peerford / Artista Management / Blake Edwards Entertainment / Ladbroke. 1982.

The Way He Looks. Director: Daniel Ribeiro. Performers: Ghilherme Lobo, Fabio Audi, and Tess Amorim. Lacuna Filmes / Polana Filmes. 2014.

Weekend. Director: Andrew Haigh. Performers: Tom Cullen, Chris New, and Jonathan Race. The Bureau / EM Media / Glendale Picture Company / Synchronicity Films. 2011.

Were the World Mine. Director: Tom Gustafson. Performers: Tanner Cohen, Wendy Robie, and Judy McLane. SPEAK Productions / The Group Entertainment. 2008.

Will & Grace (TV series). Created by David Kohan and Max Mutchnick. Director: James Burrows. Performers: Eric McCormack, Debra Messing, Megan Mullally, and Sean Hayes. NBC 1998–2006; Universal 2017–present.

The Wizard of Oz. Director: Victor Fleming. Performers: Judy Garland, Frank Morgan, and Ray Bolger. Metro-Goldwyn-Mayer (MGM). 1939.

Index

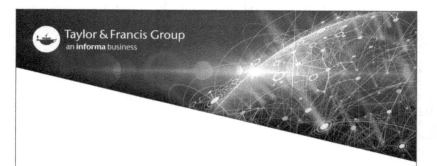